A Connecticut Yankee
in the 8th Gurkha Rifles

A Burma Memoir

=

Scott Gilmore
with Patrick Davis

Brassey's

Washington · London

Library of Congress Cataloging-in-Publication Data
Gilmore, Scott.
A Connecticut Yankee with the 8th Gurkha Rifles: a Burma memoir/
Scott Gilmore with Patrick Davis.
p.   cm.
Includes bibliographical references and index.
ISBN 0-02-881106-2
1. Gilmore, Scott.   2. World War, 1939–1945—Campaigns—Burma.
3. World War, 1939–1945—Personal narratives, American.   4. Great
Britain. Army—Biography.   5. Great Britain. Army. Gurkha
Rifles, 4/8th—History.   I. Davis, Patrick (Patrick D.)   II. Title.
D767.6.G55   1995
940.54´26—dc20   94-36337
CIP

Designed by Tanya M. Pérez

10   9   8   7   6   5   4   3   2   1

Printed in the United States of America

For Shelley, Aprille, and Peter,
who are tolerant of their old man's foibles

 **An AUSA Book**

The Association of the United States Army (AUSA) was founded in 1950 as a not-for-profit organization dedicated to education concerning the role of the U.S. Army, to providing material for military professional development, and to the promotion of proper recognition and appreciation of the profession of arms. Its constituencies include those who serve in the Army today, including Army National Guard, Army Reserve, and Army civilians, the retirees and veterans who have served in the past, and all their families. A large number of public-minded citizens and business leaders are also an important constituency. The association seeks to educate the public, elected and appointed officials, and leaders of the defense industry on crucial issues involving the adequacy of our national defense, particularly those issues affecting land warfare.

In 1988 the AUSA established within its existing organization a new entity known as the Institute of Land Warfare. Its purpose is to extend the educational work of the AUSA by sponsoring scholarly publications, to include books, monographs, and essays on key defense issues, as well as workshops and symposia. Among the volumes chosen for designation as "An AUSA Institute of Land Warfare Book" are both new texts and reprints of titles of enduring value that are no longer in print. Topics include history, policy issues, strategy, and tactics. Publication as an AUSA book does not necessarily indicate that the Association of the United States Army and the publisher agree with everything in the book, but does suggest that the AUSA and the publisher believe it will stimulate the thinking of AUSA members and others concerned about important issues.

Contents

Preface

Four of the officers I knew well in my battalion have written and published books since World War II. More challenged than daunted by this record, I set out to have a go myself, armed with the unique slant of an American with the Gurkhas (who were part of Britain's then Indian Army) and in confrontation with the Japanese in Burma. I determined to bring to the reader—likely to be more familiar with the war in Europe and the Pacific, and uninformed on Burma—a picture of some of the events and the men involved in those campaigns. Also I must tell the reader how it was I came to reach such unusual employment.

The Royal portable that I had won in a raffle in 1939 was replaced by an ornery electronic typewriter. By the end of 1991 I had knocked out fifteen chapters.

Friends shown the manuscript were polite in their praise, if holding back from all-out endorsement. My story suffered from gaps, questionable accuracy, and a tendency toward convoluted sentences sure to baffle the reader. Miss Woods, my English teacher at Greenwich High, had installed a desire to write. She had not installed the basics needed for a free-flowing rhetoric, even though Truman Capote and Francis S. Steegmuller had been her students.

What to do? A good bit of revision would be necessary before any publisher would reward my efforts with a pot of gold. I had read accounts of how Maxwell Perkins had guided the writings of Thomas Wolf and Hemingway to success, and I knew how important a good editor could be. I suggested to Pat Davis that he might be my Max Perkins. He said he would try.

Pat had spent his earliest years in India, part of a family that included a great-grandfather who won the Victoria Cross with a Gurkha regiment. Pat's knowledge of the political and historical background in India, his literary talents—which included a well-reviewed account of his own part in the Burma campaigns, *A Child at Arms*—and his subsequent career with the Oxford University Press and the London School of Economics, together with his patience with my scrawled notes, more than qualified him for the job ahead.

From mid-1992 until the present, reams of copy have gone back and forth between Greenwich, Connecticut, and Kent, United Kingdom. Pat was ever pressing me to remember places and events in proper order, to be sure of the facts, demanding accuracy and clarity.

Brassey's requests to add more coverage of the overall military picture in Burma, of the American participation in the campaigns, of the demands of the Indians for freedom, and of many other matters small and large, required Pat's historical training. And all the while he insisted that the main stream of the book, my personal account of day-to-day life with the men in a Gurkha rifle company, remain in my own style as free as possible from editing. As they say at the Oscar awards: "Without my director, I would never have made it."

For the reconstruction of my year with the American Field Service (AFS) in North Africa and of our time at the Officers Training School in Belgaum, India, both Jupe Lewis and Bill Nichols, in Stamford and Manchester, Massachusetts, respectively, have helped immensely by digging into their diaries, letters, and memories. When I visited the AFS headquarters in New York, I was made welcome by Bill Orrick and Eleanora Golobis, who spent a morning researching the archives for me.

Over in the United Kingdom, Bob Findlay, whose ancestor was one of the Scots who founded the Irrawaddy Flotilla, the side-wheelers that plied the great river from Rangoon to Mandalay and upper Burma, has supplied me with enough background for another book. Down south of the border in England, Peter Myers and Peter Wickham, both now retired and both lifelong friends, have been generous with their readings and suggestions as the manuscript progressed.

David Quaid, historian for Merrill's Marauders, and a combat photographer with that hard-fighting group, provided me with enough guidance to do another book. Unfortunately there was just not room to cover the Marauders in depth in this one.

A word about the photographs. Quite contrary to regulations, I carried a small Leica throughout the war. For permission to reproduce theirs, I am indebted to Britain's Imperial War Museum, General Sir Walter Walker, and Pat Davis. Prints of the remaining photographs were graciously loaned by Pat Davis, Bill Dodd, Peter Myers, John Peters, and Toby Willcox. Their captions lack credits because no one remembers who pressed the camera button. My thanks, no less sincere, go to the unacknowledged snappers.

Above all I thank my wife, Peggy, for her encouragement and counsel during the long writing process, and for keeping me on a low-cholesterol regime to ensure that I am still around to enjoy the royalties.

Doing this book was both fun and hard work. It will have been worthwhile if it meets with the approval of you, the reader.

SCOTT GILMORE
Greenwich, Connecticut

Editor's Preface

With some exceptions, the names of countries are the names used at the time. Thus "Siam" rather than "Thailand," "Persia" rather than "Iran."

Unless stated otherwise, "India" in this book refers to the whole subcontinent as governed by the British at the outbreak of World War II in 1939. In the years of which we write, this is what the world understood "India" to mean. After the war, in 1947, as everyone knows, that unity was split into the republics of India and Pakistan. Pakistan itself was divided geographically into two sections, west and east, with the new India lying between and below. In 1971 East Pakistan seceded from West Pakistan and became Bangladesh.

The modern love of acronyms and abbreviations presents puzzles. In a military book they cannot be avoided. Most are explained when they first appear, but for ease of reference a list is printed on page xv. In tandem with this list, we have also compiled a short glossary.

In addition to the people thanked by Scott Gilmore, I want to express my own appreciation of help to the following:

To Colonel Henry Lowe, 3rd Gurkha Rifles, who read most of the early material (chapters 3 to 6), and from his unrivaled knowledge of the Indian Army and the Gurkhas gave me much useful information and suggested many improvements.

To Evan Thomas for his permission to reproduce a passage from *Ambulance to Africa;* to Bill Nichols for leave to quote from his February 5, 1994, letter to the author; to the American Field

Service for permission to print the verses from "An AFS Guide to the Levant"; and to J. M. Dent for the right to use the casualty figures, taken from from Louis Allen's book *Burma, the Longest War*.

To Mary Davis, my wife, who has read every word of the typescript, often in succeeding versions, and has saved Scott and me from perpetrating innumerable unclear paragraphs.

Others who have helped me with information or comment on select passages are Binia Macartney, Peter Myers, Bill Dodd, Peter Wickham, Brian Irving, Russell Fairgrieve, and Bob Findlay. My thanks to them.

PATRICK DAVIS
Sevenoaks, Kent

Glossary

ADS   Advanced dressing station
AFPFL   Anti-Fascist People's Freedom League
AFS   American Field Service
ALFSEA   Allied Land Forces South-East Asia
Aloo   Potato (Gurkhali)
Baklava   Middle-Eastern cake with alternating layers of pastry, honey, and nuts (from Turkish)
Bandobast   Organization, arrangements (Urdu)
Basha   Hut, often made of wood and grass
BBC   British Broadcasting Corporation
Bhai   Brother, friend (Gurkhali)
Bidi   Cheap cigarette (Urdu)
Bihishti   Water carrier (Urdu)
Bint   Woman, girl, daughter (Arabic)
BNA   Burmese National Army
BO   British officer
BRO   Battalion routine order
BSA   Birmingham Small Arms Company, British motorcycle manufacturer
Burka   Long, sacklike garment traditionally worn by Muslim women when in public places
CBE   Commander of the Order of the British Empire
CBI   China-Burma-India theater of operations
Chaung   Riverbed (Burmese)
CO   Commanding officer
CSM   Company sergeant major (British army)

Dashera   Major Gurkha festival in honor of Durga, the goddess of war. It takes place in late September or early October at the new moon and, when circumstances allow, will last over several days.

Dhobi   Washerman (Urdu)

Dhow   Small Arab sailing vessel

DSO   Distinguished Service Order (British decoration)

Durga   Hindu goddess of war

GHQ   General headquarters

Gimlet   Gin with Rose's lime juice, a favorite tipple of the British of both sexes in wartime India

GO   Gurkha officer

GR   Gurkha Rifles

GSO1   General staff officer, grade 1

Gurungkura   Language spoken by the Gurung tribe of Nepal

Gussal-khana   Bathroom (Urdu)

Ham   Licensed amateur radio operator

Havildar   Sergeant

HQ   Headquarters

ICS   Indian Civil Service

INA   Indian National Army, formed by the Japanese

IOM   Indian Order of Merit. Until 1911, when the Victoria Cross was opened to all ranks of the Indian Army, the IOM was the highest award for bravery in battle available to the army.

Jemadar   Viceroy's commissioned officer (Indian Army), in some ways close to a second lieutenant, but by no means an equivalent.

Jiff   Japanese-inspired fifth column

KCB   Knight Commander of Bath

Kiwis   New Zealanders

KOSB   King's Own Scottish Borderers, a British regiment

Lance naik   Indian Army equivalent of U.S. private first class and British lance corporal

L5   Small, single-engine, two-seater spotter plane

LMG   Light machine gun

LOC   Line of communication

Log   People (Urdu)

Longyi   Burmese sarong or loose lower garment

Machchhardani   Mosquito net (Urdu)
Magarkura   Language spoken by the Magar tribe of Nepal
Maidan   Plain, open space (Urdu)
MC   Military Cross, a British decoration for bravery in battle
MCO   Movement control officer
Mehtar, mihtar   Sweeper, latrine attendant (Urdu)
MP   Military police
MT   Mechanical transport
Munshi   Language teacher (Urdu)
NAAFI   Navy, Army, and Air Force Institute
Nach   Dance (Gurkhali)
Naik   Corporal
Nawab, nabob   Indian Muslim ruler or chief
NCAC   Northern Combat Area Command
Nimbu pani   Lemonade (Urdu)
Nizam   Title given to the reigning prince of Hyderabad
Nullah   Streambed (Indian)
Nun pani   Literally "salt water"; hence, the sea (Urdu)
NZ   New Zealand
OBE   Officer of the Most Excellent Order of the British Empire
OC   Officer commanding
OP   Observation post
OSS   Office of Strategic Services
OTS   Officer Training School
Panji   Sharpened bamboo stake used in booby traps
Poncheechaung   Burmese priest's house attached to a monastery
Poshteen   Warm skin coat with the fur worn inside
PT   Physical training
Pukka, pucka   Proper, genuine, true (Indian)
Punka, pankha   Large fan, usually made of cloth or palm leaf, suspended from the ceiling and made to swing by pulling a rope (Urdu)
RAC   Royal Armoured Corps
RAF   Royal Air Force
RAP   Regimental aid post
Raikura   Language spoken by the Rai tribe of Nepal
Rajah, raja   Indian Hindu ruler or chief
Rumble tumble   Scrambled eggs

Rupee Indian coin, fixed at 13 1/3 to the English pound throughout World War II (1 rupee equals 1 1/2 English shillings)

Sahib Form of respectful address like "sir," but also often placed after a man's name in conversation and in writing; for example, "Ask the Colonel Sahib" (Urdu/Arabic)

Sangar Small fort or defensive wall, usually on a hilltop and roughly made of local stones

Sathi Friend or companion (Urdu)

SEAC South-East Asia Command

Shikar Hunting (of all kinds)

Solar topee Pith helmet, a lightweight sun hat made from the pith of the shola plant and worn by most Westerners in India until the 1940s (topee, topi = "hat" [Urdu])

Souk Covered market (Arabic)

Subadar Viceroy's commissioned officer, Gurkha or Indian; in some ways close to a U.S. first lieutenant or British lieutenant, but not an equivalent

Subadar-Major The most senior viceroy's commissioned officer in a battalion; no British or U.S. equivalent

Syce Groom

TEWT Tactical exercise without troops

Tiffin Midday meal, lunch; origin uncertain

Tonga Two-wheeled light carriage usually drawn by a pony or horse

Topee See "solar topee"

USAAF United States Army Air Forces

VC Victoria Cross, Britain's highest decoration for gallantry in the face of the enemy; opened to all ranks of the Indian Army in 1911

VCO Viceroy's commissioned officer

VJ Day Victory over Japan Day

WAAF Women's Auxiliary Air Force (Great Britain)

Walla, wala An Urdu word added to a noun to indicate belonging to a group or category of persons; for example, "Gandhi-walla," a follower of Gandhi

WREN Women's Royal Naval Service

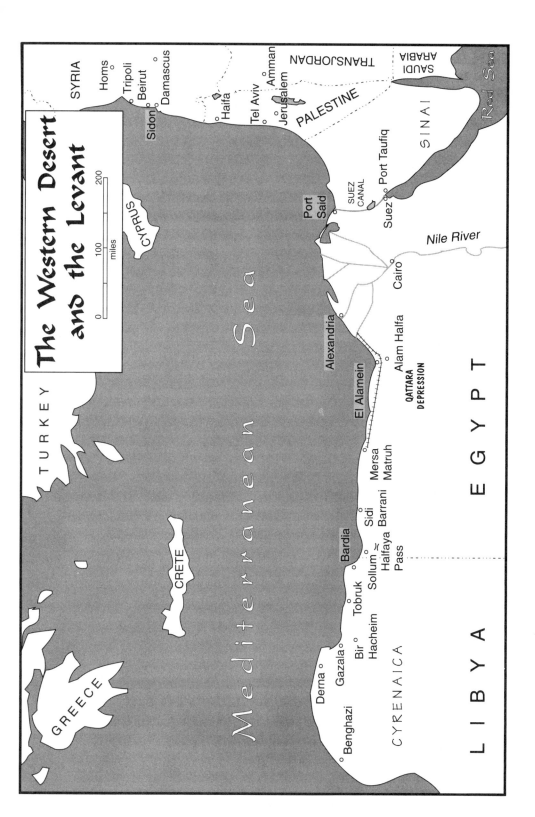

The Western Desert and the Levant

TURKEY

GREECE

CRETE

CYPRUS

SYRIA

Homs

Tripoli
Beirut
Damascus

Sidon

Haifa

Tel Aviv
Amman
Jerusalem

TRANSJORDAN

PALESTINE

SAUDI
ARABIA

SINAI

Red Sea

Port Taufiq
SUEZ
CANAL
Suez

Port
Said

Nile River

Cairo

Alexandria

Alam Halfa

El Alamein

QATTARA
DEPRESSION

EGYPT

Mersa
Matruh

Sidi
Barrani

Halfaya
Pass

Sollum

Bardia

Tobruk

Bir
Hacheim

Gazala

Derna

Benghazi

CYRENAICA

LIBYA

Mediterranean Sea

miles

0   100   200

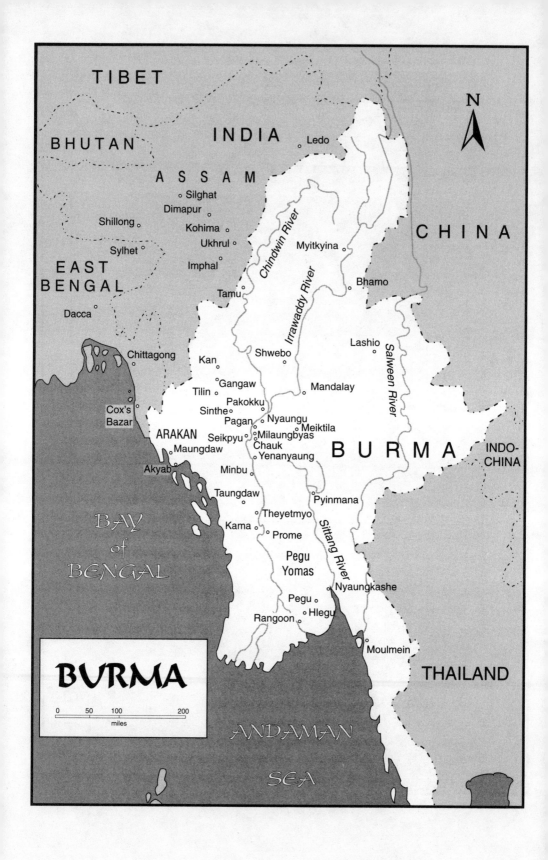

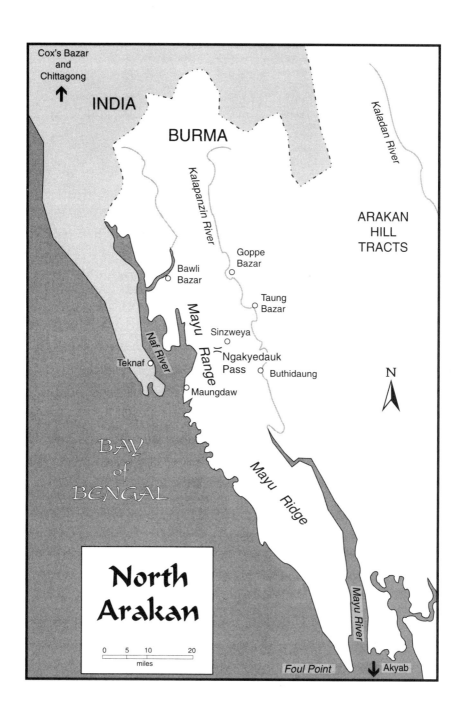

Cox's Bazar and Chittagong

INDIA

BURMA

Kaladan River

Kalapanzin River

ARAKAN HILL TRACTS

Goppe Bazar

Bawli Bazar

Taung Bazar

Mayu Range

Sinzweya

Ngakyedauk Pass

Buthidaung

N

Naf River

Teknaf

Maungdaw

BAY of BENGAL

Mayu Ridge

North Arakan

0 5 10   20
miles

Mayu River

Foul Point   Akyab

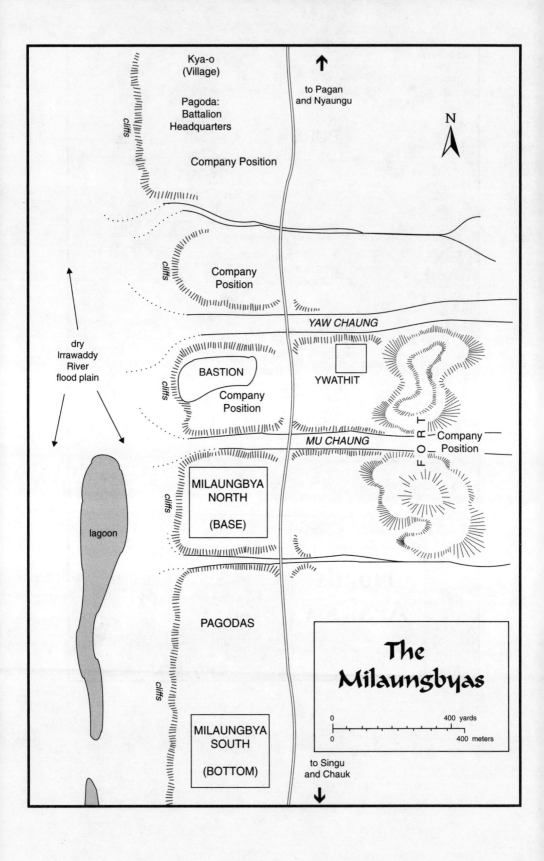

Kya-o
(Village)

Pagoda:
Battalion
Headquarters

Company Position

to Pagan
and Nyaungu

N

cliffs

Company
Position

cliffs

dry
Irrawaddy
River
flood plain

YAW CHAUNG

BASTION

YWATHIT

Company
Position

cliffs

MU CHAUNG

FORT

Company
Position

MILAUNGBYA
NORTH

(BASE)

cliffs

lagoon

PAGODAS

cliffs

MILAUNGBYA
SOUTH

(BOTTOM)

The
Milaungbyas

0   400 yards
0   400 meters

to Singu
and Chauk

A Connecticut Yankee in the 8th Gurkha Rifles

CHAPTER I

━━

A Call to Africa

I was footslogging down a track deep in powdery dust. Strung along the track with me were two young British lieutenants and a bunch of Gurkhas, doughty fighters from Nepal. On either side was bamboo forest. Ahead came the thud of artillery fire, not a continuous barrage but spasmodic bursts, as though the gunners must occasionally release pent-up tensions by firing off a shell or two. There was no other sign of war.

This was January 1944. World War II still had nearly two years to run. Place: the Arakan, Burma's most westerly province. Situation: Lieutenant Scott Gilmore was reporting as a junior officer replacement to a battalion of Gurkha infantry in action against the Japanese. I was one of the very few Americans to join Britain's elite Indian Army, and I was about to take my turn at battle in the jungle.

Decisions over the last three years, some arrived at lightly, some after tiresome brain cudgeling, had landed me at this point of no return. I might have been, I surely was, a little nervous. But I was content.

How had this come to be?

Like many Americans during the early years of that war, I read *The New York Times*'s accounts of defeat after defeat in France, listened to Edward R. Murrow's stirring broadcasts from London during the Battle of Britain and the Blitz, worried over the submarine war in the Atlantic, and wondered when we might become involved.

While not a starry-eyed altruist, by early 1941 I had begun to explore taking a leave of absence from the family business to participate directly.

I had already spent several years in our publishing company. It had been started by my maternal grandfather, William J. Johnston, shortly after arriving in New York. His forebears originated in Annandale in Scotland and had crossed to Ballycastle in Ireland several generations earlier. In 1872, still in his teens, he came to America and became a telegrapher. Early on, he invested $50 in a four-page fortnightly paper called *The Operator* that was distributed among telegraphers nationwide. By the fall of 1875 circulation had risen to 2,000 at $2.50 per year and he had bought out his partners for $250, payable in installments.

Western Union now resented his taking time from his scant leisure to contribute poetry, gossip and quips "to be read by impecunious young men with little buying power." Told to stop dabbling in this side venture, he resigned and dedicated all his time to the publication.

It became a magazine with technical articles on telephone and electrical subjects. One contributor was the inventor Thomas Alva Edison, himself a former telegrapher. By 1884 *The Operator* had become *The Electrical World*, and it remains an important publication today. During October 1886 it carried 161 pages of advertising. In 1899 my grandfather sold it to McGraw Publications, now McGraw-Hill, for $300,000.

That same year, dipping into his now modest fortune, he left his second wife—he had lost his first wife after the birth of her fourth child, my mother—and eight children comfortably installed in Greenwich, Connecticut, and went off on a six-month sabbatical to the Far East. This trip convinced him of the future in world trade. It led him to buy the *American Exporter*.

After a number of magazine ventures, at his death in 1904 my grandfather still owned the *American Exporter,* which had become a catalyst between manufacturers in the United States and importers abroad. It was then managed by two of my mother's brothers, Edwin and Franklin. They expanded the worldwide distribution of the magazine. In the boom twenties they published not only in English but also in French, Spanish, German, Portuguese and Italian. When I joined in the mid-thirties we were still struggling through the Depression but were beginning to increase advertising volume.

The uncles bent backward to avoid any show of nepotism toward me or my cousin Robert Johnston, also new to the business. With a starting salary of $14.50 per five-and-half-day week, it was some time before I would be trusted on the sales firing line. My first assignment was to work under Mr. Murphy, our circulation manager. He was an older gentleman with the habit of drifting off to his pet theory that the Americas had been first settled by Stone Age peoples crossing the Bering Strait to Alaska and gradually rubbernecking south to Tierra del Fuego.

When not listening to Mr. Murphy, Robert Johnston and I, along with several young ladies with linguistic abilities, combed commercial directories and a large inflow of letters from overseas to decide which firms seemed to be in a position to buy our advertisers' products—and might therefore be accepted as readers of the *American Exporter, El Exportador Americano,* or *L'Exporteur Americain.* Poring over directories from Oman, Angola, British East Africa, Peru and Guyana, to name only a few, not only contributed to my knowledge of geography but helped along my urge to travel.

As the training progressed I was sent via the Ward Steamship Company to Cuba and to Mexico to uncover new reader sources on the ground. In Havana I stayed at the old Plaza Hotel on the central square. I visited Sloppy Joe's, and drank frozen daiquiris at Hemingway's favorite restaurant, Floradita, where street guitarists seranaded the diners. In the late afternoon I was invited to play tennis at the Vedado Tennis Club and to swim off the Varadero Beach, near Matansas. Later, sailing through the Gulf of Mexico to Veracruz, I was the conservative fringe of a raucous three-day party enlivened by Larry Hart, who had written the music for that year's (1938) musical *I Married an Angel,* and the Dolly Sisters, musical comedy stars.

Then I joined our Foreign Service Department: four men, with secretaries, deputed to assist advertisers in locating distributors or agents in markets in any of the 120 countries covered by our magazines. As a part of this service I was given a highfalutin-sounding job—Manager, World Fair Visitors Department. We invited readers who were coming from abroad to the 1939 fair to make their headquarters with us. We sent out to advertisers a daily bulletin listing the visitors, their credentials, and their needs. This may sound like the American manufacturer was pretty helpless, but bear in mind that before passenger planes were prevalent, it might take a factory executive a year to visit all the potential markets in South America alone. A press pass to the fair went with the job, and the pass gained me entrance to such attractions as Esther Williams's water ballet *Aquacade.*

When the fair wound down in the fall of 1939, I was transferred to sales to learn from the senior salesman in New York, Gerard Kievenaar. He was a grand old Dutchman from Rotterdam, then in his eighties. In deference to his venerability, many of the advertisers came to him at our offices, where I could observe his sales technique. Few contracts involved an advertising agency. Instead the advertiser signed a simple contract form calling for a quarter, half or full page in each issue for the year and on until canceled. One manufacturer, almost within our grasp, pen poised over the contract, hesitated in order to ask "And what, Mr. Kievenaar, do you guarantee for this investment?" Kiev's reply: "The only guarantee we give is that you will receive a bill every month."

Soon the coaching was over. I was trusted to go off across the harbor to Brooklyn to start my selling career, salary upped to $160 per month. By the time I left for the war, I was paid in the order of $200, on which I occupied a decent two-room apartment on Thirty-seventh Street and Lexington Avenue at a monthly rental of $37.50. Outside on the street was parked my new Plymouth sedan, purchased for a shade over $600. My business card proclaimed that

I was indeed "Brooklyn Manager." As such it was my duty to drive my Plymouth in and out of the industrial areas over the East River from Manhattan and convince the factory owners to contract for advertising on the pages of our *American Exporter.*

I must have had some modest success because along the way I was promoted and given a second business card. This told the world that the presenter was the "St. Louis Manager." For some months before the war intervened I kept both responsibilities, several weeks in New York alternating with long swings west and south on trains like the Denver Zephyr and bumpy flights in unpressurized, rattling Ford trimotor planes. I got to places such as Memphis, Dallas, New Orleans, and Atlanta, wherever a likely smokestack suggested the possibility of an advertising schedule. My first circle through the southern cities in July and August with 100-degree-plus temperatures and no air-conditioning contributed to my readiness to go overseas.

These travels gave me the opportunity to add the telephone numbers of a few young ladies in the hinterland to the address book already containing New York listings of possible partners for an evening of dalliance in my third-floor walk-up.

On weekends I drove out to my parents' comfortable house in Greenwich, on Long Island Sound. My sister Leslie would be there. My young brother, Allen, was away at the Naval Academy at Annapolis launching his career as a submariner. There was tennis, and swimming in the sound off the rocks behind our house.

My mother was of a particularly gregarious nature and on any of these days would have invited a number of friends not so fortunate as to have saltwater swimming at their back door. Other close friends who had a standing invitation would also show up. As my father was one of a family of five and my mother one of eight close brothers and sisters, the house was always full. Some guests stayed for a few days, some for weeks.

Through 1939 and 1940, and probably for much of 1941, the majority of American citizens had no desire to enter the war. Joseph Kennedy, U.S. Ambassador to Britain, was dead against it, as was the right-wing organization America First. President Roosevelt, though sympathetic and prepared to help with munitions and supplies, was adamantly neutral in public. In secret he was prepared to sanction a good deal of more direct help. Then, in November 1940, he was reelected for a record third term. In a fireside chat broadcast over the radio at the end of December he said, "We must be the great arsenal of democracy," and began whipping up enthusiasm for our factories to supply tanks and guns and planes, first to Britain, and after June 1941, also to Russia.

Yet it still did not look as if the United States would become directly involved in the war. I wanted to help, but my tastes did not run toward a peacetime U.S. Army boot camp in Louisiana or rural Alabama. I saw myself in North Africa or England. I searched around.

My boss and uncle had connections with the navy and felt that my experience with our foreign trade magazine would qualify me for naval intelligence. The navy failed to agree. I interviewed with some success for the Canadian air force but lost enthusiasm when I was reminded how every earlier flight had resulted in my suffering from severe and humiliating air sickness.

Once I was flying over Roosevelt Field, Long Island, in a very small plane with a communications company manager and a Chinese general. We were there for a demonstration of ground-to-air communication equipment involved in a multimillion-dollar sale to the Chinese army. I completely destroyed both the demonstration and the atmosphere conducive to concluding the deal by convulsively spraying my lunch throughout the twisting, turning cabin. I did not spare the general's smart tunic.

It must have been at about this time in 1941 that one of our *American Exporter* translators, an Austrian by birth, told us that he was moving to the Windward Islands to write a novel. Sometime later it was discovered by the FBI that he had not selected his idyllic retreat to help the muse but as an observation post from which to spot shipping for Nazi submarines.

Then, in the fall of 1941, I had an opportunity to sail for North Africa with the first Middle East contingent of the American Field Service (AFS) sent to serve with the British in the desert. I had heard about this organization from two sisters in Greenwich. The AFS had been launched in August 1914 by a group of Americans living in Paris to care for French wounded. During the Battle of the Marne this group made numerous trips to the region northeast of

Paris. The first section sent to the British front, on November 7, 1914, contained ten ambulances donated by the Ford factory in Paris. It was attached to the Indian Army Corps, which had arrived in France only a couple of weeks earlier. By a small coincidence, forming part of that corps was the 2nd Battalion of my future regiment, the 8th Gurkha Rifles.

After the entry of the United States into the war in 1917 the AFS was officially militarized and its 1,220 donated ambulances were taken over by the American army, but it continued to serve the French. Over the course of that war 2,500 drivers signed on for a minimum of six months each. Between the wars the AFS was active in sponsoring fellowships at French universities.

Under the leadership of Stephen Galatti, Director General, the AFS had a section on its way to the front in France in May 1940. On the fall of France, the AFS continued to be active with the Free French. During the spring and summer of 1941 fund-raising and recruiting drives were being held in America in forty states and thirty-five universities.

Galatti looked like a chubby Napoleon. He was no chicken: during World War I he was number two to the then Director General, Colonel Andrew. He was an expert at fund-raising, not through mass advertising or on the radio, but by word of mouth via a network of contacts. Many members and friends of the AFS were well-heeled. All funding was voluntary.

We were a hundred assorted types in that first Middle East bunch, the majority keen youths fresh out of prestigious universities such as Harvard, Brown, Yale, California, Virginia, Princeton, and Dartmouth. A number of our drivers were the sons and nephews of World War I drivers. Despite my less than illustrious Greenwich High School education, I had passed the screening by Galatti at the AFS Headquarters on Beaver Street in New York.

Were we clean-cut idealists? Maybe some were. Perhaps many were to some degree. But I guess there was wanderlust, a yearning for excitement, a need to escape the constrictions of the tedious present, a wish to test oneself against the wider world beyond the horizon. Who knows? Motives are usually mixed. Our group of youngsters was leavened with a few overage adventurers, one or two incorrigible delinquents, a painter, one actor (David Wayne), two lawyers, and a professor. In the main they were a cast of characters who were stimulating and amusing to be with.

After a long, uncomfortable night train trip to Halifax, Nova Scotia, we boarded the U.S.S. *West Point* and sailed three days later, on November 10. Formerly the S.S. *America,* the *West Point* was a fast luxury liner converted to a troopship, and now was part of a large convoy taking British reinforcements by this roundabout route to General Auchinleck's forces in the Western Desert of North Africa.

Certainly the average American who had not seen such an armada spread out for miles over the ocean—passenger ships, freighters, and U.S. Navy fighting ships in awesome power—had no concept of the commitment that Roosevelt had made to the war effort that early on.

We know now that from the time the Germans gained control of the coastline of France, in the summer of 1940, the American government had operated, unannounced, a "short of war policy" that included protection of the shipping of Britain and her allies. It was in September 1941, three months before we sailed, that the American navy began direct convoy escort in the western Atlantic, and it was in October that the first American warships were torpedoed.

It was as well for our nerves that we were not aware of the ups and downs in the Battle of the Atlantic and knew nothing of the somber statistics of merchant ship sinkings through 1940 and 1941. It so happened that by late 1941 when we sailed the struggle had swayed briefly in favor of the Allies. The German U-boat packs and long-range Kondor bombers operating from the French Atlantic ports had been countered by fighters catapulted from the decks of merchant ships; by the quantity, quality, and training of the convoy escort vessels; and from mid-1941 by the speed and accuracy of the decoding of the messages to and from the German submarines (even though the Germans were simultaneously reading the British naval code). These developments for a time transformed the odds.

A month or two on, in January 1942, after Pearl Harbor and after America's war against Germany became official (December

11, 1941), there was another "happy period" for the U-boats. Heavy losses in the eastern North Atlantic forced a change of German strategy. Submarines were ordered into the Mediterranean and told to give attention to the west coast of Africa and to the huge convoys rounding the Cape. A small number were allocated to the Canadian and American eastern seaboard, which until then had been forbidden territory.

Unbelievably now, it was not until May that a blackout of the North American coast was ordered and the aids to navigation such as lighthouses and light beacons were doused, and in July that a coastal convoy system was instituted. The German submariners could not believe their fortune. There were rich pickings, nearly five hundred boats sunk in North American waters in the first six months of the year.

Had our convoy from Halifax sailed during January 1942 rather than November 1941, the dangers would have been powerfully expanded, both at the start of the voyage and when rounding the Cape.

For six weeks we slept sixteen to a fetid stateroom, portholes tight shut in the blackout. We stopped over at Trinidad on November 17 (no shore leave). In mid-Atlantic the British navy took over as convoy guardian. We got ashore at Cape Town. I remember enjoying a dance at a roadhouse outside the city with the young ladies of a welcoming committee, and being introduced to the new combination of steak and eggs with no thought of cholesterol.

At some point in the Indian Ocean the British battle cruiser *Repulse* passed close by, plowing and rolling through a heavy swell. Our troops lined the rail to cheer and were saluted in return. She was on her way to reinforce the British presence in the Far East against the looming menace of Japanese aggression.

Then, on December 8, came the startling news of Pearl Harbor. Suddenly the war was drawing closer.

The *West Point* changed destination to make toward India. The many thousands of troops on board would not now go to the desert but four thousand miles eastward to Singapore. They arrived there just in time to become prisoners of the Japanese. Fortunately this change did not apply to us AFS.

For the Japanese had made impressive progress in those first few days after their attack on Pearl Harbor. Their forces, which had landed in southern Thailand unopposed, now eliminated the weak British air defense and landed on the northeast coast of the Malay Peninsula. They began to move inexorably south. On December 10 carrier-borne bombers sank the *Repulse* and the battleship *Prince of Wales* with heavy loss of life. Only a few days had passed since we had cheered the *Repulse* on her way. The Japanese reached Penang on December 16 and Ipoh on December 26. In the Philippines, within three days they had destroyed American airpower and had begun landings on Luzon. The American garrisons at Shanghai and Tientsin on the China coast were taken. Bangkok, capital of Thailand (Siam) was occupied on December 9, and most of the rest of the country fell by the end of the month. They began landings in Sarawak and Brunei on December 16. On Christmas Day Hong Kong surrendered after two weeks of fierce fighting.

There was more, much more, to come. It was going to take many weary months to organize effective resistance.

So we sailed on to our various destinies. Mid–Indian Ocean the finals of the boxing championship took place. Boxers from the Sherwood Foresters, Beds and Herts, Cambridgeshires, gunners, signalers, and a few AFSers had competed in preliminary rounds earlier. Seas were calm, flying fish skipped along the gentle waves, the destroyer escorts sailed our flanks offering reassurance. The warm sun gave a healthy color to the five thousand troops who crowded every perch overlooking the ring that had been set out on the upper deck. The ship's captain and the brigadier commanding the troops were in the front row.

The hopes of the AFS rested on Bob Sullivan, a product of Boston and Ireland, matched in the heavyweight finals against CSM Southgate of the Kings Own Yorkshire Light Infantry. Sully's good friends Bill Nichols and Andy Geer were his seconds. Southgate was taller and longer of reach than Sully. His arms were covered with tattoos and he looked formidable. But if the Tommies had any doubts about the soft, effete Americans, these were soon dispelled when, after two rounds of all-out slugging, Sully dispatched the CSM. For that moment Sully was the center of all attention. Standing in the ring, his face slowly relaxed into a smile.

Sully, the big fearless Irishman, by then a U.S. marine, was killed in the landing at Saipan.

On the *West Point* reveille was at five-thirty. After that there was nothing more strenuous than three meals a day eaten standing at wooden shelves and listening to the "housey housey" numbers called over the loudspeakers and leaning on the rail to watch the water go by. "Housey housey" was Tommy language for bingo or lotto in the British army of that time.

Here is an extract from a diary kept by one of the AFS men: "We have wonderful weather, each day like the one before. Desultry reading, chess, looking at the sea, looking at the sky, talk (mostly foolish) . . . lectures on the British Army, lectures on first aid, poker. An hour before sunset portholes are shut. Smoking on deck a major offense. At 9pm all lights go out and portholes are opened. Stand-to bell at 5.30am. Hang around in life jacket until breakfast starts at 7am. To relieve the monotony a group of twenty-eight have signed on to work in different capacities with the ship's crew."[1]

Our AFS men and some tank corps and artillery units were off-loaded at Bombay in late December. While awaiting transport to Egypt we were installed in the transit camp at Deolali, high up on the Western Ghats and about a hundred miles inland. Here we were introduced to the life of the British army in India. Little had changed since Kipling's day: servants to polish the boots, fetch tea, and wash clothes even for the lowliest private. The barracks were constructed from woven matting on concrete floors. To celebrate the holiday season some of us favored a punch that was served at the hotel down the road and was made with buffalo milk and local whiskey.

During our weeks at Deolali (December 20, 1941, to January 26, 1942) the authorities made some attempt to keep us busy. We learned how to march, how and when to salute, something about first aid, and something of what goes on under the hood of a vehicle. Eventually space was found for us on an ancient P & O steamer, the *Talma.*

Once more we embarked for Suez. By comparison our accommodations on the *West Point* had been palatial. Now we were well belowdecks in what must have been a cargo hold. Each man was allotted a hammock, to be strung from the rafters. The only other furnishings were fixed tables and benches arranged underneath the hammock area.

A lucky few, chosen by lottery, were installed in two empty staterooms off the upper deck. Those of us not so lucky would sponge on our friends for a bath with running salt water. Meals were fetched from a distant galley perhaps better not investigated too closely. At breakfast oatmeal was lugged across the deck and down companionways in a large pail to be ladled in dollops onto our tin plates. For the main meal the lascar cooks concocted a sort of stew. None of the ingredients were readily indentifiable. Nor did this vary from day to day.

Alongside the living quarters, and not five feet away, visible through an opening to the engine room below, two enormous pistons, each with a twelve-foot arm fixed onto the gasping steam engine, rose and fell incessantly in a rhythm that in earlier days had turned side paddle wheels. The cages that had housed the paddles were still in place, but the driveshaft now led to the stern and a somewhat updated system of propulsion. Each thrust of the pistons was accompanied by a clang and followed by a hiss of escaping steam.

Engine heat and noise, body heat, the smell of oil and sweat— sleep was a rare prize in such quarters. The teak deck gained favor. Here it was cool. Lying on the deck one could marvel at the vastness of the universe as the star-filled sky swung slowly back and forth and the old ship rolled gently up the Red Sea to Egypt.

CHAPTER II

—

With the AFS in the Western Desert

We were met at Suez by Colonel Richmond and Major Benson, from AFS HQ, who had flown up from Cape Town to prepare for our arrival. From February 10 to 17 we were in tents southeast of Suez at El Tahag, the giant mobilization center for the Middle East. Tahag was a desolate, windswept encampment on the fringe of the desert.

Here we were issued our winter battledress, sixty-six Dodge four-wheel-drive ambulances, two lorries, and several motorcycles. Each ambulance was equipped with a sun compass mounted on the hood, sand tires, jerry cans for spare fuel and water, metal sand tracks five feet long and fourteen inches wide to go under the wheels if we got bogged in soft sand, and four stretchers, an upper and lower for each side of the back. The stretchers were removable and a bench could be dropped down as seating for the walking wounded. Any chrome on the ambulances, and as much glass as possible, was covered by a mixture of sand and oil to limit reflection that could be seen by prying eyes.

We were organized in two platoons of thirty-three ambulances, broken down into six sections of five ambulances each with three in reserve. There were roughly forty-five drivers in a platoon.

During that week at Tahag we received special training in map reading and desert navigation, neither easy in featureless sand or flat, stony desert. We heard lectures on what goes on underneath the vehicle's hood. With so much sand constantly blowing into all parts, vehicle maintenance, especially lubrication, was vital. A good deal of time was spent crawling under a Dodge with a grease gun. There was driving practice, on both ambulances and motorcycles. There were talks on the organization of the British army and on the medical setup from RAPs (regimental aid posts) to field hospitals.

There was not much to do in the evenings. We might wander over to a circus-size tent that housed the NAAFI (Navy, Army, and Air Force Institute) to throw darts and get to know the Tommies over fried eggs, chips, and tea.

When ready to move we were told that we would not be going straight to the fighting in the Western Desert (this term had come to mean any area west of Alexandria), but would spend some time with the Australians in the Levant, one platoon in Damascus (Syria) and mine at Tripoli, Lebanon (Map 1, page xix).

Both Syria and Lebanon had formed part of the Ottoman Turkish Empire until 1918. In 1920 they were placed under French mandate by the League of Nations. Against rising national-ist movements, the French remained in control into World War II. In both countries, when the Germans overran France in 1940, the French army—some 45,000 men, ninety tanks, and an air force of fighters and bombers—remained loyal to the new pro-Nazi Vichy government of France.

The British were nervous at having this considerable hostile force at the back door of their army fighting the Germans in North Africa. The Germans had just overrun Greece and Crete to the west. To the north Turkish neutrality was uncertain. Eastward a coup d'état by Rashid Ali in April had brought hostile leadership to power in Iraq and the revolt there had only just been quelled. Threats to the Suez Canal and the lines of communication to India, and to the vital oil supplies of the Middle East, pressed from all sides. Evidence that German planes were landing on Syrian airfields did not soothe worried brows.

It was to neutralize the French forces and to forestall the establishment of German air bases that the British fought a fierce little five-week war through June and July of 1941, a campaign that has been overshadowed by Hitler's invasion of Russia on June 22. A mongrel force of Australians, British, Free French, Indians, and Gurkhas was scraped together and in the circumstances did a creditable job. To look ahead, Allied troops withdrew from both Syria and Lebanon in 1946.

Driving north through the Sinai Desert and into what was then Palestine, I drew the assignment of riding one of the BSA motorcycles. At first this was a thrill. It became less of a pleasure after I had been thrown several times by running into small sand dunes drifted by the wind across the road. At a stopover in Haifa we were treated to a good meal, including an English trifle, by the volunteer ladies who ran the canteen (by our reckoning, mature ladies, strong on motherly solicitude, and no doubt married to local British functionaries). Then once more off north up the coast road through Sidon and Beirut to Tripoli. Here we spent a good many quiet weeks near a crumbling Crusader castle overlooking the sea.

During this static period in our military experience there were no battle casualties to deal with, only a few Aussies with VD to be driven to the hospital in Beirut. Broken Lebanese heads, from the scrapping over lorry loads of wheat being distributed in Tripoli's central square, were not our responsibility. The Aussies would tell us of the sweeps they were making through the hill villages to suppress interclan hostilities. Both we AFS and the Australians had little grasp of the fierce tribal and religious divisions, which were as explosive then as they proved to be later. There cannot have been many of those rough, cheerful customers from the sheep stations of the Outback whose fluency in Arabic extended much beyond *"Shuffti bint?"* ("Where are the girls?"). In my own case, it was not until twenty years later, in the 1960s, when my company opened an office in Beirut, that I began to get a grip on the myriad factions within the Muslim and Christian communities.

Contacts with the locals in Beirut were few. The occasional unveiled good-looking woman was usually in the company of one of the Free French officers who had landed a civilian job in the city.

I became friendly with the son of the editor of the leading Arabic newspaper, and he introduced me to a nightlife not open to the military. In a run-down theater a jam-packed audience, exhilarated by the belly dancers and by slugs of arrack—the local drink, similar to anisette and reported to deteriorate the brain—stomped on the floor and yelled encouragement to the grinding belly dancers, tossing coins on the stage. Tarbooshed spectators who emerged from the smoke in the pit to climb onto the stage, hoping to embrace the dancers, were roughly thrust back.

It made a sobering change to this side of Arabic nightlife to be invited with Jupe Lewis, a fellow AFS volunteer, to enjoy the hospitality of the genteel missionary couple who lived in a modest stone house in a village by the sea near Tripoli. We stayed for supper and conversation, which included some of the history of the Crusader castle on the heights above our camp. Winter in Lebanon turned out to be often cold and wet. It was too cold for swimming in the sea. On the occasional warm, sunny day we wandered among the ruins of that castle and imagined how the fearless Saracens might have assaulted the now crumbling walls.

From Beirut sometimes we took the roundabout route back to Tripoli via Damascus to visit its huge covered souk, then up to Palmyra and back via Homs. One jaunt digressed as far as Aleppo.

A souk is a permanent marketplace, a dense agglomeration of shops and stalls. Souks exist in every Middle Eastern city. Souk Hamidieh in Damascus was one of the oldest and most interesting of these forerunners of today's shopping mall, a labyrinth of cobbled alleys under a vaulted corrugated iron roof. Throughout the day the hawkers and tenacious merchants would hope to entice the crowds with exotic descriptions of their wares. Lively bargaining was a satisfaction for both sides. Shoes, spices, silks, inlay work, jewelry, pottery, carpets, damasks, brocades—all the necessities and the luxuries of life were on display. At one end of the souk the roof gave way to two huge Corinthian columns, remains of the Roman temple of Jupiter.

The shoppers were a microcosm of the Levant. There were peasant women with black veils and full-length dresses (when the veils parted one could see foreheads circled with gold coins), country men in dark blue pantaloons, Turks in tarbooshes, Bedouin from the desert in flowing white, Iraqis in brown cloaks, and a sprinkling of Druse from their mountain villages. Druse women covered their hair with a gauzy white veil much like a medieval wimple; their long dresses were girdled at the waist and overlaid by a loose jacket. Though many of the Druse have straw-colored hair and blue eyes, geneticists do not accept that their sect originated with the lust of the Crusaders.

Our serious purpose in strolling the souk the first time was to negotiate the purchase of a Primus stove. Those compact cookers were simply round containers for petrol, with a hand-operated pump fitted to one side with which to create pressure in the container. The gaseous mixture then fed into a copper tube and out through a pinhole beneath a round frame on which the cooking pot, or billycan, sat. In the treeless desert, and lacking a supply of the camel dung used for fuel by the Bedouin, a genuine Primus from Sweden or a knockoff model from India was carried by almost every vehicle as an essential for brewing tea. In default of this luxury, petrol mixed with sand could be made to burn adequately in a pierced can.

Considering our low pay, the stud poker stakes of up to five dollars a card were high. The most avid players were the Californians. Losers were able to prop up their finances by cabling the folks at home.

One indulgence was the honey-sweet pastry served along with thick Turkish coffee in the cafés of the neighborhood. Jerry Maloney, a diabetic with a craving for sweets, carried a sizable box of baklava with him at all times. After leaving the AFS Jerry was torpedoed in the Mediterranean and suffered the double torture of sharing a lifeboat with an ex-driver with whom he was on unfriendly terms and of doing this without his favorite pastry.

Another delicacy was lemon meringue pie of a very superior flavor that was available at a certain roadside stop run by an American-Lebanese woman returned from Columbus, Ohio.

Among the cedars at the end of a twisting road in the mountains, we tried out the local skiing. So late in the spring the snow was far too soggy to compare to the snow in New England, but we did enjoy showing off our Arlberg technique to a couple of girls from Baku. Their husbands watched complacently from the hotel terrace.

Two of the AFS delinquents, soon shipped back home, were found to be selling tires to illicit traders when not smuggling hashish into Palestine or driving loads of prostitutes down the road to Tel Aviv.

Here is a poem that appeared in an AFS newsletter[1]:

AN AFS GUIDE TO THE LEVANT

Damascus has some swords and silk
And substitutes for Liebfraumilch.

Aleppo boasts a citadel
And missionaries, as well.

Near Merj Ayoun there is a castle
And quite a lot of wassail.

Sometimes we go to old Beirut
To quench the passions of our youth.

The gate receipts at Baalbek's ruins
Are somewhat less than the Boston Bruins.

Palmyra has a bath of stone
But Queen Zenobia has gone.

In Raqqa there are scorpions—
The big ones and the bigger ones.

Ras Baalbek is a hopeless spot;
To go there I would rather not.

There's a lot of love in Tripoli
But almost none of it is free.

A little more of Syria
Will give me hysteria.

In April an incoming contingent from the States took over our vehicles and our assignments in Lebanon and Syria. We were transported back to Egypt and El Tahag to be refitted for the desert.

There was only one surfaced road from Alexandria to Tobruk. It ran roughly parallel to the coast, was a single lane, and was heavily used around the clock. It was, of course, a magnet for enemy bombers and fighters. Driving it at night without lights included the hazard of wandering off the road and onto one of the many unmarked mines lying beneath the sand. As successive campaigns rolled back and forth across the land, the population of mines had blossomed. Sometimes there were pockets of loose sand deep enough to stop the best four-wheel-drive or tracked vehicle. Safe routes were marked by empty fuel drums, difficult to spot when the sand was blowing. Intersections were identified by nostalgia names such as Picadilly, Knightsbridge, and Oxford Circus. Often they were discernible from the rest of the desert only by keeping a sharp eye for the denser tread marks.

The desert here was not all billowing sand dunes as depicted by Hollywood. There were miles of rolling flatness cut by an occasional wadi and in places surfaced with hard stones, sometimes with boulders. The coastal escarpment, and low ridges and minor undulations, rose out of the plain and became the coveted objectives of both sides, with names that became familiar worldwide—Ruweisat Ridge, Halfaya Pass, and many more. Vegetation? Where there was any, it was usually camel scrub.

Wind and water shaped our lives. There was too little water, too much wind. The wind was almost constant, rising to frequent and sudden sandstorms that cut visibility to a few feet. Desert navigation with map, milometer, prismatic compass, good memory, and instinct became a much-prized skill.

With almost no civilians to get hurt, this worthless land was the most humane location over which to conduct battles.

The war had come to North and East Africa on June 10, 1940, during the German blitzkrieg campaign across France and the Low Countries, when Italy declared war on Britain and France. "The hand that held the dagger," said President Roosevelt in his broadcast to the Americans that day, "has struck it into the back of its neighbor." Italy ruled Eritrea and the recently conquered Abyssinia (Ethiopia). British-controlled territory bordered these lands to the northeast (British Somaliland), to the south (Kenya and Uganda), and to the west (Anglo-Egyptian Sudan). The Italians were also sovereign in Libya, owning 600 miles of common border with Egypt. Egypt was nominally independent, but British troops had been in the country continuously since 1882, chiefly to safeguard the Suez Canal. From Libya an enterprising army was well within striking distance (450 miles) of the canal, Britain's lifeline to India and to the vital oil of the Middle East.

There had been immediate small-scale actions, border raids, by the two British armored brigades on the Libyan frontier. In September 1940 Italian forces had invaded Egypt. They had occupied a strip of coast from Sollum to Sidi Barrani, and showed no inclination to go farther. On December 9 the British armor and the 4th Indian Division, joined later by an Australian division, attacked the Italians—two divisions against seven—and defeated them. They advanced across the whole of Cyrenaica to the Tripolitanian border at El Agheila, and captured 130,000 prisoners for the loss in killed, wounded, and missing of under 2,000.

Then, in March 1941, the experienced Australians and the recently arrived 2nd New Zealand Division, plus much of the slender air resources and admin backup, were transferred to Greece, where a German invasion was imminent. These forces were virtually destroyed during April in Greece and then in Crete during late May. At the same time Hitler had sent General Erwin Rommel to North Africa (he landed on February 12) with a smallish force of Germans to bolster the Italians.

Rommel soon took the offensive with the result that by mid-April he was back on the Egyptian frontier and beyond. The substantial difference was that the port of Tobruk was held by the 8th Army and became a major irritation eighty miles behind his front line.

Cyrenaica, that great bulge of territory from the Egyptian frontier to the Gulf of Sirte, became familiar to tens of thousands of soldiers over the next three years. The Mediterranean provided a northern constraint. To the south the waterless wastes of the Libyan desert precluded all but long-range patrol penetration.

Several abortive offensives throughout the summer failed to dislodge Rommel, who was reinforced by three German divisions and more Italians. It was not until mid-November 1941, while I was sailing across the Atlantic, that the new British commander in chief in the Middle East, General Auchinleck, felt strong enough to launch another major offensive, Operation Crusader. After very tough fighting this campaign succeeded in relieving Tobruk and in driving the Axis army back again to the Tripolitanian frontier. However, it was lack of supplies and reinforcements as much as the British attacks that forced Rommel to retreat. That autumn a large percentage of his supply ships were being torpedoed or bombed.

So for the third time the two armies had traveled and fought across the entire width of Cyrenaica. This process had come to be called the Benghasi Handicap. Tanks and lorries that survived the battles became worn out. So did some of the soldiers.

By comparison with the enormous armies locked in battle across the frozen wastes of Russia that winter, the numbers involved in North Africa were small. Nevertheless, here was the only land area where the free Western powers were fighting the Germans, for in May the campaigns in Ethiopia and Eritrea had ended with Haile Selassie's victorious reentry into his capital, Addis Ababa. The disasters and triumphs of the desert war held deep symbolic importance for the Allies, especially for the British. The strategic prize—control of Egypt and the Suez Canal—was far from symbolic.

Rommel did not rest in defense for long. Once more outside events controlled local fortunes. During the winter of 1941–1942 the British naval and air forces lost control of the mid-Mediterranean. Thus at the turn of the year several convoys reached Tripoli with their supplies for the Germans unscathed. Over the same period reinforcements intended for Auchinleck were diverted to India, Burma, and Malaya.

My own troopship, full of men expecting to fight in the desert, ended up in Singapore. The 17th Indian Division in India, earmarked for the Middle East, was sent to Burma. An armored brigade was actually withdrawn from the desert and sailed for Rangoon. It was a replay of the situation a year earlier, when troops meant for the desert had been sent to Greece.

The formations that remained were either new and inexperienced or worn out, thin in numbers, and inadequately equipped. And it was now the British whose lines of communication were overstretched.

Rommel attacked on January 21 and rapidly regained territory up to Gazala. He was held in a forty-mile line west of Tobruk that arced from the oasis of Bir Hacheim in the southern desert to Gazala on the coast. The Gazala line was a series of "boxes," fortified areas linked and surrounded by minefields. Here, and as far back as Tobruk, the British, Aussies, South Africans, Indians, Gurkhas, Free French, New Zealanders, Poles, and many others—infantry, armor, engineers, and artillery—were concentrating for their own attack. The armor had some newly arrived American Grant tanks, more powerful than the older British Valentines and Crusaders and a match for the tanks on the German side.

It was at this point that Scott Gilmore joined the pageant. We left the reinforcement center at Tahag in convoy on May 17 and three days later arrived at a campsite at Pilistrino, on a ridge five miles southwest of Tobruk. Tobruk was the first port of any size on the Mediterranean coast traveling west from Alexandria. As was already noted, it had become well-known for a gallant defense the year before as the German and Italian forces swept past the garrison and besieged it for nine months. The town was now a battered cluster of roofless and ruined white buildings. The harbor was cluttered with masts and stacks of sunken vessels rising above a sparkling sea. Around us the hard desert plain was strewn with the debris of earlier battles: burned-out lorries, destroyed guns, the rusting hulks of tanks. Pilistrino was well within the defensive arc of Tobruk's fortifications; in places the earth was a warren of abandoned diggings rapidly filling with drifting sand.

The camp was near some South African artillery—not the most muted of neighbors—and my section was assigned to a South African brigade in the north of the defensive line. We had an ambulance with each of the three battalion regimental aid posts

(RAPs). An RAP consisted of a lorry, one doctor, a few order-lies/stretcher bearers, and an AFS ambulance to evacuate casualties back to an advanced dressing station (ADS). Other ambulances ran the seriously wounded farther back to a main dressing station.

I must add that in the spring of 1942 I knew little of the history just outlined. Most soldiers operate within a fog of ignorance much of the time. Of course, we heard individual anecdotes of what had happened to people in the recent past. We certainly knew of General Rommel, our opposing commander. Probably we noncombatants picked up some of the apparently general dissatisfaction with the commanders on our side, and with the weapons and equipment our troops were given. But we were not deeply affected by such matters. It was enough to have a job to do and to be trying to do it efficiently.

The first days were relatively quiet, so long as you could ignore the constant traffic of supply vehicles through the swirling dust, sporadic booms from the twenty-five-pounders, and occasional attention from the enemy's air force. One day a flight of Stukas came diving low with sirens screeching and unloaded their bombs, which were followed by machine gun strafing. Some nights the sky was as spectacular as a Fourth of July celebration: searchlights sought out the German bombers over Tobruk and ack-ack guns showered the heavens with their bright explosions; parachute flares like sinking moons unveiled us all with impartial brilliance; the intersecting light paths of tracer bullets shot briefly out of nowhere and arced into the void.

Spring was the time for the oven-hot khamsin winds to blow out of the Sahara, and we soon got used to a life seasoned by sand. Food was ladled into our mess tins by the British army cooks assigned to us. Swirling clouds of sand flavored the boiled tinned bacon and hard biscuits in the morning and the bully beef and hard biscuits at midday. Sometimes there was tinned jam and butter. These delicacies were eaten squatting on the ground.

One change from this diet came when the cook announced that, from God knows where, a shipment of leeks had arrived. This vegetable was unknown to most of us Americans, but apparently it was highly esteemed by the Tommies. The coveted treat unique to

British cookery turned out to be less than delicious. Dumped into the mess tin was a pallid, flavorless, stringy, watery mess shot through with tooth-grinding, abrasive grit.

We were not left in relative peace for long. It is known now that the British advance was planned for June. It was a slow business building up supplies over what had become very lengthy lines of communication. Almost everything from replacement pullovers to sacks of flour to clips of bullets to Grant tanks had to sail from Britain or the United States across the Atlantic (where so many ships were torpedoed), around the Cape of Good Hope, up the east coast of Africa, and over the Red Sea to Suez; or it came from India across the Indian Ocean. Either way, it must then be carried by truck over hundreds of miles of desert road. Water and petrol were always short, as were the lorries that carried them. The administrative burden of organizing these extraordinary lines of communication must have been a nightmare.

So what happened? German General Erwin Rommel (promoted to field marshal June 22) struck first. His lines of communication were long enough (from Germany and Italy across the Mediterranean to Tunisia and Libya) but were not comparable with ours. On May 26 his Afrika Korps attacked at night and during a sandstorm. In a monumental two-day battle outside Gazala he destroyed the bulk of the British armor. The new Grants had done well, but their tactical distribution was poor and there were not enough of them to replace those knocked out or broken down.

It was a busy time for us ambulance drivers. Naturally we knew little of the overall strategic and tactical situation as it changed dramatically from hour to hour. Did anybody? We had to ignore the uncertainties of such a fluid war and forget the rumors.

There were many wounded—carried on stretchers, hobbling in on foot—to be packed into our ambulances and driven back to the ADS tents for amputations, transfusions, and complex operations tackled by tired doctors at short notice and under great pressure. Men lay on the bare desert covered with bloodstained blankets while waiting their turn for the surgeon. The sand blew around and over them, the flies gathered. Some of those able to talk were surprisingly cheerful: "Glad to be out of it, mate." But in the Western Desert the fog of war was always thick: panzers might appear from any point of the compass at any time, and you were never "out of it" until you were back in Cairo.

To be cut off and captured was a possibility that lay at the back of the mind as a constant threat. This had happened to many thousands of others on both sides. Yet somehow one believed it would not happen to oneself. Anyway, we were too fully occupied and preoccupied to become obsessed with shadows.

Farthest inland, the Free French in the Bir Hacheim box were pounded day and night from the ground and from the air. After an epic defense, the survivors broke out at night. At Bir Hacheim we had our first AFS casualties. The twelve ambulances with the French were destroyed; two drivers were killed, two were wounded, and two were taken prisoner.

The fall of Bir Hacheim (on June 12) opened the way for the destruction of the remaining boxes and the armored reserves. A detailed account of these battles is not to be a part of this book, but the rout that followed became known as the Gazala Gallop, and we AFS galloped with the rest. Lorry loads of troops, tanks and tank carriers, cook wagons, ambulances, signals trucks, field artillery, and Bren light machine gun carriers all bounced hugger-mugger down the coast road and in clouds of dust over the scrabble tracks inland. I don't think there was panic, or not much; just a determination not to be caught in whatever traps the agile Germans might be laying. Tobruk fell on June 21, and with it were captured many of the South Africans.

Using fuel from Tobruk, Rommel advanced across the Egyptian frontier and beyond to Mersa Matruh. We AFS were reassigned to the 2nd New Zealand Division. The Kiwis got embroiled in a series of rearguard actions to slow Rommel's advance, and we with them. They suffered considerable casualties.

I do not remember feeling much in danger during this long retreat; just excitement and some confusion. There was one night with the New Zealand 5th Brigade when we drove until the early hours and then stopped to form a well-dispersed laager in the middle of empty desert for some much-needed sleep. Joe Gaynor and I were no sooner unconscious beside our two ambulances than there came a loud voice out of the dark: "Stand by for ground attack." This was not a command I had previously encountered. It brought visions of a bayonet charge out of the gloom, and I was suddenly very awake. Lying prone on the sand, peering into the starlit night with no trench, no weapons, and no idea from which direction the attack might come, left Joe and me with a strong feeling of helplessness.

Fortunately the alarm proved false. Perhaps a German column had passed us by in the dark. As dawn broke we brewed up in a hurry and again headed east. Over toward the distant coast we could see other clouds of dust that we hoped were rising from similar convoys rushing toward El Alamein. One could never be entirely sure that such clouds were formed of British dust.

During this time there were even periods of tranquillity. One driver, Hod Gilmore (no relation), carried his violin with him and on more than one evening played beautifully for all within earshot. My friend Cliff Saber, an artist of talent, had time to sketch caricatures of the troops and of us drivers. His other talent was imitating the sound of a muted trumpet by puffing up his cheeks and blowing out of one side of his closed mouth. That is how battles are won.

By early July the battered and depleted army was back at El Alamein, only sixty miles from Alexandria. Auchinleck had sacked General Ritchie and had taken over direct command. At El Alamein it was possible to build up a defensive position across the forty miles from the Mediterranean to the impassable wastes of the Qattara Depression. Here in early July, Auchinleck himself fought the successful defensive battle known as First Alamein, which was a tough one for the Kiwis. And here Rommel ran out of steam. With only fifty-five panzer tanks operational in his German formations and with even fewer Italian runners, short of infantry, with his lines of communication now stretched over hundreds of miles of desert, low on fuel and almost every other commodity of war, and from the sheer fatigue of his surviving men, he was forced to halt.

He had come within a whisker of taking Egypt and the Suez Canal. In Cairo documents were burned in the British embassy, HQ civilians headed for Palestine, and the shoe boys began to polish up their German. There was a run on Barclay's Bank. We heard there was even a plan to split the 8th Army in two, one half to Palestine, the other up the Nile.

Of the Allied forces at Gazala in late May, seventy thousand had been lost (the majority prisoners), and there had been a punishing loss of tanks, artillery, transport, and all the supplies of war. It is remarkable that the morale of the men in the 8th Army did not deteriorate to the point of collapse. The historian Barrie Pitt attributes this in part to anger: "They were not in any way angry at their opponents—to whom in fact they gave little thought—but they were furious at those who had sent them into battle with what they believed were inferior weapons, with what they knew to be inferior training and techniques—and, most important of all, under leaders who quite obviously were incapable of discharging their responsibilities."[2]

And from the same source: "The men knew that they were as tough physically as their opponents; they believed (rightly) that their adaptation to desert conditions was better than that of the Germans . . . and they knew that their own native intelligence and shrewdness was enough to withstand enemy onslaught, if they were not shackled by impracticable precepts imposed from above. And this they had seen happening at every turn of the battle."[3]

I read now that there were other cracks in the unity of the Allied force. There grew to be a bitter contempt for the armor, felt by the infantry, that was almost crippling to the prosecution of battle. It was a contempt based upon some searing experiences. This was aggravated by the fact that the armored divisions were British, while much of the infantry was Australian, New Zealand, South African, and Indian. The Aussies and New Zealanders tended to decry most British troops, infantry, and armor.

I was not fully aware of these mutual hostilities, though one could not escape some knowledge. We American AFS, being few and noncombatant, and being volunteers with a job that was appreciated by all, escaped lightly. Our relations with the Australians and New Zealanders were warm.

Through these weeks of retreat and during the long period from July through to October of regrouping, reinforcement, and retraining on the El Alamein positions, during which two major battles were fought and minor activity was continuous, I was mostly with the Kiwis. During First Alamein I do recall feeling sorry for some newly arrived white-skinned British Tommies, huddled in trenches with their wool blankets propped over them to give some shade from the furnace heat of the desert sun in July. But although we moved with and around many units, making friends in the 51st Highland Division, the 50th Northumbrian, and the 44th Home Counties—as well as the 7th Armoured, the veterans of the desert—it was the down-to-earth Kiwis and their Maori battalion from far-off New Zealand whom I got to know best and admired most.

Much of the fighting and patrolling was at night. Time and again the men went out on night raids and in the morning our ambulances were busy carrying back the wounded. Bill Nichols and Bob Sullivan (the champion boxer on our voyage) accompanied a reconnaissance patrol out for a prisoner and for information on enemy dispositions. All were armed except for Bill, who carried a medical knapsack. Sully had a tommy gun. He was a fire-eater. In his ambulance, which he shared with Bill, there was the tommy gun, a .303 rifle, a Beretta pistol, and half a dozen hand grenades—not a good advertisement for the Geneva Convention.

Bill Nichols wrote recently:

As I recall there were about twelve of us led by a lieutenant. We left at 11pm. There was no moon; the tricky part was going through the minefields—first ours, then theirs—walking in two files in the steps of the leaders, the Lieutenant and a Staff Sergeant. Then there was a long lonely wait sitting in no-man's-land while two German-speaking soldiers and the Lieutenant and Sully crawled forward as close to the German lines as they could.

Mission accomplished (without a prisoner), we headed back about 2am. I remember that the moon was coming up as we returned through the minefields. One felt naked and vulnerable for those few minutes.

My last memory was of us all—except Sully, who did not smoke—lying under a blanket, heads toward the centre, feet on the outside, smoking those ghastly "V" cigarettes we received each week.

This was not Sully's first patrol nor was it his last. For me it was both. He was still fuming the next

morning as he pulled himself out of his slit trench because the Lieutenant had not let him shoot the German soldiers he had in his sights.[4]

The Kiwis would speak of fishing the streams on their islands
and of their families back home. We watched their rugby games behind the lines. In matches against the Aussies it was a shock to notice that the ruddy, well-built twenty-year-olds of both teams
removed false teeth before the game. Dentistry in the Antipodes
had yet to reach the level of that in the United States. I admired the
brigade padre, a tall, smiling, youngish man whose mission it was
to counsel and cheer all who might be suffering anguish, fear, or
homesickness. He walked around the positions with little thought
of personal danger.

There were times when the battlefront was quiet and leave became available to visit Cairo and Alexandria. In Alexandria I became friendly with a group of rich young people, mostly Greek,
who seemed to live a jet-set life. They could have been characters in
Lawrence Durrell's *The Alexandria Quartet,* that rich novel of
Egyptian life so popular in the 1950s. These people had lavish
apartments, endless funds, and time to enjoy the best foods and
wines. The contrast with the dirt and teeming poverty of the
streets, and with the austere discomforts and dangers of the desert
war, was abrupt.

In Cairo, Groppi's was the equivalent of the Café Dome in
Paris or the Automat in New York, a place to idle over coffee and a
pastry, to wait for a friend, or just to sit and observe people and life
in the big city. It was spacious and airy, a hubbub of waiters and the
clattering of cups.

Later the scene might be moved to Shepheard's Hotel, either
to the Long Bar or to the terrace overlooking the sidewalk. Here
was a place to gossip, read the news, drink seriously, or speculate
on likely spies. Shepheard's was restricted to officers, but the AFS
paid little attention to such limitations. Upstairs, Joe Gaynor, one
of our bons vivants, had booked a suite and might be entertaining
up to fifteen casual friends with drinks and a procession of waiters
bearing plates of shrimp. Loans to Joe to subsidize his largess were
always promptly repaid after a cable to his father.

I have wondered how we AFS appeared to the rest of the army. Officers probably recognized the intellectual status of our average member, but the British at least may have been puzzled, perhaps shocked, by our failure, despite efforts from our leaders, to acquire a serious discipline and a passable dress code. The Tommies may have resented the fact that we ragtag Americans made ourselves at home in places denied to them by the class distinctions of their military hierarchy. Out of battle there were separate messes for officers, sergeants, and corporals, and in the fleshpot cities many of the amenities were out of bounds to "other ranks." I never heard a Tommy complain. But the 8th Army was a great medley of race and language. It included troops such as the anarchic Aussies (who might well greet an officer with a "Good on yer, mate sir") and the ebullient Free French, and Britain's own Northumberland Fusiliers ("hard, uncompromising men" who "obeyed their own officers but treated anyone else in authority with contempt"[5]), as well as the most tightly stratified Guards regiments. So a handful of free and easy gringo ambulance drivers was never likely to cause an international incident.

My sister Leslie had attended the Alliance Française in Paris with René Harari, now a young lawyer in Cairo. On such a slight link he was generous enough to invite Jupe and me to a birthday party for his younger sister. This was in the family home in Heliopolis, an upscale suburb. The girls, fourteen and fifteen, were all from the same French school, quite sheltered and somewhat at a loss for small talk with a couple of ancient Americans.

Also in Cairo I introduced myself to the owner of the Westinghouse distributorship, a reader of *American Exporter*. He had us for lunch and tea with his wife and several children. The meals were served on a porch underneath a vine-covered trellis overlooking the city.

Such was our social life in the midst of war, made possible only because Rommel had been so successful in bundling us back eastward close to the Nile. Looking back, I must have been very pushy, not loath to use the weakest excuse to introduce myself.

For most of September a small group of us was back at Tahag helping to train new arrivals from the States. We relative veterans were supposed to pass on our experience of the desert. And we really did attempt to instill some discipline into what so far had been a particularly spirited collection of individuals.

One day at Tahag a smooth-faced young British lieutenant marched his platoon of Cypriot soldiers into our area to remind us that we had promised to instruct his men in the art of baseball. The Empire had not yet shrunk. The British forces still included many (to me) exotic peoples: Singhalese, Mauritians, Sudanese, Indians, Fijians, and these Cypriots. To teach baseball to men brought up on kicking a ball was difficult. To transmit the complications of the game to men whose home-base language was Greek or Turkish proved hopeless. We compromised: we made lesson one the art of throwing and catching. When the experiment was over, they marched back to their camp in obvious relief.

On return to the front, Bill Nichols and I were put in charge of sections. By now sand in our food was not the main discomfort. It was the friendly flies: flies by the billion as soon as the sun rose, flies swarming into every orifice, clouds of flies settling on the food before one could whisk furiously with the hand not occupied in the eating process.

On shorter lulls within reach of the sea, it was possible to trudge through the deep sand of the dunes for a cleansing swim. On one such outing we encountered a lone Arab fussing over a tangle of netting mixed up in the gorselike shrubs on the dunes. He was setting a trap for the birds migrating south from Europe's winter. Exhausted after their flight over the Mediterranean, the birds sought shelter in the first bit of greenery—only to find themselves trapped. They would end on the table of some Alexandrian pasha.

We seldom saw the nomadic Arabs. No doubt they gave the battle zone a wide berth. Occasionally we encountered a small band making across the desolate landscape. One such family consisted of a father, older children, and wife on foot; an aged parent and some chickens riding a donkey; and a camel carrying the family's possessions, including a black goat-hair tent. We bartered with them for a few fresh eggs as a change from the tasteless powdered egg in the British rations. When the winter rains fell along the coast we saw families like this set up tents and plant small plots of wheat, miraculously soon to sprout.

One day we stopped at the side of the track to brew tea on our

Primus, the stove bought so many months back in the Damascus souk. Near us was a lorry with its hood up. We could not have failed to observe that the British Tommy customarily used an old English substitute for *copulation* to express disgust. But when this driver, perhaps from Liverpool, said "Fookin' fooker's fooked," that was the first time we had heard a complete sentence constructed from the "f" word.

Often petrol was less scarce than water. Petrol was more effective for washing the sweat out of a shirt. Petrol and sand mixed and heaped over a rare issue of tinned beer cooled the beer in no time.

Once I was dozing in the midday heat under the shade of an ambulance when a German Stuka began to take an interest in our patch of desert. Like a hawk selecting its victim, the plane circled the targets below—vehicles, guns, dumps, men. I jumped into my personal, formfitting slit trench. Suddenly the plane wheeled and dived. Its wings glinted in the sun; the unnerving screech grew rapidly louder until it seemed to fill the world. The plane was surely aiming at my burrow. From five hundred feet a small silvery barrel tumbled out of the Stuka's belly, turning over and over as it fell directly at us. Those last fear-filled seconds seemed an eternity. Then the *ssshwumph* and concussion of an explosion just feet away. A golf-ball-size bit of hot iron too spent to do any damage landed on my lower leg to emphasize a close-enough call.

Several times a day we looked up quickly at the roar of a Hurricane streaking back to base. Once, before our eyes, an unsuspecting pilot no more than a few hundred feet off the ground was jumped from above by a machine-gunning Messerschmitt. The Hurricane crashed in a mushroom of black smoke.

Reminiscent of World War I, there were daily dogfights in the clear blue sky. Perhaps one of the scarce Spitfires would climb toward a German Focke-Wulf Kondor circling at 35,000 feet to photograph our positions. Squinting into the sun, we could just make out the puffs of white as the guns opened up. The plane would spin out of control and perhaps a parachute would emerge. Another cloud of oily smoke rose from the desert.

And every day and all day under the hot sun a vast and varied collection of vehicles rolled back and forth along the web of tracks. Clouds of brown dust trailed this unending flow, which transported rations, water, ammunition, mines, wire, petrol, people. Trucks fitted with sprinklers tried to lay the dust with a weak drizzle of Mediterranean water. The attempt proved futile.

In mid-August Churchill replaced General Auchinleck with General Alexander as commander in the Middle East, while General Bernard Montgomery took charge of the veteran 8th Army. More and more one heard the name "Monty." It seemed that the men needed a figurehead to tell them that the enemy who had given them such a bad beating was not invincible, that very soon under his guidance they would give Rommel hell.

One morning I joined a crowd of perhaps a hundred soldiers beside the coastal road in time to see Monty make a jaunty exit from his car and climb onto a platform of sorts. Self-assured and cocky in his funny hat, he waved in the assorted troops and launched into a short spirit rouser: "There will be no withdrawals. Everyone is to stay put and fight to the last bullet. We are going to hit Rommel for six." To me he seemed to be too obviously putting on an act, a performance. As an American, I could only be puzzled by his cricketing metaphors. Nevertheless, there were many who valued such chances to see and judge their new commander for themselves. Morale began to rise quite remarkably quickly. The earlier generals of the desert war had not often made time to visit their fighting troops, and so were known to the majority only at second hand, as remote figures who got them killed to no purpose.

At the end of August, Rommel made his last attack, his final desperate attempt to reach the Suez Canal. This was the Battle of Alam Halfa (named for a key ridge in the British defenses). Short of petrol, battered from the air, and meeting stubborn resistance, he was forced to withdraw after taking heavy losses. For the most part it was an artillery and tank battle. Two of our New Zealand brigades were among the few infantry formations heavily engaged, being required to cut the retreat corridor of Rommel's panzers. They failed, and lost nearly three hundred men. Our ambulances were busy.

Alam Halfa was Monty's first major victory. There had been no retreat and Rommel had been hit for six. Both sides then settled down to prepare for the climactic collision that everyone knew was to come when the British were ready. Monty did not rush things.

Much has been written on the Battle of Alamein. Although the forces engaged on both sides were not large compared with those slogging it out in Russia, the strategic rewards were not small. Victory for the Allies removed the German threat to the oil wells of the Middle East and safeguarded the most direct route from Britain to India and the Far East. The 8th Army's subsequent chase west eventually freed the north shore of Africa as a launching pad for the invasion of Europe from the south. Above all, a clear victory would be a boost for morale among the troops, while back in Britain it had an enormous effect among the civilians. It must not be forgotten that by late 1942 Britain had been under aerial bombardment for over two years and was enduring severe shortages of food and of almost every necessity.

There was no way for the British to outflank Rommel's forty miles of defensive works, just as at the Battle of Alam Halfa he had been unable to outflank ours. The soft sands of the Qattara Depression to the south, and the Mediterranean to the north, set inflexible boundaries. After Alam Halfa, while Monty trained his troops, built up his stores, perfected and rehearsed his plans, and put into operation elaborate deception measures, the Germans and Italians had seven weeks to thicken up their defenses. Rommel himself was sick and was in Germany, though he returned as soon as battle opened. His armies were short in almost every department—tanks, guns, men, and above all fuel. He could not plan a mobile battle. He was forced to rely on fixed defenses. These were now formidable. It is reported that his engineers laid half a million mines.

Accounts vary as to the numbers involved. One source gives: men—8th Army 195,000, Panzerarmee Afrika 104,000 (50,000 German, 54,000 Italian); tanks—8th Army 1,029, Panzerarmee 489; artillery (field, medium, and antitank)—8th Army 1,403 pieces, Panzerarmee 1,219; airplanes (fighters and bombers)—8th Army 750, Panzerarmee 675.[6]

So, on the night of October 23 at 2140 hours, under a full moon, a thousand Allied guns opened up with a barrage more powerful than any in the history of warfare to that date. The sky was lit as if it were day, and the noise pulverized the senses. "It was a shattering fantastic sound . . . like gigantic drum-beats merging into one great blast of noise."[7] Soon the fog of war, metaphorically and literally, shrouded the battlefield, for each bursting shell and bomb scattered a cloud of drifting dust, and thousands upon thousands of shells were falling, hundreds of bombs were being dropped by the RAF.

This is not a work of military history and I do not propose to detail the progress of the battle. Many of our AFS sections were attached to the Kiwis of the 2nd New Zealand Division, which was part of the main northern assault force attacking the Miteirya Ridge. To their right was the Scottish 51st Highland Division (new to battle); to their left was the 1st South African Division. On the previous evening the Maori Battalion with the Kiwis had put on a stirring war dance, the Haka, as a warm-up. On the night of the battle the Highlanders went in with their pipes playing. Several of their pipers were killed.

The official history of the New Zealand forces in World War II has the following paragraph as part of its account of the El Alamein battle:

> The medical organisations of the British and Commonwealth forces, though retaining their individual entities, were also integrated in a master plan so that wounded could be evacuated and treated with a minimum of delay. For this, the lines of evacuation of each division were carefully planned from advanced dressing stations to field and base hospitals, with check posts linked by radio or telephone so that the wounded could be distributed according to the degree of injury and a heavy influx at any one point might be spread over several of the medical channels. Cab ranks of ambulance cars were set up well forward so that an empty car could be dispatched at once to take the place of every loaded car coming back through the check posts. In this work the drivers of the American Field Service were prominent, greatly easing the strain on the medical corps' staff at the height of the battle.[8]

We AFS were insignificant cogs in a vast cauldron of mutual destruction. We depended on the medical staff and the wounded for snatches of rumors on what was happening in the noise, fire, and smoke. Surely Rommel's men would not be able to withstand the pasting they were getting from the ground and from the air? Surely this chaos must end in the victory Monty had promised?

Victories are seldom won cheaply. Casualties at Alamein were heavy, some 13,000 killed, wounded, and missing. As an NCO in charge of a section of six ambulances, the wounded were my concern, and it was my job to detail and dispatch the drivers. Decisions were not always straightforward. I rode along on some runs to help with the navigation. It was nighttime (though moonlit), and we had entered unfamiliar territory. There were mines, there was wire, there were trenches; there were tanks and carriers and trucks on the move, some stationary, some burning; there were men walking, running, hobbling, shouting; there were men who were dead.

Here is Evan Thomas, an outstanding person (son of Norman Thomas, several times Socialist candidate for U.S. president). He was with the New Zealanders. He describes the opening barrage, its enormous impact, and how, during a lull, he could hear the wailing skirl of the bagpipes from the Highlanders.

> It wasn't until 1.30 that our Field Service ambulances were called upon to go to work. Five were ordered to the 24th Battalion's RAP. I went along as spare driver for Brook Cuddy. We drove westward on a dusty track crowded with tanks and Bren carriers getting ready to move up at dawn. It was touchy work by-passing the concentration of armour, at times leaving the track and running a chance of hitting a mine. We found the 24th's RAP truck without mishap and loaded three cars quickly when a very excited padre came rushing up to tell me that the 25th Battalion, a few hundred yards to the west, needed ambulances in the worst way.
>
> It took us two hours to find the 25th Battalion, working ourselves around the tanks and through the German mine fields. When we got there we found that neither the MO nor his truck had put in an appear-

ance. The Battalion had just taken its second objective and the wounded were scattered all over. I found a young captain and told him we would be glad to evacuate as many casualties as our ambulances could carry. "Ambulances!" he said. "We haven't had time to collect our wounded. Perhaps you'd see to that? I'll send a guide. Better hurry up and get those ambulances away."

We drove back to the ADS at dawn, fighting our way past the tanks in the narrow mine field lanes. At the ADS there was a great rush of work as the casualties poured in from the battalions. Scotty Gilmore's boys were busy shuttling between stations.[9]

Farther south and a week later Bill Nichols and one of his drivers, Eccy Johnston, had been under heavy shell fire all day with a battalion of the Durham Light Infantry of the 44th Division. Three battalion doctors were killed that day, including the doctor Bill and Eccy were working for, as the infantry got caught in the midst of a tank battle.

George Lester, with the Scots Greys of the 7th Armoured Division, saw exciting work during the first three days of the battle. At one time under heavy shell fire they dug forty-odd slit trenches for patients who could not be evacuated. Then he made six successful runs through the shelling to the ADS, getting the whole lot out of danger. Late that afternoon he was sporting a large hole through his back door from a shell that had failed to detonate.

When the 8th Army finally broke through, after eleven days of slogging battle, tanks, armored cars, and lorry loads of infantry raced across the desert in a chase that would not stop until the whole of North Africa had been cleared. Large pockets of Germans and Italians were encircled and taken prisoner.

Meanwhile, in the world outside, the battles at Stalingrad roared on and into the icy Russian winter, consuming men and equipment on a scale that would have seemed incomprehensible to us had we known of it. The fighting was continuous from September to the end of January. In the Pacific the first Allied counteroffensive, the long pain of the fight for Guadalcanal, was at its height. The amphibious landings had begun on August 7, and the island was not to be cleared until February of the year ahead. In early November, as Rommel ordered retreat, Operation Torch—the landing of over 100,000 American and British soldiers on the shores of French North Africa—began, threatening his rear.

In the Western Desert we AFS went along with the chase westward, back over familiar ground. We saw plenty of prisoners. I was impressed by the defiant expressions on the faces of one group of German officers who sat haughtily upright in their open staff car. Probably they had run out of petrol. They looked unrepentant and proud as they waited to be collected. Our New Zealand column was too busy moving west to oblige them.

Later I spoke to some of the prisoners coming in on foot. They were in their heavy greatcoats, for by November the desert night is cold. They did not seem too dispirited, perhaps thankful to be alive. One of them told me that he had worked for Anderson Meyer, a big German trading company, in its Shanghai office. I remembered this outfit as being on the reader list of *American Exporter*. Sure enough, he told me that he had been a regular reader and hoped to be again.

The New Zealanders were sent on a hook south and west through the desert to the coast back near Mersa Matruh, and their progress was much slowed by heavy rain. But I missed out on the later stages of this sortie. I had contracted jaundice, and late in November was flown courtesy of the RAF to the hospital on Gezira Island in the Nile off Cairo. The jaundice had somehow caused a hard lump, which refused to go down, to form under my jaw—to the bafflement of the doctors and despite a diet of assorted drugs. Finally they operated. Within a reasonable period I was able to amble over to the Gezira racetrack in hospital pajamas. On January 20 I was free to leave.

I was free to leave both the hospital and the AFS. My contracted year was finished. Most of the group had signed on for another tour and I was asked to do so. The AFS was expanding. But I felt it was time to change the course of my military career.

CHAPTER III

We Shift
Our Talents

In time of war it is often easier to change jobs than you might suppose. Uncertainty, fluidity, is in the air. There is always somebody who knows somebody. And Americans are used to breaking camp and recasting their lives. Cairo, the hub of wartime activity in the Middle East, presented several opportunities.

Some of us considered returning to the States by signing on with one of the merchant vessels off-loading at Suez or Port Taufiq. One of us telegraphed home for $350 and flew to Lagos in West Africa, from where, presumably, he had heard it would be easier to find transport across the Atlantic.

My friend Joe Gaynor had already transferred to the American army, which was rapidly expanding its skeleton staff in the city. His job, he whispered over coffee at Groppi's, was hush-hush. He could tell me only that it involved plain clothes and undercover investigations of spy plots among the polyglot civilian population. The scene of intrigue was more often than not one of the seamy

Cairo nightclubs. The agents of both sides ran from exotic belly dancers to Greek generals. Joe let drop that with the job, in his case, went a flat and ample opportunity to install a mistress. The setup sounded interesting. He offered to introduce me to his boss, a major. I accepted the offer without hesitation.

The major, desperate for staff, put me to work that Monday morning. I would start with the rank of sergeant and soon be commissioned. I could not be sworn into the U.S. Army until Thursday, when my physical was complete. "But," said the major blithely, "don't worry about details. We need you *now*."

By Tuesday it was apparent that my job was not as described by Joe. I was not to entrap belly dancers in the pay of the Nazis. I was to sit in a hot office in central Cairo from 8:00 A.M. to 6:00 P.M., six days a week, sifting through records of traffic violations. That afternoon I announced to the major that a desk job in Cairo was not my idea of war: "I'm sorry, but I have decided to leave." He was understandably apoplectic.

Once more I examined the alternatives. What appealed the most was the drive put on in Cairo to sign up potential officers for the rapidly expanding Indian Army. How did I hear of this? God knows—probably over a coffee at Groppi's. Everyone took coffee at Groppi's, and that is where one always went for information, whether on General Montgomery's latest plans for "hitting Rommel for six" or for the names of the most alluring houris.

HQ Delhi was after British infantry NCOs (noncommissioned officers) with battle experience. I did not quite fit. Nonetheless I was interviewed by a Major Carr and another officer who said that Americans could be enrolled without loss of citizenship and that four of my AFS compatriots (Ralph Muller, Al Wright, Pat Pattullo, and Bill Nichols) had already been accepted.

The physical was cursory. Ralph Muller was almost blind in one eye. He passed the eye test by first covering his sightless eye with his left hand and then, when asked to use the other eye, covering the same eye with his right hand.

I still have a copy of a letter dated January 24, 1943, from our AFS Major King to Major Carr recommending me for a place in an Officers Training School in India. It reads:

Conforming with arrangements made by Major Hirrichs, who is at present away, I am sending Scott Gilmore to see you as he is interested in getting into the Indian Army Officers Training School.

He has had a good deal of experience with the American Field Service and has at all times done a first-rate job. He has a letter of recommendation from Captain Ives. Subsequent to the date he left Captain Ives's Unit, he did an excellent job as an NCO in the formation and training of a new unit. I spent some time with his Section during a period of intense activity at the beginning of the recent push and was very favourably impressed by the way in which he handled the work. I recommend him to you with great confidence.

Thus, with the approval and blessing of the U.S. embassy in Cairo, we swore obedience but not allegiance to King George VI and were committed to a future in the prestigious Indian Army.

What was this Indian Army I was about to join? At that time, in the Cairo of early 1942, none of us AFS knew much about it, so what I write now was learned subsequently. We had been impressed by what we had seen and heard of the Mahrattas, Punjabis, Baluchis, Dogras, Gurkhas, Rajputs, Sikhs, and other soldiers of the 4th and 5th Indian divisions, formations that had been in the Western Desert—and in Eritrea, Abyssinia, and the Sudan—since the early days of the war. Some of the men were already veterans of four campaigns. The 4th Indian Division was reckoned by many to be the most experienced formation in the area, though it was not given its due by the new General Montgomery.

The British first came to India in the early seventeenth century to trade. The merchant adventurers of other European nations were already there, particularly the Portuguese, Dutch, and French. For similar reasons, reinforced by religious zeal, the Spanish and Portuguese crossed the Atlantic to South and Central America, and the French and British quarreled over North America. In India, trade came first; conquest and colonization came at the hands of later generations.

It was in the year 1600 that Queen Elizabeth I granted Britain's East India Company an exclusive charter to trade in the eastern seas. Twelve years earlier the Spanish Armada had tried to invade England and depose Elizabeth. Spain had been defeated. British seamen were now confident and determined not to be excluded from the lucrative spice trade of the East Indies.

In India the Europeans found a developed civilization and a somewhat anarchic political situation. The Mogul Empire at its zenith controlled much of the country. The Moguls were Muslims and had been the most recent conquerors of that faith to reach northern India through Afghanistan. Their first leader was Bābur (1483–1530), an attractive and remarkable man thought to be of mixed Turkish and Mongolian blood. He was a warrior-statesman, but also a poet, sportsman, hunter, lover of gardens, and writer of a memorable diary, which survives.

His descendants, including Shāh Jāhan, the builder of the Taj Mahal, expanded Mogul power. But by the time of the English ascendance in the eighteenth century, this empire was breaking up.

Successor states expanded and contracted according to the skills of local leaders. These rajahs, nawabs, princes, petty chiefs, and regional warlords depended on paid armed forces to retain authority. The Europeans in their small trading stations or "factories" were forced to protect their property by similar measures. This was not new for them. Most merchant ships of the time were armed against pirates.

The tendency to anarchy was compounded by European rivalries. The French and English, so often at each other's throats in Europe, often supported competing Indian claimants to a particular domain. It was the French who were the first to raise and train significant bodies of Indian soldiers on European lines. Small numbers of European soldiery were imported. These influenced events in disproportion to their numbers, but they were expensive, and proved a rapidly wasting asset as disease killed them off.

In this way through the seventeenth and eighteenth centuries the European enclaves came to dominate local politics, and themselves grew to be centers of power.

So began Britain's Indian Army. The men were mercenaries in the employ of the East India Company. They served for pay. That is how it began and how it ended. In India the profession of mercenary was not disparaged. For centuries it had been an honored craft among both Muslims and Hindus.

We cannot linger on the story of the expansion of British rule over the whole of India and the consequent development of the Indian Army. But 1857 was a crisis year. This was the year of the great Indian Mutiny, when a number of regiments, mainly from the Bengal army, rose against their British officers. There was savagery on both sides, not easily forgotten. Some modern Indian historians think of the Mutiny as the first patriotic war. In some sense perhaps it was. There was still local loyalty to the old Mogul emperor, in Delhi, whose powers now were tightly restricted.

Over India as a whole there was no general movement that could be called nationalist as we understand that word today. Regiments in the army that did not revolt in the Mutiny outnumbered those that did. The British would never have regained control without the help of regiments that were recruited from the Punjab, the frontier provinces, Gurkhas from Nepal, and others who felt little kin with the mutineers.

Horrified by the Mutiny, the British government withdrew political authority from the East India Company. From then on power was wielded in the name of the monarchy (Queen Victoria, at that time) and the elected Parliament of Great Britain. Men serving in the Indian Army now swore loyalty to the Queen Empress and her successors. It continued to be an army made up of men of many races, of several religions, and of diverse language.

We need to distinguish between the Indian Army and the army in India, a nuance likely to confuse. The Indian Army was made up of the units of cavalry, infantry, artillery, engineers, and other specialties raised in India and composed largely of Indians and Gurkhas. The army in India included the Indian Army—and also the considerable number of British regiments of all arms stationed in India at any one time. From 1895 the whole medley was put under one commander in chief.

The relationship between the Indian Army and the British regiments serving in India was fairly close, with the Gurkhas usually very close. Over the generations thousands of British army soldiers served in India and alongside Indian troops.

The army in India came to be more than a police force available for internal security, though it was that. Between 1860 and 1914 units of the army, British and Indian, were on active service in China (twice), Abyssinia, Burma, Malaya, Egypt, Sudan, East Africa, India's northwest frontier (repeatedly) and her northeast frontier (less often), Afghanistan, and Tibet. An ambitious British officer keen to find action, learn his craft, win decorations, and gain promotion was more likely to succeed while stationed in India.

When World War I started, the Indian Army consisted of some 240,000 men, including reservists. During the war it expanded to 1,500,000, though not all were combatant soldiers. Between the wars it returned to its old strength or somewhat less. By 1945, at the end of World War II, it had grown to 2,500,000 and was probably the largest volunteer army ever raised.

By 1914 the Indian Army was a very professional force. However, it was not designed to contribute to a major European conflict; it was designed to keep the peace in India and to send small temporary forces as required to trouble spots in the Middle East and Far East. It was not heavily armed, nor was its weaponry up-to-date. This was partly by design, partly because it was always short of funds. The Indian Army was paid for out of taxes raised in India. In years of peace there is a reluctance on the part of almost all governments to spend revenue on armies. This was particularly so in India, with its huge impoverished population.

It is often forgotten that two Indian Army infantry divisions and a cavalry corps were thrown into the fighting on the World War I western front at a very early stage. War was declared on August 4, 1914. They were in the front line in Flanders from October, during those critical weeks when the Germans were still pressing hard to achieve a quick victory in the west. The Indian infantry remained there until November 1915, the cavalry until 1918. Casualties were at times horrific.

This is what happened to the 2nd Battalion of my future regiment, the 8th Gurkhas. The battalion embarked from Karachi in September 1914 and disembarked at Marseilles on October 13. None of the Gurkhas had been overseas before, and neither clothing nor scale of weapons was adequate for European campaigning in winter against the Germans. Nor had they been trained in any way for the trench warfare into which they were so abruptly pitch-forked.

On October 29 they took over a section of the front line near Neuve Chapelle. Next morning they were repelling a heavy German attack. By the end of the fighting two days later, 9 British officers, 5 Gurkha officers, and 206 other ranks were killed, wounded, or missing. The battalion had landed in France with 11 British officers.

So it continued for a year until the Indian infantry divisions were withdrawn (the cavalry stayed on). By then 40 British officers, 27 Gurkha officers, and 1,356 other ranks had been killed, wounded, or were missing. Not one of those officers who had disembarked at Marseilles remained. If we assume that the total strength of the 2nd Battalion was about 750 when it landed, probably very few of the original muster saw that year through unharmed.

In World War I, Indian Army soldiers also fought at Gallipoli and in Egypt, Palestine, Syria, Mesopotamia, Persia, and East Africa. It was Indian Army units that formed the largest component of the forces under General Allenby that captured Damascus and knocked Turkey out of the war. Without the Indian Army, Britain would have been pushed to hold the Suez Canal and the Persian Gulf with its oil.

In brief, for a century and a half or longer, "It was the Indian Army that made possible control of Asia and of the Mediterranean and Cape routes" for the British Empire.[1]

But here is another interesting quote from the historian F. W. Perry: "What the war of 1914–18 did was to underline the ambiguous status of the Indian Army and, indeed, of India itself. Neither fully independent nor fully subordinate to London, India and the Army followed policies partly originating in India, partly in London, and with no clear responsibility or control of events."[2]

Just as the imposition of British rule over the whole of India was a gradual business achieved over a couple of centuries, so the Indian Army was not created in a day, but evolved during the same long period to meet changing needs and circumstances.

When I joined in the middle of World War II, infantry battalions were grouped into regiments, each regiment with its own training unit, which came to be known as the regimental center. Some regiments were composed of a single class or race, like the Dogras, the Gurkhas, the Garhwalis, the Mahrattas, and some Sikh battalions; others were mixed. Within a mixed battalion, each company would recruit from a single class.

Basic identification was by numbers. For example, there were ten Gurkha regiments, and my future regiment was the 8th Gurkha Rifles. The 8th Gurkhas had two battalions in peace, but expanded to four battalions in both world wars. The battalions were also numbered—hence 1/8th, 2/8th, 3/8th, and 4/8th. In addition to their numbers, some regiments had titles. For example, the 3rd Gurkhas were the 3rd Queen Alexandra's Own Gurkha Rifles. The numbering of the Indian battalions was a little complicated and need not be detailed here.

Between the two world wars men tended to be recruited for the Indian Army from certain areas of India only. The specter of the Mutiny inhibited recruitment from Bengal and Bihar. And there had grown to be a prejudice (not shared by every Briton) against enlisting from southern India, for example, where men were small and black, and were thought to be amiable but bloodless, not of the "martial classes." Yet the Madras Sappers and Miners were as good as the best—intelligent, brave, highly rated by all who worked with them.

The martial classes were believed to lie in western and northwestern India and along the rugged Himalayan fringe of the northern borders. Men here were favored because of their larger physique and fairer skin, or because they were hardy men of the mountains, and because they were of peasant or yeoman stock, simple men, not too intelligent.

Here is one postwar British historian: "Those selected by the British as 'martial' were considered by the bulk of Indian opinion as rather bone-headed"; and "These were the men with the most inert political outlook, conservative and willing to conform to the established order."[3]

Also it has to be remembered that regiments recruited from the north and northwest had remained loyal during the Mutiny. They fought happily against the mutineers and alongside the hard-pressed British battalions. It would be natural for the British to look on them with a kindly eye.

Regiments tended to perpetuate their makeup by seeking recruits from the same areas year after year. This was perfectly possible in peacetime, when the numbers required were small. Recruiting was usually done by pensioners, men who would surely get the best results in their home districts among people they knew. So regiments became "families" in a more literal sense than in most armies.

F. W. Perry states bluntly: "From a British point of view the Indian Army was a means of policing a dependency or acting as an Imperial Reserve and the martial classes concept was one of identifying the groups from which mercenaries could be obtained. . . . What the British needed from the Indian Army was a force which would fight, if necessary, for causes that were British rather than Indian."[4]

Another matter of controversy was "Indianization." By the outbreak of war in 1939, some Indians were in positions of the highest responsibility in the Indian civil service and other branches of the administration. In the army things had moved more slowly. Indianization in the army meant granting the King's Commission to Indians. These officers would then expect to command bodies of troops larger than a platoon. With the passage of time the British must be prepared to share the higher command structure.

This policy was agreed against opposition from a minority of British officers convinced that only they could lead their troops and organize the staff work with the necessary degree of efficiency and courage.

Britain's training academy for infantry officers was, and still is, at Sandhurst in southern England. The initial batch of ten Indian cadets was accepted at the Royal Military College in 1918. The strain on those young men, living for the first time in a foreign country, some with an imperfect grasp of the English language and customs, must have been severe. They did not have the toughening background of a boarding school that would have inoculated almost all the British entrants. Thirty percent of the first eighty-three Indian cadets failed.

Things went better when an Indian Sandhurst, the Indian Military Academy at Dehra Dun, was started in 1932. By 1939 there was a leavening of Indian officers in selected regiments of the Indian Army. Different accounts give different statistics, but one author reports that there were 3,031 British and 697 Indian officers serving in October 1939. By the war's end there were 18,752 British and 13,947 Indian officers, plus about 14,000 officers seconded from the British army.[5] The word *British* is used loosely. As well as myself and the other five AFS Americans, there were Australians and surely more.

Here we have to make an exception for the ten Gurkha regiments. In these, King's Commissioned officers remained "British."

Battalions grouped into regiments made up the peacetime structure of the infantry. Within this regimental framework proceeded the time-honored traditions by which raw young recruits straight from the villages were transformed into soldiers. For battle formations, battalions from various regiments were grouped into brigades, divisions, and corps, as in every army. In the Indian Army during most of World War II the standard infantry brigade of three battalions had one British battalion and two Indian or Gurkha battalions.

There were exceptions to this norm. For example, the 2nd Battalion of the 8th Gurkha Rifles (the 2/8th), which we have already met in France in 1914–15, from early 1943 until the end of World War II was part of a brigade composed wholly of Gurkhas, the 43rd Gurkha Lorried Brigade. It saw little of its lorries, but much hard fighting up the interminable succession of rivers and ridges that form the Apennines, the mountain spine of Italy. This was the battalion to which my compatriot Jupe Lewis was sent.

"Men come to the colours for pay but it is not for pay that they earn the Victoria Cross." So wrote Philip Mason in his fine history of the Indian Army, *A Matter of Honour*.[6] The Victoria Cross is Britain's highest decoration for gallantry in the face of the enemy. Why did Indian and Gurkha soldiers willingly and repeatedly face death in battle in the service of the British Crown?

Their officers were men of another faith, or no faith, and from a distant and mysterious land; men who looked different, spoke another language, ate strange foods, and followed customs and ways of behavior that must have been often puzzling, sometimes unappealing, occasionally repellent.

The Indians were not being patriotic. They were not dying for their country. India was not a nation in 1939, much less in 1914. Few of its myriad constituent peoples thought of themselves as part of the British Commonwealth. As for the Gurkhas, they came from the independent kingdom of Nepal, which had never been conquered by the British (though its army had been defeated in 1815 when it tried to extend Nepalese power into India—see Chapter 6).

The threat of foreign conquest can breed patriotism, but India was used to conquerors. The British were but the most recent of a long succession of them. Once the British were settled, there was never a serious danger of a new conquest from outside, not even when the Russians were in their most expansionist mood, not even in 1944 when the Japanese came across the borders into the Indian state of Manipur. Indian nationalist agitation against the British never inhibited enlistment in the army.

As to the causes of the two world wars, these must have been remote to the average soldier, probably unintelligible. No young Indian recruit went to war because the Germans resented the 1919 Peace Treaty of Versailles, because Hitler fancied Poland, or because the Japanese needed oil and space and bombed Pearl Harbor.

So why was it that these soldiers of India were willing to risk limb and life for very modest wages and were happy to assist in keeping the peace over an area of a million and a half square miles? They belonged to a population of their brothers many times larger than that of the ruling masters. Why were they ready to join in overseas wars fought for shadowy, incomprehensible reasons?

Here are some of the answers.

Training has much to do with it. First-class training is a prerequisite of a first-class army. Soldiers who are well trained; adequately paid, fed, and housed (and India has always teemed with millions who are inadequately fed and housed); and who are kept busy and interested, will have no incentive to rebel.

Then you must have good officers. The old adage that there are no bad soldiers, only bad officers, will always remain true. Officers should be dedicated to their men and thus earn loyalty. In India the system encouraged this bond, demanded it. A weakening of the bond in the decades before 1857 was a major cause of the Mutiny. Probably every subsequent instance of desertion or rebellion, and there were not many, can be put down to a failure of regimental officering.

"The safety, honour and welfare of your country comes first, always and every time. The honour, welfare and comfort of the men you command come next. Your own ease, comfort and safety come last, always and every time." These are the words that were inscribed on the walls of the Indian Military Academy at Dehra Dun when it was opened in 1932. Fine sentiments for any army, though it would be interesting to know what both the British instructors and their Indian cadets understood by the words *your country*.

So we have sound training and dedicated officers. But at the heart of Indian and Gurkha steadfastness probably lay a man's personal concept of honor, of self-respect, his *izzat*. Honor prefers death to shame. Honor entails never acting to bring shame on one's kin and one's village, nor on one's comrades, one's regiment, or one's class. Honor demands that a man gives good value and beyond for his pay.

Pat Davis, my companion in war and assistant with this record, wrote twenty-five years ago, at the conclusion of his book *A Child at Arms:* "Whatever first drove us to war, it was friendship, trust and loyalty to one another that kept us at it long after we might have preferred to be elsewhere."[7]

Honor keeps a man fighting when every instinct tells him to crouch in a trench and let others cope with the terrifying world outside. For the men of the Indian Army personal honor was a cardinal element in the business of living.

The Indian Army in early 1943, when I was sailing down the Red Sea to join it, was at a critical juncture in its wartime expansion and reorganization. It had already contributed substantial forces to the fighting in the Western Desert, the Horn of Africa, and throughout the Middle East. Soon it would be embroiled in Italy. But from December 1941 its main focus had turned to a nearer enemy, the Japanese. In Africa and the Middle East the army had achieved some remarkable successes. In Malaya and Burma it had suffered some demoralizing defeats.

These defeats were due to a complex of causes, among them

lack of suitable training, inexperience, dilution due to expansion, poor administrative organization, and a series of political, strategic, and tactical blunders due mainly to the failure of politicians and commanders at many levels to evaluate the Japanese army. But lessons had been learned. Much was in preparation that would bear fruit later. I was joining at a good time.

On February 9 I sailed from Suez on a creaking old tramp steamer, the *Salween*. In a couple of hours we were rolling down the Red Sea. I shared a first-class stateroom with Jupe Lewis. The other Americans had sailed earlier. Jupe was from Long Island, a graduate of Dartmouth, and by chance he was later to end up in the same Gurkha regiment as I. By further coincidence Jupe (Roscoe is the name preferred today by his wife) now lives in the next town to mine in Connecticut and is helping to sharpen my memory.

A brass plate under the bridge told us that our comfortable but aged ship had been built on the Clyde more than fifty years earlier. From the stern flew a large balloon dragging a steel cable a thousand feet in the air. This was our antiaircraft protection.

In the late afternoon, to freshen up after the heat of the day, one bathed in a huge tub from the Edwardian period. Freshwater being in short supply, salt water gushed from the tap. Lather it would not, despite the special seawater soap. Somewhat revived, we took up positions on the aft deck for the predinner drink. Cockney stewards—colonial Britain even in adversity never lacked for servants—tendered drinks in a shady corner on the port side. Unexpectedly the ship had a substantial supply of Guinness. Even served warm, this inky liquid helped toward enjoying the scene.

On the barren shores of the Red Sea we passed occasional clusters of white adobe houses reflecting back the still-bright sun. Each house was topped by a sail-like wind scoop intended to funnel air down to the interior. Dhows sailed in and out of small ports. Some of these dhows were said to be used by smugglers. It was rumored that they still brought slaves from Africa for the feudal rulers of Arabia. Inland rose the heights fought over by Lawrence in World War I as he skirmished with the Turks retreating back through the Hejaz to Sinai.

After a five-course evening dinner we escaped once more to the deck. By now the sun had set behind the rust-colored escarpment on the African side, and the early moonbeams were bounding off our phosphorescent wake. An ancient out-of-tune upright piano was hauled on deck. Soon the words of so many sentimental songs of the times were floating astern: "Girl of My Dreams," "Long, Long Way to Tipperary," "Lights of London," "Down by the Old Mill Stream," "Lili Marlene," "Troopship Just Leaving Bombay"—all nostalgic, beery songs, more's the pity seldom sung today.

The days passed rapidly and pleasantly. Out on the Indian Ocean we stood turns at submarine watch, even though there had been only rare appearances of enemy subs in these waters. We saw none, but schools of flying fish skipped the tops of the sun-flecked waves.

Then one morning we found ourselves in a procession of ships and dhows of all sizes converging on Bombay. Soon we were near enough to catch the unique pungent odor, carried on the morning haze, of thousands of cow dung fires. At the dock stevedores in loincloths climbed on board and the off-loading began.

Jupe and I were scheduled to join the other four Americans at the OTS (Officers Training School) at Belgaum, but were detoured to a transit camp at Colaba, a short way along the seafront. We were there for three weeks. Since we could not be permitted to float free in the military machine, we were enrolled into the East Yorkshire Regiment. Did that no doubt distinguished unit ever discover its good fortune?

With our new status as officer cadets neither the sergeant major nor the camp commandant seemed to know what to do about us. The commandant was a crusty colonel too old for active service. He appeared each morning on his charger to inquire about "those Americans." As a result we led a life of complete idleness: games of snooker, the cinema, the races, visits to the Army & Navy Stores on Hornby Road. Jupe had a craving for an American milk shake but the Bombay version, made with water buffalo milk, never quite measured up.

At the races we admired the Parsi women in their saris and devised a betting system. Our system involved isolating the three least-favored horses in the race, studying them carefully in the paddock, and betting on the one that appeared most likely to complete the course. Our one winner in several visits to the track was at such outside odds as to cover all earlier losses as well as numerous gin-and-limes at the Harbour Bar in the Taj Mahal Hotel.

Finally we were given orders to entrain on the Poona Mail for Belgaum, some three hundred miles to the south, there to join our compatriots for the four-month course that would convert us to second lieutenants in the Indian Army. From the comfort of a first-class compartment, while the train climbed the Western Ghats, we contemplated this future with contentment.

CHAPTER IV

An Officer of the Raj

"Never! Never in the hool of my twenty years in India! Never have I seen such a shower of shite hawks! You lot should be ashamed to wear uniform."

While I have long forgotten most of the commissioned instructors at our Officers Training School at Belgaum, I will long remember gruff Welsh Sergeant Major Phillips, who I suspect was largely responsible for its smooth running. This pillar of the Empire seemed always to be present and observant. From dawn to dusk his scornful voice boomed across the parade ground.

Belgaum was a sleepy city not far inland from the then Portuguese colony of Goa. Belgaum's altitude of 2,500 feet is sufficient to insure a climate that is benign but less humid than that of Goa and Bombay. It is built on laterite rock, whose characteristic red dust was apt to coat us and our clothing whenever we ventured out.

The villagers in the area were brown, slightly built Mahrattas.

They were Hindus. And despite their small size, they were rugged fighters. Once formidable in resisting the British (there had been three Maratha wars between 1775 and 1819), they had supported British rule for many years by enlisting in the Mahratta Regiment, whose cantonment was on the far side of the town from ours.

I had already discovered that India is not inhabited by one homogeneous people. The land has filled with many races, tribes, and sects, overlapping, intermixing, or fitted around and between each other like the pieces of a jigsaw puzzle. Many languages are spoken, many and varied religions are practiced; cultural diversity ranges from remote and primitive hill and forest peoples to representatives of some of the most ancient and sophisticated civilizations on earth.

This genetic and intellectual patchwork was spread over a vast peninsula, a subcontinent, at that time undivided under one ruler, the British. It embraced the widest variety of climate and physical landscape—from the high Himalayas, along the northern rim, across vast plains, deserts, and rolling forests to the rich, lush tropical lands of the south.

Over the centuries successive waves of conquerors, mostly from the northwest, had produced this confusing human jumble. As I was to discover, and as subsequent history has repeatedly demonstrated, all was not sweet harmony among its peoples. Yet so long as the British sat at the top, relative peace prevailed.

At the Belgaum OTS our group was divided into two companies, with about thirty officer cadets in each. My Long Island compatriot, Jupe Lewis, and I shared quarters. Servants were cheap and plentiful. Misled by tattered remnants of letters of recommendation written in weak moments by past employers, Jupe and I took on a Goanese bearer. With no duties after the morning bath except to polish our second pairs of boots and take laundry to the *dhobi,* and with wages of less than five dollars a month, perhaps it was not surprising that he spent his days removing our few personal possessions one at a time to sell in the bazaar, only returning in time to help us change for dinner.

Most of our fellow cadets had been British army NCOs and were already onto the dodges of army life. Others had been clerks or junior managers in the jute mills or tea plantations of India and

Ceylon. They were referred to as "India-wallas." Presumably because we all went in with a bit more experience, our commissions were to be granted after four months instead of the normal six.

I have been asked how the British with whom I worked in India and Burma reacted to having an American within their ranks. There was not a problem. In India I was not aware of that oft-quoted tag about my countrymen in England: "Overpaid, oversexed, and over here." In Britain there were hundreds of thousands of American soldiers and airmen awaiting the invasion of Europe. It is surprising the island did not sink. Their smart uniform, their better pay, their access to Hershey bars and nylons, gave them an unfair advantage.

In India the British were accustomed to being surrounded by a polyglot crowd. They were themselves a foreign minority in someone else's country. I doubt that there were ever enough Americans in India (except maybe from time to time in Calcutta) to create widespread jealousy and animosity. I do not recall that in Belgaum we six Yankees were made to feel unwelcome. After Belgaum, when we were distributed to our various units (and were paid the same as everyone else), we were no threat, not in the social field. I like to think I fitted in. I am an easygoing guy.

Each day started with rigorous PT. There was the usual arm waving and knee bending. Then there might be a grueling obstacle course—jumping off towers and down into pits, crawling over red ground on elbows and stomach—urged on by sadistic sergeant instructors. Or there might be a cross-country run from which I returned gaspingly at the rear. My handicaps were age—at thirty I was the old man of the class—and weight. The 215 pounds I then carried were to melt to 160 by VJ Day through boring food, heat, a good deal of walking, and some anxiety.

After exercise and in the few minutes left before breakfast, one would attempt to remove the red, sweat-soaked grime in the too-small galvanized tub filled by the bearer. Refitted with freshly starched shorts and bush jacket, appetites sharpened, we bicycled over to the mess for breakfast. Breakfast was served by red-sashed and turbaned mess waiters: porridge, eggs, bacon, and toast, all washed down with strong tea. Never did a meal taste better.

At Belgaum the four rupees a day messing fee docked from our pay to supplement army rations got us surprisingly good food. Surprising because in many establishments of this size mess fees disappeared into the pocket of the cantonment contractor with no great improvement in the food.

Three hours later, back from the morning lectures on military organization, troop movement by rail, working with tanks, or whatever, we were again storming the bar, scribbling a blizzard of chits for orange squash or *nimbu pani* (lemonade—literally, "lemon water") in the minutes before lunch. Beer, whiskey, and gin we saved for the evening.

Except for Wednesdays and Saturdays we had classes after lunch from 2:30 to 4:30. Then the bearer would bring tea and sandwiches to our quarters. There followed more study, then another bath, and dinner at 8:30. After dinner we might have a visit from our *munshi* (tutor) in Urdu.

We were treated to a number of training films on such subjects as "Control of the passes into Afghanistan" or "Treacherous tribesmen." They were masterpieces of cinematic drama, with actors from the Bombay studios playing stealthy hook-nosed Wazirs slinking from boulder to boulder below a stone *sangar* (fort) on a hillcrest. The sangar was held by a thin force of Kiplingesque guardians wearing solar topees.

One film featured a sneaky-looking Pathan of an unfriendly tribe crawling under cover of darkness into a camp to steal a Tommy's rifle. The lesson: to avoid falling to such unsporting behavior, the stupid soldier must chain his rifle to his person. When the screening was held after a curry lunch, attention was incomplete.

India's North-West Frontier with Afghanistan was seldom wholly at peace. In the nineteenth century the tide of British conquest had halted at this rugged mountainous barrier. It was a barrier that stretched from the Pamir Mountains in the north—where China, Russia, India, and Afghanistan all converged—southwestward for a thousand miles to the border with Persia (Iran).

British policy was to keep Afghanistan neutral, but friendly, as a check against Russian expansion. From time to time there were scares concerning the growth of Russian influence. Spies of all colors ranged the mountains, or so it was believed. Of the two British invasions of Afghanistan (1839 and 1878), the first had been a disaster and the second could just about be called a draw. British generals, who tend to know their history, could have warned the Russians what to expect when the latter moved into Afghanistan in 1979.

For centuries the tribesmen of the frontier reckoned to make a part of their living from plundering caravans, from eliminating careless military posts, and from raiding the settlers on the plains of the Punjab and Sind. When they thought that government was weak, they descended in numbers. A minor war could follow.

Defeating such incursions was made easier by the intense intertribal enmities. Seldom did the Pathans of different tribes combine to attack the British. Within each tribal society blood feuds also weakened the common front against outside foes.

The army in India developed a considerable respect for the Pathans. The tribesmen were bold, skilled guerrilla fighters, expert at concealment, at ambush, at the quick knife rush. Romantic legends proliferated, mythology flourished.

"As far as the military men were concerned, it was no bad thing to have a frontier where a state of virtual warfare was in existence. Training merged into real operations. Sentries had to be alert. Precautions could never be neglected. There were opportunities to show efficiency, zeal and gallantry. There were medals, awards, and distinctions to be won, and colonels and generals could earn their knighthoods if involved in successful operations on a large enough scale."[1]

Frontier operations were often poised on the edge of disaster, and sometimes disaster came. In the Waziristan campaign of 1919–21 a battalion of Mahrattas in one morning lost 95 men killed, 140 men wounded, 10 Lewis guns, and 131 rifles. In two months' fighting, the column in which that battalion was serving suffered 639 dead and 1,683 wounded. But casualties on that scale were exceptional.

Defense of the North-West Frontier became one of the army in India's primary roles. Battalions served their turn there in rotation.

Another lecture hardly of use on the Burma front or in the

Western Desert was "Coping with Civil Disobedience." We cadets were asked to imagine that we were in command of a platoon of His Majesty's forces vastly outnumbered by an unruly mob. We were on the *maidan* (open square) of one of India's teeming textile cities. The agitators, described as Gandhi-wallas, were in a nasty mood, shouting, pushing, hurling rocks. Our job was to stop the spread of the riot and restore order.

The drill called for the officer to have at his side the police chief and the highest civil authority, the magistrate. The magistrate—and the whole plan went astray if he had skipped town—was called upon to read the riot act. In a quavering voice, without benefit of loudspeaker, he was to warn the mob that they were illegally congregated and must disperse, otherwise the troops would fire. Should this message fail to mollify the surging, chanting crowds, a single soldier must be ordered to fire for effect at a specific target, usually the ringleader. He would most often aim at the legs.

We were reminded of the infamous incident at Amritsar in 1919, when General Dyer ordered troops to fire into a crowd, killing hundreds, to provide a potent rallying cry for opponents of British rule until independence in 1947.

To us novices, the Indian political scene seemed peaceful enough. Unarmed and without anxiety, we wandered the streets of the bazaar in Belgaum surrounded by the teeming, lively crowds common to any Indian city. If there were people in those crowds who hated us, they did not show it.

I believe that most of my British companions, few of whom knew much more about India than myself, would have agreed that India should be allowed independence of British rule one day, and some would have said tomorrow. None of us would have forecast a date so soon as 1947. It was hard for a soldier to bother himself about such matters in time of war. The British had been ruling parts of India for two and a half centuries, and all of it for nearly a hundred years. Everything was so settled. Self-government by the Indians certainly must come, but not now, when there were enemies at the back door.

Self-government, independence—there were still British about who did not believe that Indians were capable of running their own affairs. On the other hand, there were plenty of British who knew that independence must come sooner than their own pensions, men who conscientiously trained their successors, aware that by doing so they were burying their own careers.

At the highest level, under the viceroy, India was governed by the members of the Indian Civil Service (the ICS). This crème de la crème numbered around a thousand men. It was recruited through stiff, open competition, and was famous for its incorruptibility and its efficiency. Its members administered the districts into which India was split, manned the provincial and central secretariats, and provided personnel for the higher reaches of the political, judicial, customs, and other branches of government. Below the ICS in the hierarchy of administration were the other imperial services such as the Indian Forest Service, the Indian Medical Service, the Public Works Department, and the Indian Police.

In 1923 Indians in the ICS numbered about 10 percent. Until the end of World War I, Indianization moved slowly. By 1947, the year of independence, the ICS was 50 percent Indian, and the supporting services almost wholly so. The last recruitment of Britons into the ICS was in 1939. It had ceased earlier for the other services. Only with the Indian Army, as has already been described, had Indianization been slow, and with the advent of war that was expanding swiftly.

Geoffrey Moorhouse states that by 1947 in the other professions there were 92,000 registered Indian doctors trained in Western medicine, nearly 100,000 university teachers, and many thousands more teachers in the schools. There were engineers, pilots, printers, industrial tycoons (a few), lawyers by the gross, and a myriad of politicians, some of whom were immensely able and were governing provinces.[2]

Along the twin tracks of political freedom and material progress, the British could be accused of traveling too slowly, but they had covered some distance. There was now a well-educated layer of Indian professionals and intellectuals at the top and a growing band of middlemen who between them were already handling much of the country's government and its law and order. Except at the highest level, Indians conducted the commerce. Those who had benefited least looked to be the mass of peasant farmers, too many of whom were still debt-ridden and stuck in a Stone Age agricultural technology. Progress since Akbar's day had been patchy and slow.

As others have found out, it is virtually impossible to change a people's ingrained social and cultural habits except through violent revolution. And the revolution has to be conducted by the people's own leaders. The British had neither the inclination nor the means for violent revolution.

Then there was the India of the princes, the rulers of the semi-independent princely states. The maharajas, the rajahs, the nizams, and the nawabs still ran their principalities and maintained their state forces. Some were tiny, one or two vast. Hyderabad had an area of 83,000 square miles and a population of fourteen and a half million. Some were poor, others rich. There were 562 princely states, each bound to Britain by its own treaty. They accounted for about one third of the land area. This land was never under direct British rule; Britain was the protecting power. The princes governed with a British resident at their elbows (the smaller fiefdoms might have to share this paragon). They were left alone if justice and the state accounts were in good order, but there was no doubt as to the ultimate boss.

The princes tended to favor British rule, to fear independence, and with good cause. What place was there for them in a democracy? By the mid-1940s they were an anachronism, their future a cause of much heartburn. They did not long survive the British departure.

The interwar years in India have been called the period of reform. Those twenty-odd years between 1918 and 1939, which throughout the world started with so much hope and ended with such despair, witnessed a seesaw of events and emotions on the Indian political scene. In 1917 Edwin Montagu, Britain's Secretary of State for India, told the British House of Commons that his government would take "substantial steps as soon as possible" to effect responsible government in India. There lay hope, partly realized.

In 1915 Gandhi arrived from South Africa with his preaching of nonviolence, his rejection of caste, and his growing power over the Indian National Congress. The Indian National Congress had been founded in 1885 by an Englishman, Allan Hume, a retired member of the Indian civil service. It had the support of the viceroy of the day. Its aim was to promote the regeneration of India, concentrating first on political reform. Through the early years there were regular expressions of loyalty to the British Crown; only gradually did the congress become confrontational.

The dreadful Amritsar massacre of 1919 was a setback to amicable progress. Throughout the period political India alternated between bouts of unrest, even of extreme disturbance, and of renewed political advance.

In 1931, for example, with a new, get-tough National government in power in Britain, civil disobedience in India resulted in 36,000 Congress followers in jail, including Gandhi. Yet the 1935 Government of India Act brought in changes to the central and provincial governments that "meant that India was bound to become independent within a generation at most."[3] After the provincial elections of 1937, Congress-led governments controlled the majority of the huge provinces (eight out of eleven). The franchise now included about one sixth of the population, including women for the first time.

On September 3, 1939, the first day of World War II, the viceroy, Lord Linlithgow, immediately declared that India, too, was at war with Germany. He did this without consulting a single Indian and without giving any political assurances as to the future of the country. The eight provincial Congress governments resigned and refused to support the war effort. Understandably, Congress was not prepared to fight for Britain's freedom, unless offered freedom for itself. There were civil disturbances in 1940, and again on a large scale in 1942.

In 1942 the British government had offered India complete independence when the war was over and increased participation in the government immediately. Congress came close to acceptance. In the end, swayed by Gandhi, they thought they could do better. Malaya, Singapore, and Burma had fallen to the Japanese. Their forces were on the eastern borders of India and were expected to invade when the monsoon died. This had to be a good moment to strike for complete and immediate independence. Congress started the Quit India campaign in August. Despite Gandhi's nonviolence, this released widespread murder and destruction, much of it carefully organized. Gandhi himself said it was rebellion.

He and the Congress leaders were promptly interned (in a palace) until the end of the war. More than a thousand people from both sides were killed, sixty thousand arrested. Over much of India, but particularly in the United Provinces and Bihar, there were attacks by gangs of saboteurs on the railways, the roads, the post and telegraph systems, police stations, and other government installations. In some areas all forms of communication were cut except for horses and feet. It was a difficult and nerve-fraying time for district and police officers (many of whom were Indian). For the first time since the 1857 Mutiny, troops were called out on a substantial scale.

With hindsight it can be seen that Congress miscalculated. They had rebuffed an opportunity to get most of what they wanted within a united India. Congress was predominantly Hindu. India was predominantly Hindu. However, there were large Muslim minorities, particularly in the northwest and in the east. The word *minority* may be misleading. In a total population of 400 million, we are talking of 90 million Muslims, a huge number. In 1942 the Muslim League under Muhammed Ali Jinnah might have settled for some form of federal arrangement within a central government and an undivided country. When next the chance came to negotiate for independence at the war's end in 1945, the Muslim League's mood had hardened. Jinnah saw to it that India was split. Pakistan was born.

Many Britons with knowledge of India still look with deepest disappointment upon this failure to keep the country a political unity. Their forefathers had brought unity and stability to a land that was divided and unstable. With firm government and a unified army, with roads, railways, telegraphs, and education, they had united the many languages, religions, and races of this vast area. The last-minute division hurt.

Back to 1943. The months of unrest and the calling out of troops had not only seriously disrupted communications to the eastern front, it had delayed training schedules for the fresh units being readied for the winter campaign season, and had interrupted reorganizations and preparations of many kinds. Yet by the time I reached Belgaum in March 1943, everything seemed normal.

Humphrey Trevelyan (Lord Trevelyan), in his delightful memoir *The India We Left,* writing as a former member of the ICS and a man on the spot, says: "In a large part of the country the political struggle hardly ruffled the surface until the end of British rule was in sight, when the machine began to run down and communal pressures could no longer be kept in check."[4]

As I have said, we officer cadets were given some instruction in what to do if the army was called in to help with quelling a civil disturbance. Looking back, I am astonished at how little we cogs in the military machine were touched by the political dramas. British and Indian, military and civilian, we got on with the jobs that fate had assigned to us, happily consuming our rumble-tumble (scrambled egg) for breakfast each morning and downing our beer or our gimlets (gin with lime juice) each evening. The disastrous famine in Bengal during 1943 was another horror about which I, insulated in distant Belgaum, heard little. Around two million probably died. I do not think that we even knew. It was not difficult to bury our heads in the sand and hope that riot and famine would never arise on our own patch.

Political disturbance appeared to have virtually no effect on recruitment into the army; and disaffection within the army, when it occurred, was not often traceable to political causes. I deal with the one major exception, the Indian National Army, in Chapter 13, as this organization was unknown to most of us until 1944 and does not seem to have been a factor on the political scene in India until 1945.

Communal pressures were another story. Every year intercommunal hatreds, hunger, caste rivalries, religious touchiness, local political ambitions, and British insensitivity caused outbreaks of violence somewhere, usually in the teeming cities. Normally the police coped. Indian politicians of my day and earlier blamed the yoke of British imperialism and accused the British of practicing "Divide and Rule." Perhaps there was something in this. But I notice that riots and mayhem of every kind seem about as common now as ever they were. The tensions between India and Pakistan, which have occasionally burst into war, seem permanent.

Anyway, as the lecturer droned on through the swish of ceiling fans and in the postluncheon heat, the riot scenario lacked reality. We aimed to be soldiers, not policemen. Our targets would surely be German or Japanese, not the smiling, amiable Indians among whom we happily wandered in our hours of leisure.

Continued bad news from the Burma front did little to hurry the pace or update the content of our training. Many hours were set aside for the elementary drills of weapon training: changing the barrels on the Bren gun, sighting the Lee-Enfield rifle, ranging the two-inch mortar. Some of this had not advanced much since the Afghan wars of the nineteenth century, but one concession to topicality was antiaircraft drill.

This involved quick-aiming the rifle at a miniature Zero plane that the instructor swung in circles from a string at the top of a pole. He would shout "Enemy plane left . . . enemy plane overhead! Look sharp, you fool!" Our veterans from the Western Desert seemed skeptical of this lesson.

"Knocking out tanks" was a subject demanding even greater faith. If confronted by one of these steel monsters while armed only with a rifle, have no fear, advised the instructor. Stand your ground, fire at the slots. The slots were minute peepholes and the firepower of a tank was awesome. Only blind confidence could suggest survival.

Another plan called for the fearless rifleman to dash alongside the tank and plant on its side a magnetized "sticky bomb." Eight seconds later the bomb would detonate the tank into shredded metal. All this asked for considerable imagination: neither tanks nor magnetic bombs were available.

We moved into more advanced areas of learning, including TEWTS—tactical exercises without troops. These required us to wander over the countryside in small groups, or syndicates, consulting our map cases and deciding how to deal with a notional enemy confronting our notional position while apportioning our own hypothetical troops, guns, and supplies. Usually one of the zealous ex-sergeants, destined to waste his talent for battle plans in the Service Corps, would come up with a brilliant solution. This allowed the rest of us to ride on his glory.

My only failing grade was in map reading. The instructor was unimpressed with the sketch map I made of the area known as "Leper Asylum." Fifty years on I shall attribute this lapse to one of those hot afterlunch sessions that inspired dozing rather than good work.

Toward the end of the course we were sent on a jungle penetration exercise. Midday, with a column of six, I found myself slogging uphill along a narrow path through dripping forest. We hoped soon to reach our objective, an abandoned Buddhist temple deep in the jungle to the south of Belgaum. Suddenly the silence was broken by the clattering of hooves, fierce snorting, and a rush of wind as two tons of brown hide topped by a dangerous span of horns charged down the center of the trail and we dived to either side. With the speed of a locomotive the gaur was past us and around a bend, as terrifying as anything in the Madrid bullring. The splintered gunstock held by a fellow cadet confirmed our luck. There could easily have been another headstone in one of India's forgotten Christian graveyards: "Died when gored by a bison."

We cadets were accorded guest privileges at the civilian club in Belgaum. It was a particularly gloomy clubhouse administered by a sour secretary. A bearer in a floppy turban shuffled into the library with a tray of orange squash. We leafed through year-old copies of the *Illustrated London News,* the *Sphere,* and the *Tatler,* and enjoyed pictures with captions like "Lady Wilburton-Warwick at the Mirabelle with Lt Jukes-Baring, Brigadier Wilburton-Warwick is overseas." Here in the enclave of Englishness the members could withdraw from contact with the natives and the cow-dung-scented world of the clamorous bazaar, from the petty criminals, the beggars, the land disputes, the incipient famines.

On sectors of the globe once controlled by the British, wherever there were four possible players, a golf course was laid out. When I ventured onto the Belgaum course with Jupe or with Bill Nichols, each of us was provided with a caddy and we had an extra caddy whose job it was to lurk out ahead to spot balls that might hook into the rough. The caddy's fee was considerably less than the cost of a hard-to-obtain new ball.

Parched fairways sloped off both sides of a ridge. While a roll of three hundred yards on the drive was not unusual across the hard-packed surface, it was unlikely that the ball would stay on the same fairway. Smack in the middle of one par-five hole was a temple, creating a hazard of some magnitude, demanding a shot of both loft and distance with mandatory use of the third caddy on the far side.

Bill Nichols was originally from Brookline, Massachusetts, a strong center for racket sports. He located the only squash court in Belgaum. I played several times with him until he dropped me (which he now denies) in favor of a regular game with the wife of a Sikh officer instructor. I can't blame him. Her game was probably quite up to mine, and it is likely that Bill found this emancipated lady who played in a Punjabi blouse and baggy pantaloons a more interesting part of the Asian experience.

Female diversion at Belgaum was provided by the daughters of the small Anglo-Indian railway community. Over the years some term-expired British soldiers, rather than return to an uncertain future in Britain, chose to stay in India and take Indian wives. Many found work with the extensive railroads crisscrossing the subcontinent. With their half-caste children, these people occupied a unique place, neither Indian nor British, and accepted socially by neither community.

We heard that should a British officer of one of the elite regiments be seen too often with a Eurasian girl, a stern warning from the CO would certainly reach him. Failure to drop her might result in banishment from the regiment, or at the least would hurt his chance for promotion.

In the OTS at Belgaum and in this time of war, the lines were less sternly drawn. Several of my fellow cadets made sallies into the railway community, and a lucky few arranged to escort one of the pretty and supposedly hot-blooded girls on a Sunday afternoon bicycle picnic. A blanket would be carried to serve both as a picnic table and as a couch should the hoped-for dalliance materialize.

Some of us were invited to tea by well-meaning missionaries, treated to discussions on the weather and the postage rates and exhorted to attend church.

On Saturday evenings we cycled into town where the bazaar

cinema allowed us, despite rasping sound and numerous reel changes, to enjoy the latest Ginger Rogers film, or to glimpse the war outside our remote outpost through Fox Movietone News.

My favorite instructor was a captain of dashing appearance and considerable charm recently returned from serving with the Tochi Scouts on the North-West Frontier. From the Tochi Tiger, as we nicknamed him, we heard with fascination of the perils of keeping order among the treacherous tribes of that area. His stories of constant patrolling, intrigue, and even shootouts among the Muslim Mahsuds, Afridis, and Mohmands charmed us greatly. But he endeared himself even more for his ability to put on a first-class *bandobast*.

Bandobast, meaning "arrangement," was a word much used in India. In Gurkhali, which I had to learn later, one often heard the phrase *ramro* ("good") or *naramro* ("bad") *bandobast*. The Tochi Tiger was a master of *ramro bandobast*.

On one exercise under his command we were resting during the heat of midday in the shade of a grove of mango trees heavy with ripe fruit. The school oxcart creaked into our midst guided by two turbaned mess waiters. On the cart was the usual keg of lemonade. In addition the Tochi Tiger had somehow arranged for baskets filled with Cornish pasties.

That one of these delights—the ripe mangoes or the pasties— was responsible for a subsequent unease of digestion did not dim our gratitude.

Some months later the *Gazette of India* carried the notice that the Tochi Tiger had died "of wounds sustained in the Arakan."

To communicate effectively with the men in the ranks of the Indian Army we were given intensive lessons in Urdu, understood over much of the subcontinent. We had evening tutoring with a *munshi*, or private tutor. Our *munshi* was unique in that he was Jewish. A man of about thirty, as Indian in appearance as Gunga Din, he was part of a small and ancient community founded hundreds of years back by a wandering Jew who had settled, surrounded by Hindus, in a village near Goa. As a teacher he had talent. Jupe and I passed the written and oral test after 90 days instead of the permitted 120. Thus we qualified for a grant of 90 rupees, at that time worth all of twenty-five dollars, from the Raj. In passing, when we became second lieutenants, our pay shot up to the giddy heights of 446 rupees per month.

The Indian who oversaw the Urdu classes in the school congratulated Jupe and me on passing the tests. He assured us that we "would take back with us the means of becoming a powerful link in the chain of understanding between the Orient and American civilization." Our reply was probably inadequate, and I fear that our lives did not exactly fulfill his prediction.

My newfound command of elementary Urdu proved of value in bazaar negotiations, in ordering tea through a railway carriage window, and in demanding hot bathwater at the Grand Hotel in Calcutta. However, it was of little use to me in the military. The moment I joined a Gurkha regiment, I was forced into a new linguistic experience, learning Gurkhali. I forgot much of my Urdu.

With the Gurkhali I somehow missed out on formal classroom instruction. No one taught me a basic understanding of verb declensions, genders, or sentence structure. I learned through what is now called total immersion. With about a hundred Gurkhas in a rifle company, and only rarely accompanied by another officer, one was condemned to silence and uselessness until the struggle to pick up the language had begun to bear fruit.

The Indian Army was recruited from many peoples. It was during one of the Tochi Tiger's lectures on the makeup of the army that I first became intrigued with the story of the Gurkhas. For 150 years—in the Indian Mutiny, through scores of minor wars on the borders of India and in Burma, and not least in World War I in France, Mesopotamia, and at Gallipoli—these short, stalwart Mongolians had fought for the British Raj in return for adventure, pride, money, and escape from the hard life of their villages in the Himalayas. My interest was fueled by the romance of their coming down from mysterious Nepal, at that time a country forbidden to Westerners.

On July 4, American Independence Day, and toward the end of our course, a document arrived from GHQ in New Delhi listing the postings we had drawn to fill the officer requirements of the moment. I had indicated a preference for Gurkhas. I drew Indian

Army Ordnance Corps, a formation no doubt essential to the war effort but far from my idea of a *pukka* posting.

I appealed to the good Sergeant Major Phillips. I found him not only sympathetic but willing to bend his usual strict adherence to regulations. He shuffled the papers so that some other less romantic soul was able to spend the rest of the war quietly supervising the manufacture of mines while Jupe and I headed for the more elite 8th Gurkha Regimental Center in Quetta. I never regretted the choice.

At the passing-out parade we were addressed by the commandant, Major Courtney-Hood. He made it clear that he did not really approve of commissions for other ranks, although, so he told us, he tried to face up to this unsatisfactory necessity. After all, there was a war on. He hoped that some of the better qualified among us would convert our emergency commissions to regular ones and that we might become more than temporary gentlemen. His closing admonition was this: "Do remember, gentlemen, that when things become confused, as they inevitably do both in war and in peace, an other rank will say there has been a 'fuck up'; an officer will always refer to a 'foul up.' "

Probably the commandant was right to be suspicious of our competence. I have since read that there was a critical shortage of suitable potential officers in 1943 and 1944, to the point where it inhibited further expansion of the Indian Army. So now I marvel less that so many of us were commissioned, and that six Americans were slipped in.

Postscript: Of the other four Americans who left Cairo and went through Belgaum with me and Jupe Lewis, Bill Nichols was posted to the Royal Garwhal Rifles and then transferred to Mars Force, the new American infantry unit operating in northern Burma. Pat Pattullo joined the Frontier Force Rifles. Al Wright joined the 5th Gurkhas, to be wounded in the Mediterranean theater. Tall, lean Ralph Muller distinguished himself before an appreciative gathering of cadets at the bar of our Belgaum mess by tearing a cartilage in his knee while demonstrating how an about-turn (or, in American parlance, an about-face) should be performed. On recovery he joined the Jats and was posted to Italy and the 4th Indian Division. He was wounded at Cassino (seven months in the hospital in Caserta, six months' convalescent leave in London), and then found himself Assistant Military Attaché with the Indian legation in Washington. From there he transferred to Lord Louis Mountbatten's staff, traveling through Ceylon, Indochina, Burma, Indonesia, Cambodia, and Malaya. He left the army in October 1946, and his subsequent adventures are summarized in the epilogue.

CHAPTER V

I Join the Gurkhas

On July 8, 1943, we were officially commissioned. We were converted to gentlemen, however temporary. Proudly we put up on each shoulder the single pip that proclaimed the new status. Now we were ECOs, Emergency Commissioned Officers, second lieutenants in the Indian Army. The following day we boarded the Bombay Mail and headed for a few days' leave before reporting to our regiments.

Jupe and I shared a gigantic room in the Taj Mahal Hotel that cost each of us the equivalent of $4.50 a day, including meals. Through the chatter of diners and the clatter of cutlery both midday and evening meals were accompanied by the Taj string quartet playing Richard Addinsell's Warsaw Concerto and the like. Outside it was monsoon time: gray skies, bursts of heavy rain, maximum humidity. It was a more intense version of the heat common to summer in Saint Louis or New Orleans, even New York, conducive to raising heat rash on the body and green mold on the shoes.

Supplied by the hotel, a bearer sat on his haunches at our door ever ready to shine shoes, run baths, or press trousers in preparation for social encounters. These were not too spectacular. We were competing with senior officers for the vastly outnumbered nurses and WRENs (members of the Women's Royal Naval Service). I did once enjoy a dance with an attractive Italian lady, a refugee from the recent Abyssinian campaign. Perhaps she mistook my single star for a major's crown.

After ten days of sparse socializing, a lot of buffalo milk shakes during the day, and too many gin-and-limes at night, we were not unhappy to board a train for Quetta, far to the northwest. Quetta was home for the training center of the 8th Gurkha Rifles. The journey would take three days and two nights.

After leaving the confusion of Bombay station the train climbed slowly through the jungles of the Western Ghats and then rolled through Rajputana and into the principality of Baroda. It made numerous stops. At each we gazed out of our compartment window at the multitudes of Indians milling in every direction. Skinny, mangy dogs roamed the platforms, not always with four legs, fighting over scraps dropped by the grimy vendors seeking to sell to us passengers. Tea, cakes, chappatis, and fruit were shoved through the window in exchange for a few annas. Water-sellers paraded, some with Hindu water, others with pails for the Moslems, all chanting their willingness to pour into the cupped hands of the customer. Unbelievable numbers of poorer Indians packed into the third-class carriages. Suitcases, tin boxes, crates, roped bundles, and bodies of every age were jammed solid on the wooden benches, the floor, the baggage racks, hanging out of the windows, clinging to the roof. Judging from the photos I see now as the century draws to a close, this has not changed. Most stations had a cow or two wandering on the platform. Sometimes monkeys would clatter down from the station roof.

At the city of Baroda the gauge changed. Red-turbaned coolies attacked each compartment for the right to carry luggage the few hundred yards to the wide-gauge train waiting to take us north. The coolie successful in cornering my business led off with my tin trunk on his head, my bedding roll under one arm, and a suitcase under the other. He was two thirds my size, barefoot, skinny, legs like beanpoles; still I had difficulty keeping up with him as we hurried to establish rights to lower berths and, if possible, a compartment to ourselves.

Some stops were long enough for a meal in the station dining room. Occasionally there was tasteless river fish, more often watery soup followed by stringy chicken. Like station restaurants anywhere in the world, those in India served indifferent food. However, due to foresight in laying down large stocks early in the war, they were an oasis able to provide the thirsty traveler with a wide variety of alcoholic refreshment.

Flies were everywhere, and they hardly stirred in response to the movement of the *punkas* (fans). Sometimes the *punkas* were turned languidly by electricity. More often they consisted of cloth flaps hung from the ceiling and swung by the hand or toe of a lowly *punka-walla*, paid a few pice to tug on a rope.

Finishing the baked caramel custard, the usual dessert offered, with a third cup of tea, we heard the whistle of the train tooting impatiently. A harried stationmaster entered the dining room to inquire if the sahibs were not ready to leave as the engineer was anxious to get under way.

In the afternoon, still in hill country, the locomotive gasped to a halt to take on more coal. Passengers traveling with their bearers (who rode in the small servants' compartment adjoining first-class) had them dash along the track to the engine to tap hot water from the steaming boiler for tea.

On the second morning of the journey the rails dropped from the jungle down to the stony desert of Sind. Left behind were the overflowing skies of the monsoon. Dust seeped through every crack in our carriage. The thermometer soared to above 118°F. Now an ingenious air cooler was put into operation. A feeble electric fan was aimed at a slab of ice melting in a tub placed on the floor in the center of the compartment. This caused faint puffs of cooler air to bounce off the shrinking ice and into the stifling atmosphere. Wooden blinds cut off the blazing sun.

Because of another variation in track width we changed trains again at Hyderabad. This city is just north of Karachi in what is now Pakistan. Here we were warned of the danger of attack from brigands, the Hurs. These bandits had been terrorizing the countryside ahead, holding up trains, chopping up the passengers with hatchets, removing the booty, and riding off into the sunset. Their leader, the Pir Pagaro, was an almost mythical figure in 1943, a combination of ruthless fanatic and Jesse James. He preached independence for the province of Sind and financed himself by pillage. Substantial reward was offered for his capture dead or alive. It was rumored that two brigades of troops were tied up in his pursuit.

Picking up *The New York Times* in 1977 and reading of the difficulties of Prime Minister Bhutto of Pakistan, to my surprise the Pir Pagaro again figured in the news. It was not my 1943 friend, who was caught and hanged for murder. It was his spiritual descendant (the title is hereditary), apparently a respected and potent force in settling Pakistan's problems.

We cleared the desert without incident and entered the long Bolan Pass. A second powerful locomotive was added, for the line now tunneled and climbed some five thousand feet to the plateau where Quetta lay, and beyond which was the famous North-West Frontier. On the plateau, stops might be at no more than a cluster of sun-baked mud huts, sometimes only at a post in the ground marking the distance to Quetta, with a few surly Pathans outstaring the passengers. Tall, tough Baluchis, brothers to the hostile tribesmen farther west, displayed beneath black locks their prominent noses and blue eyes, throwbacks to Alexander's army, which had swept down into northern India so many centuries ago.

At length we reached Quetta. Much of the train's freight was loaded onto camels attended by raffish bandits identified as the Army Camel Corps. But Captain Peter Rawson, who came to meet us, had more modern transport—a truck driven by a Gurkha. At this point Jupe discovered that he was never again to see his tin trunk, which he had checked in at Bombay. The retrieval stub he had been handed was made out to a gentleman from Karachi entitling him to twelve baskets of dates.

Even in late July the early morning air of Quetta's five thousand-foot altitude was cool, dry, and invigorating. The city (of under fifty thousand people) had been rebuilt after a devastating earthquake in 1935. Donkeys, cattle, and camels roamed in and out of the open bazaar, set amid low, uninteresting shops and warehouses. The men milling about inspecting the merchandise ranged from short, dark traders from the south to tall, pale, rifle-carrying tribesmen from beyond the frontier hills. The women, and there were not many about, were enshrouded within the head-to-toes shapeless *burka*, a garment prescribed by Moslem custom to hide their every feature from lecherous eyes.

Capital of Baluchistan, Quetta has always been an important mart on the trade route between Kandahar, in southern Afghanistan, and the lower Indus valley. Armies tend to follow trade routes. Like the even more spectacular, wild, and fabled Khyber Pass to the north, this highway through Quetta and down the Bolan Pass has been a traditional path for invaders entering India.

Outside the town to the north, and sprawled over a stony plain, were the barracks and parade grounds of the military cantonment. Some miles off across the plain to the east and north rose the first of the mountains, barren, and looking close in the clear air. The cantonment comprised a number of establishments. The best known was the staff college, attended by many of Britain's famous army commanders, including Field Marshal Bill Slim (as a student in 1926) and Field Marshal Bernard Montgomery (as chief instructor, 1934–1937).

Halfway between the town and the army were the club (now earthquake proof), a row of shops including tailors, and a cinema catering to the military.

Our inexperienced driver handled the lorry as though it were a live and unruly beast. He was determined to keep the upper hand, driving with aggressive verve. It was a relief to achieve a jolting halt outside a whitewashed one-story structure on the edge of Kuch Lines.

The building was a row of five or six rooms. It was made of mud brick with a corrugated iron roof, and had a wide communal veranda along one side. There was not a bush or a tree within view. As I soon discovered, one of the main camel routes into Quetta from the mountains of the frontier passed within a few yards of the rear of the building. Senior officers had superior quarters nearer the mess. Itinerant juniors such as Jupe and I shared rooms in this desolate spot a mile away up a hill.

Peter Rawson saw us unloaded and left. Posted to the 3/8th

Gurkhas in Burma, he won an MC (Military Cross), and then was killed in action on March 1, 1945.

Soon I had curled my six-foot-two frame into a metal tub three feet in diameter to wash off that part of the Sind desert still with me. Each room had a bath cubicle attached, the *gussal-khana*. I sat soaking, half overflowing onto the matted rope floor cover, and took in our quarters. The furnishings included two rope beds, a dresser, a chiffonier, a desk and chair each, and a fireplace (which we never had time to enjoy). The walls were whitewashed, the floor was concrete. Such was my introduction to the regiment of my choice.

In addition to its starkness, Kuch presented the inconvenience of a cycle ride back and forth to the mess and parade grounds. Each parade seemed to require a change of uniform. The cycles were rented out by the cantonment contractor, a Pathan scoundrel with a monopoly to purvey goods and services to the regiment. They seldom retained air in their scarred tires. Nor had I, an American more accustomed to riding the Madison Avenue bus than cycling, the muscles necessary for uphill pedaling. After a late evening in the mess, the long grind until the squat white building at Kuch stood out in the moonlight did have the benefit of burning off excess alcohol.

In the mess that evening I met my fellow officers. One was the rakish young Huxley-Duggan, whose patched-up nose pointed sideways at an alarming angle. This was an early clue to the unusual importance Colonel Willasey-Wilsey, gruff martinet and commandant of the center, placed on the success of his boxing teams at the All-India championships and other contests.

We juniors hardly saw Colonel W-W. By day he evidently did not feel the need to concern himself with our affairs. He must have spent his evenings at home with his family. And why not? But rightly or wrongly, some of us had the feeling that he took a jaundiced view of the emergency officers and was happy when he could dispose of us to the battalions. On the plus side, when he was with the 1/8th in Palestine in 1918 he had won a Military Cross for bravery, and he was now said to run one of the most efficient and effective regimental centers in India.

In the fifty-page "A Brief Outline History of the 8th Gurkha Rifles," which Colonel W-W wrote and had published in 1944, and which was intended for young officers such as myself on first posting to the regiment, he described the regiment's occupation as "Killing Huns and Japs" and listed as the regiment's hobbies "Any sport that toughens for war."[1] Those phrases reveal a lot about the man, and also about the times in which we then lived.

It was soon clear that I had joined a "sporty" regiment. Sport was encouraged "because it is considered that all the activities that are developed in sport and in training for sport, are of the utmost value in war and in training for war."[2] Football, hockey, athletics, and boxing were the favored activities. Naik Lalbahadur Thapa became the Junior Provincial Athletic Champion in 1943, and All-India Amateur Flyweight Boxing Champion in 1944. Behind him was a host of keen sportsmen, all trained up in a year or so from men who had mostly never played any sort of sporting game until they joined the army. My preferred activities of squash, tennis, and golf were not among those taught to our recruits.

While the British officer in India was quite capable of living under the most rugged conditions if necessary, he saw no point in suffering needlessly. Unlike his American counterpart, he felt no guilt while enjoying comforts not available to his men. There were no egalitarian doubts. Whenever possible he surrounded himself with whiskey, books, good food, and numerous servants. Extra delicacies for the table were covered by a mess fee of a few rupees each month deducted from each officer's pay. His pay, which came from the Indian treasury, was more generous than for the equivalent rank in Britain.

Customs and rules in the Indian Army had evolved to support men who were there for a career, not merely for the duration of a campaign or a war. God willing, they meant to be around for twenty or thirty years. "Going native" was frowned on. It was not merely from a conviction of racial superiority: health, mental and physical, for the Westerner probably depended on a measure of separateness from the way of living to which his men were accustomed. In battle it was another matter. An officer looked after his men before he looked after himself, and shared their hardships.

Our regimental officers' mess in Quetta, some two thousand

miles as the hawk flies from the nearest Japanese, seemed to me particularly sumptuous. On that first evening I found my fellow officers being served before-dinner sherries and whiskies in the subdued and opulent atmosphere of the billiard room and lounge, where a blazing fire cut the evening chill. Moving to the dining room, we were surrounded by silver trophies and horned heads along the wall, reminders of past triumphs on the fields of sport, battle, and hunt. Seated at a long polished mahogany table set with quality Spode, we were served an excellent meal.

On that first evening I fell short of making quite the right impression. I had not known that in addition to the regular mess waiters, it was customary for personal bearers to stand behind our chairs to insure that needs were promptly satisfied.

This is how Jupe described such service in a letter home:

> My bearer Ali Khan (brave king), serving his first stint in the mess, was outfitted at my expense in spotless white, broad green sash, neatly wound turban, jacket sleeves too long. I sat down at my place and looked around to see approaching slowly up the aisle my bearer carrying a bowl of soup as though it was a silver bowl of rubies that he was about to have the honor of laying at the feet of the Viceroy. When eventually he arrived he placed the soup before me with such extreme care, concentration and dignity, I doubted that the rest of the meal would reach me by breakfast time. He stands behind my chair watching like a hungry hawk. When a potato falls off my fork I want to turn round and apologise. At breakfast he is constantly pushing more butter and marmalade toward the toast than is prudent.

Later that week I witnessed a more formal dinner, my first mess night. That occasion brought in the married officers (who normally dined in their cottages) and the commandant and the second-in-command. Guests were drawn from whichever high-ranking officers or civil administrators were in the area.

The evening provided my baptismal exposure to the serenading of the diners during dinner by Gurkha bagpipers. I have to presume they played well, but *din* is the word to describe the pipes a few feet from one's ear.

Toward the end of the meal as the clatter of china was superseded by the chatter of wine-loosened voices, a cut-glass decanter of port moved in the traditional leftward direction around the table. Then came the solemn toast to the King Emperor. On this first occasion it struck me as an amusing, old-fashioned rite, though impressive. Similar pledges were no doubt being made at the same moment in other regimental messes in every corner of the Empire.

More than two years later I was again in Quetta prior to demobilization. I was present for another mess night, and this time happened to be the senior officer present. Protocol dictated that I must call on Mr. Vice to propose the ritual toast to the Crown. I remember with even more amusement, and at the same time a sense of privilege, that moment when I, a Republican Connecticut Yankee, led this symbolic royalist rite.

After dinner the more senior officers retired, either to their bungalows or to the billiard room. The younger ones sometimes launched into a form of rugby in the lounge. Special rules protected the furniture and the trophies. From this roughhouse I excused myself, preferring to inject myself into the snooker game.

On Sunday morning before *tiffin* (lunch) the band played on the lawn in front of the mess. The regimental band had earned an impressive reputation between the wars. Even the much reduced wartime band was considered very good. Round-faced Gurkhas, newly schooled on the cornet and Western music, puffed into their instruments a valiant version of "You Are My Sunshine" while numerous gin-and-limes were downed by the officers and wives. The hot Madras curry that followed insured deep somnolence through the early afternoon.

After the nap and before tea, the thing to do was to cycle up the slope to the swimming pool at the outskirts of the cantonment and plunge into its icy mountain water. Here, too, we could enjoy ogling the few unattached wives left behind by officers on active service. One or two of these had a reputation for availability, but their interest in dalliance leaned toward those officers more permanently on the scene.

Three distinct cliques gathered each evening in the mess to talk over the day on the parade ground or to leaf through year-old copies of *Punch* and *Country Life*. A small minority were the older regulars, career soldiers who had been commissioned into the army in peacetime, long before the expansions of war. Many of these, like the grizzled quartermaster, were past active service. The regulars clanned together, drinking and talking local gossip.

A second group comprised the younger training staff. They were mostly emergency commissioned and included the eager boxers. Their concern was with the firing range, the drill square, and the upcoming championships to be held at Lahore. It sometimes seemed to us that the boxers could stay at the center indefinitely. It was this second group that tended to monopolize the snooker tables.

In the third group were those like myself and Jupe, mostly newly commissioned, who were destined soon to be posted to one of the active battalions. It was our job to learn as much as possible about the men and weapons while we had the chance.

One officer fitted none of these categories. This was Ian Mac-Horton. He had recently returned from hospital to convalesce from wounds received while with the first Wingate expedition deep into Burma behind the Japanese lines.

Orde Wingate and his Chindits—the name was said to be a corruption of the Burmese word for their mythical griffin, the *chinthe,* guardian of their pagodas—had received wide press coverage. Older readers will recall that during World War II the news was more closely controlled than has sometimes been the case subsequently. In the interests both of operational security and of national morale, censorship was strict. There was probably a measure of agreement for this both in America and Britain. While no one expected to be fed lies, it was understood that revealing the whole truth might on occasion endanger lives.

The paeans of praise for Wingate and his men were carefully orchestrated by the military command in Delhi, desperate for a victory. The press was encouraged to paint Wingate's pioneering sally as a huge success deserving world admiration. Wingate himself, gaunt and bearded, an unconventional, charismatic character who was already planning a second more ambitious foray, knew exactly how to reap the most reward from the publicity.

The world was not told that of the three thousand men who had set off, nearly one thousand were lost. So were most of the mules and equipment. Nor was the world informed that of the battered remnants who returned to India in dribs and drabs, scattered across several hundreds of miles of frontier, many were half starved, suffering from beri-beri and malaria, and were never again fit to fight.

"What did we accomplish?" asked Bernard Fergusson, one of the column commanders, in his classic book, *Beyond the Chindwin*. "Not much that was tangible. What there was became distorted in the glare of publicity soon after our return. We blew up bits of a railway, which did not take long to repair; we gathered some useful intelligence; we distracted the Japanese from some minor operations, and possibly from some bigger ones; we killed a few hundreds of an enemy which numbers eighty millions; we proved that it was feasible to maintain a force by supply dropping alone."[3]

Fergusson was writing his book in June 1944 while the war was still on, and his next sentence reads: "But we amassed experience on which a future has already begun to build."

This clear-eyed and perhaps overharsh summing-up omits the propaganda bonus. The conclusion drawn by the rest of the army in India was that as soldiers we were the equal of the Japs, and that with suitable training and generalship we could fix them. This feeling spread with remarkable speed. And looking back now one can see that although the Chindits endured horrendous risk, heavy casualties, and great hardship for rewards that were of no strategic and small tactical value, psychologically their deeds proved to be golden, a marvelous story of courage and endurance by ordinary men to set against the catalog of failures elsewhere.

Fergusson's paragraph mentions air supply, though he does not stress it. It was in the pioneering of air supply that Wingate's first expedition made its most lasting contribution. For many weeks a number of widely separated mobile columns were fed and resupplied with weapons, ammunition, new wireless sets, clothing, mail, whatever was required. The experiment did not always work well. Bad weather, unexpected Japanese movements, and temperamental wireless units sometimes left men hungry and short of essentials. Everything depended on the ability of the wireless operators to tell the air-transport people, hundreds of miles distant over jungle-clad hills, what to drop and where to drop it. Every column had a Royal Air Force officer marching with it.

On the way back to India, after the columns had split up and most of the wireless sets had been lost in battle or dumped for lack of mules to carry them, the supply system failed, which is why so many of the survivors starved.

> Unless they can be fought over a long time scale, with the whole-hearted support of indigenous populations, Chindit-style operations do not win wars.[4]

> The hard fact was that Wingate had changed the nature of jungle campaigning for good.[5]

These two extracts from relatively recent accounts of the war in Burma show that Wingate still evokes contrasting judgment. I think my vote comes down with Louis Allen, who wrote the second extract above. It is true that Wingate did not win a war. He did not set out to. He did change the nature of jungle campaigning. Sending out formations, small and large, in deep penetrations and wide sweeping encirclements, unhampered by the need for the umbilical cord of land communications, became a feature of the Burma war. This was the factor that most contributed to the defeat of the Japanese in 1944 and 1945. It was, of course, a tactic possible only for a land force that also had command of the air. Shortage of aircraft and hostile weather set the limits.

There were three young 8th Gurkha officers drafted into the first Chindit expedition. Ian MacHorton, Alec Gibson, and Harold James were sent down from Quetta in January 1943 to join the 3/2nd Gurkhas. This was almost at the last hour. "Do you know why you are here?" asked the adjutant when they reported for duty. They confessed total ignorance. "You're going into Burma in a few days' time." And he added, "I suppose you have made out your wills."[6]

All three were recently commissioned second lieutenants, two of them still teenagers, and none of them could speak more than a smattering of Gurkhali. They knew none of the men they were to command, most of whom were wartime recruits without active service experience. They had been through none of the special training the battalion had just completed. This was not the best introduction to what proved to be (as expected) a tough and highly dangerous operation. Both Harold James and Ian MacHorton have written books about their experience (see the Select Bibliography at the end of this book).

Alec Gibson was captured while trying to recross the Irrawaddy and spent the next two years as a prisoner of the Japanese in Rangoon Jail. Two thirds of his fellow inmates died of wounds, brutality, or malnutrition.

It was only a few months before we met him that Ian, wounded in the hip by a mortar blast and unable to walk, had been left behind on the wrong side of the Irrawaddy. The safety of each column depended on its mobility. There could be no passengers. Stretcher parties slowed progress and drained energies. If a man was not able to keep up on his own feet, he was left. That was the harsh reality.

In poor shape, Ian was discovered and hidden by some Burma-Gurkhas until he could hobble with the help of a rough crutch. He set off alone to cover perhaps 150 miles of inhospitable, enemy-dominated territory that included two major rivers, the Irrawaddy and the Chindwin. He was alone for several days. Then by extraordinary fortune he met with another group and with it recrossed the Irrawaddy. This group got split still further. He crossed the Chindwin at night and was again alone. He struggled on, now close to death from starvation and exhaustion. Once more luck intervened. He was found by a patrol of the Mahrattas.

We regarded him with some wonder.

After dinner on Sunday evenings in Quetta a couple of open touring car taxis, driven by Sikhs, took us to the cinema. Seats, booked by telephone, were in a row of sofas and easy chairs reserved for the sahibs. As we made an entrance, some of us noticeable in bulky sheepskin poshteens, lower ranks from the numerous British army and RAF posts around Quetta, already seated on hard benches, would be relentlessly stomping for the picture to begin.

Poshteens were thick cloaks or pelisses evolved for use in the winters of Afghanistan. They were worn with the wool inside. Even in July and August the dry, thin atmosphere lost its heat rapidly. Those of us not sporting poshteens would shiver.

On the first Monday after my arrival in Quetta I began to learn about the factory for the manufacture of soldiers called a regimental center. Ours was one of the ten Gurkha regimental centers spread over northern India. There were similar establishments for all the other regiments of the Indian Army.

The Gurkha centers were very new. It had not been until 1940, a year into the war, that a decision was made to raise another ten Gurkha battalions and permission to do so was obtained from the Maharajah of Nepal. Later a further ten battalions, and various ancillary bodies, were raised.

It was known that something better than the individual battalion training companies would be needed to process the vastly increased flow of recruits. Replacing the heavy casualties of the 1914 and 1915 battles in France had been a nightmare, achieved initially only by milking the battalions still in India, a destructive solution. It had to be expected that in this new war casualties from sickness and battle might again be heavy. So on November 15, 1940, the 8th Gurkha Regimental Center was born. The birth took place in Shillong, eastern India, under the supervision of the redoubtable Colonel Willasey-Wilsey. From instructors to warm blankets, everything was in short supply.

In May 1942 the 8th Center moved across the width of India to Quetta. Shillong was too close to the Japanese incursions along India's eastern border, its facilities too valuable to be occupied by a training center.

By the time of my arrival the center had developed, and went on developing, into

> an enormous and, of necessity, somewhat impersonal "sausage machine" with thousands of raw recruits [from Nepal] pouring in one end, and thousands of "trained" men emerging from the other. Each intake of recruits was sifted on arrival, and then, or as soon after as was practicable, those with more than average

ability or education were earmarked for specialist training. The best were chosen as potential non-commissioned officers, and as often as not gained their first stripe within eighteen months of enlistment. By this means alone, it was possible to provide junior instructional staff and ensure a reasonable turnover with the four active battalions. A similar procedure was adopted with most "intakes" of British officers, although their retention at the Centre, naturally, for all wanted to be off to the front, was unpopular with many, and the subject of much heart burning.[7]

The 8th Center was not seriously geared to the training of new junior British officers. Its energies were almost all directed toward the transformation of illiterate peasant hillmen into skilled infantry soldiers. Green young second lieutenants were a side issue to which neither Willasey-Wilsey nor anybody else appeared to have given more than half a passing thought. From time to time we were sent away to other parts of India on specialist courses. They could be useful. Otherwise we just spent a great many hours watching the recruits at their training. Of course, until we had learned some Gurkhali, we could not communicate. It happened that on this first visit Jupe and I were in the center for only a few days before we were sent off. Most of what I record here about the center was learned after our return.

By the autumn of 1943 there were some six thousand Gurkhas in the center, divided among three training battalions and a holding battalion. In the latter were stored the trained recruits, now proudly classed as riflemen, while they awaited impatiently their dispatch to an active battalion.

Equipment had improved, but remained short: only one Bren gun per platoon, for instance; only three rifles per five men; only three or four mortars for the whole center.

The center did more than train recruits. It had centralized and now kept up-to-date the accounts and records of every man, woman, and child (there were Gurkha families attached) in the regiment, many many thousands of bodies. It organized the sports. It ran a boys company of about 250 promising young Gurkhas, educating and training them to a higher level than was usually possible in the standard five-month course given to the ordinary recruit. It kept track of men on leave, and of the sick and wounded in hospitals.

On the grassless, dusty parade grounds spread out on the plain in every direction, and overlooked by the distant mountains, through the following days and later I watched some of the recruits at various stages of their training. I could see how they were being instructed, toughened, molded into soldiers.

By seven in the morning the sun already beat down with a relentless glare. The only rest for the eye was a single line of trees along one side of the road to the mountains. These trees flourished because they were watered by a snow-fed stream flowing beside the road. It was part of this stream, diverted for an hour or two each day along a branch channel, that was responsible for the trees and bushes around the officers' mess, and that fed ice-cold water to the swimming pool.

Companies of squat, stocky young men in starched shorts and gym shoes ran or marched in every direction. Their high cheekbones and almond-shaped eyes suggested their origins in central Asia. The color of their skin ranged from light brown to dark. Their heads were close-shaven except for the *tupi,* the scalp lock by which God would haul them up to heaven when they died. This flopped from side to side as they moved. They were shepherded by tough-looking Gurkha NCOs and Gurkha officers. It was these men who carried the burden of training and discipline.

I was watching PT. Lots of arm waving, knee bends, push-ups, and running. What the men and boys really enjoyed as part of PT were the games. A relay race or tug-of-war would be accompanied by shouts of glee and raucous laughter. They could never get enough of Simon Says and would play in their own time in the evening.

For the rest of the day the recruits worked relentlessly at the increasingly complicated arts of soldiering. Far from complaining, they reveled in it. This is what they had aspired to from the time they were young boys and had listened to their fathers and uncles telling stories about the honor of serving in the armies of the British king.

I could see that those who had but recently arrived were often underdeveloped, anxious youngsters bewildered by the strangeness of almost everything around them, some of them still baffled by the complexities of marching in step, of "presenting arms" with a rifle, of sleeping on a bed. After a few months of good food, regular exercise, and a growing catalog of skills learned, there were remarkable transformations. Even after a week or two a squad of recruits radiated confidence, cheerful vitality, a new robustness.

From dawn to dusk these youths were exercised, drilled, educated, fed well, and taught the rudiments of soldiering. Most of them were trained as riflemen, the basic unit of every army. Those with aptitude might be designated signalers, mortarmen, machine-gunners, snipers, drivers, and mechanics. Officers who had doubted that the hill Gurkha could learn to master the intricacies of the wireless set, or the petrol engine, were proved wrong. But I would not maintain that every Gurkha was a genius in waiting.

Education included an occasional talk on the geopolitics of the world struggle, but it was doubtful whether the individual rifleman was much concerned that he had been selected to fight Fascism. He was loyal to his friends, to his Gurkha officers and NCOs, and in time perhaps to the pale-complexioned, round-eyed officers who stood on the parade grounds looking important, the visible face of the Raj. That was probably the scope of his awareness. He was earning good money. Life was a lot more exciting than back in the village. He was experiencing trains and toilets, bayonets and boots, electric light, the bicycle, the cinema, the mysteries of reading. He took them all in his stride, joked, and transformed himself, with a little help, into a soldier.

Every army formation assumes, with justification, that newly posted junior officers are in need of brushing up on their proficiency with the basic hardware of war. The 8th Gurkhas was no exception. My own background in this respect was definitely thin compared with that of my companions. Soliciting advertising through the eastern United States, and driving an ambulance in the desert, were hardly to be compared with time in the ranks of the British army and, for many younger wartime officers, several years in school cadet corps. Pat Davis tells me that he was target shooting (with a .22 rifle) from the age of nine, and scampering about the English countryside with a .303 rifle and bayonet from fourteen.

Therefore it was good that on my first morning I was placed in a junior officers' small arms cadre under solidly built, mustached Captain Frank Crouchman, recently transferred from the Guards. He proved to be an excellent instructor. Unfortunately, three days of the course had already passed, and since I was to be dispatched elsewhere at the end of five more days, it was little wonder that I did not become too speedy at stripping and reassembling the Bren gun, or that my proficiency with the rifle and two-inch mortar was not markedly improved. My shortcomings included forgetting to pull the pin when throwing my first grenade.

CHAPTER VI

The Gurkhas

Throughout the time I was in India and Burma, none of us officers got to travel in Nepal, homeland of the Gurkhas. To us it was an unknown, mysterious kingdom, a forbidden country.

For generations Nepal had followed an isolationist policy. British recruiting personnel were barred. Travelers were barred. Each Gurkha regiment in India employed retired Gurkha officers to tour the hills and pick out candidates. In peacetime the number of men required to keep the battalions at strength was not great. During the war, of course, the trickle became a flood.

The young aspirants, as young as sixteen and seventeen, might march for several weeks, certainly for many days, from their villages down to the recruiting centers in India. Here the recruits were checked out by the British for physical fitness and intelligence (and many were rejected) before proceeding to their battalions.

Gurkhas were mercenaries, paid to kill. They were marvelous people, happy, braver than most, trustworthy, loyal—but mercenaries. It is doubtful if those of our day reflected on king and empire. George VI of Britain was not their king (they had one of their own), and Nepal was not part of the British Empire.

The Gurkha soldier is renowned for his courage, and this is the quality he himself values deeply. On a level with courage he might set loyalty. He is intensely loyal to his friends, to his regiment, and to officers whom he trusts. We officers had to earn this loyalty by demonstrating a reasonable competence at our job and by doing better than our best for the safety and welfare of the men in our care.

Pompous behavior, selfish behavior, devious behavior by superior officers is noted and remembered. Much is forgiven, for he does not expect perfection. But he will not care to be shamed before his fellows, to have his self-respect, his honor, discredited. Sarcasm is a weapon never to be used.

Gurkhas are shrewd judges of character. And they are great mimics, of each other and of their officers. At company and battalion entertainments, we Westerners could count on watching ourselves on stage, with sharp caricatures of mannerisms and idiosyncrasies.

Gurkhas love to laugh. Life is a joke. Of course war is serious and death is not one of God's better jests. Yet Gurkhas nearly always contrived to grin. Often their's was banana skin humor. Should a comrade or their officer trip on a tree root, no one would disguise the laughter and the five-minute barrage of caustic repartee that would follow. But it was kindly laughter, accompanied by practical help; the victim could not help but join in.

This had no effect on discipline. Gurkhas seem to have an innate sense of discipline that is linked to their independence. Every Gurkha is his own man. If he chooses to become a soldier and obey the orders of superiors, this in no way diminishes his individuality. He is a volunteer, and outside the necessary professional hierarchies, he is no one's inferior. There were very, very few "old soldiers," those sour-faced, persistent complainers in most other armies who live by the book and hate the world.

Gurkhas are, or were, an extraordinarily direct and honest people. It did not seem to occur to them to steal, cheat, lie, or prevaricate. They had no wish to score off their fellow men. I am writing of a time that is now fifty years gone, and I do not know whether the tidal wave of tourism and the insidious flow of cultural invasion from India and the West may have changed things.

Their bravery is legendary. Britain's highest award for courage in battle is the VC, the Victoria Cross. Queen Victoria and Prince Albert instituted the medal by a Royal Warrant on January 29, 1856. British soldiers of all ranks were eligible from the first, but it was not opened to Indians and Gurkhas of the Indian Army until 1911. Over the longer period thirteen VCs have been won by British officers of the Gurkha Brigade. Since 1911, thirteen have been won by Gurkhas, ten of these during World War II.

Nepal, the Gurkha homeland, is a small landlocked country of 54,000 square miles and a population in 1943 of around 5.6 million (1991 estimate, 20 million). It is set in the southern Himalayas, sandwiched between India to the west, south, and east, and Tibet to the north. At the time of which I write Tibet was independent, India was still controlled by Great Britain. India became independent in 1947; Tibet became a colony of China in 1950.

Nepal is about 520 miles from west to east and some 100 miles from north to south. It can be divided into three east-west strips.

In the south is the Terai, a low-lying area up to thirty-five miles wide of open fields and forest on the fringe of the Gangetic plain. Fifty years ago there was more forest than field. The population has been growing.

Next come the foothills, 42 percent of the area, grazed in summer to thirteen thousand feet, inhabited up to around eight thousand feet. "Foothills" is a kind name for a severe landscape, deeply carved by large, snow-fed rivers running in precipitous valleys. The rivers flow south into India to join the Ganges. Traveling from east to west entails a series of ascents and descents of three thousand to four thousand feet.

The foothills merge northward into the snowy peaks of the high Himalayas for which Nepal is famous. There are seven mountains over 26,000 feet. The highest mountain on earth, Mount

Everest (29,028 feet), is one of them. (For comparison, the top-most peaks of the Rocky Mountains do not reach 15,000 feet; Mont Blanc, king of the European Alps, is 15,771 feet.) Through this barrier of ice and snow there are a dozen or so passes of varying difficulty by which a hardy traveler may reach the Tibetan plateau.

The men we recruited came from the foothills area. The Gurkha is a mountain man, a village man, a farmer.

The capital of Nepal is Kathmandu, population in 1943 about 100,000, in 1989 300,000. It lies in the Valley, a substantial saucer of land at about 4,500 feet. It is the only town of size. With few exceptions, our soldiers did not come from the Valley.

Nepal is inhabited by a number of races and tribes. By no means all Nepali are Gurkhas. To give one example, the Sherpas, who live to the south of Mount Everest, and who have made such a name for themselves as high-level porters on mountaineering expeditions, are not Gurkhas, and few were enlisted into the army.

A Gurkha is a man or woman from the so-called martial tribes. These are Chhetri, Thakur, Gurung, Magar, Rai, Limbu, Sunwar, and Tamang. It is from these peoples that the majority of soldiers have been enlisted. In the 8th Gurkhas we took mostly Magars and Gurungs from western Nepal. The tribes are further divided into clans, and clans into kindreds.

In our time a recruit would probably have thought of himself first as from such and such a village and this or that kindred and clan. He might not have been too conscious of his citizenship of a country called Nepal. Schools, roads, and tourism must have changed this, but perhaps not so much as might be expected. In 1992 one of my fellow officers from the 8th Gurkhas, walking through parts of eastern Nepal, found that he was the first Westerner seen by many of the villagers. Very few spoke a word of English.

We officers would often speculate on the distinctions and relative merits of the clans and tribes from which we enlisted. It was a harmless pastime, unhampered by much anthropological or sociological evidence.

In the army a Gurkha's tribe was added to his given name: thus Manbir Rai, Shamsher Gurung. There was one exception: individual Magars were known by their clan names: Thapa, Rana, Roka, Pun, Ale, Bura, and Gharti. This may have been because the Magars are a large group, nearly one third of the total population.

First, or given, names were limited. *Bahadur* (meaning "brave") was often part of the name. Kharakbahadur, Ranbahadur, and Lalbahadur were common names. There were so many Lalbahadur Gurungs in my battalion that, to avoid confusion, the individual was often identified by the last one or two digits of his army serial number. During their favorite game, basketball, one might hear the exhortation *"Ja char bisi panch"* ("Go, eighty-five!").

The Gurkhas are of Mongolian origin. Their tribal languages (but not Nepali, the lingua franca) support this. They are short, thickset, generally hairless on the face, and fair-skinned, with the high cheekbones and epicanthic fold at the eyes that are so typical of the Mongolian races. On the other hand, their cultural inheritances—religion, music, dances, literature, and food, for example— are mostly of Indian origin.

There are exceptions to be seen, taller men, dark-skinned men. The Chhetris, much favored by the 9th Gurkhas, are often of this kind. Chhetris are also stricter in their observance of Hindu and caste laws. It is believed that they originate from an intermix of local hill women and high-caste Rajput refugees fleeing Muslim invaders.

The official religion of Nepal is Hinduism, with 89.5 percent of the population classified as Hindu. Six percent are Buddhist (Buddha was born in Nepal). Most Gurkhas tend to carry their religion lightly. Our men in the 8th Gurkhas did not believe that they or their food were defiled if we, their officers, entered the cookhouse or squatted down to join them in a meal.

Although relations between the Nepalese and British governments were amicable, and each respected the other, the Nepalese maintained their policy of seclusion until after the end of World War II. Few foreigners were allowed into the country, and those few were seldom permitted to travel outside the Kathmandu Valley. Until an air service began in 1950, British legation officials walked or rode. There was no motorable road until 1957. The legation became an embassy in 1947. America established a separate embassy in 1959, China in 1960. Suddenly Nepal was joining the world.

Myth envelops the early history of Nepal. However, we know that by 1768 what is now Nepal was more or less united under Prithwi Narayan, tenth king of the House of Gurkha. Through much of the later eighteenth century this expansionist dynasty clashed repeatedly with Britain's East India Company. Nepal refused a British resident, would not agree on borders, and continually raided down into the rich plains of Bengal.

The war of 1814–1815 was the result. After hard fighting and several defeats, the British forced the Nepalese to accept a treaty. The former had no wish to occupy and rule Nepal. The kingdom retained its independence, though stripped of some of its more recent conquests. What is important for this story is that the East India Company obtained the right to recruit Gurkha soldiers, and thus the first three Gurkha regiments to enter British service in the Indian Army date from 1815. The records show how Gurkha and British had come immediately to like and respect the qualities of the other. By the turn of the century there were ten such regiments, each of two battalions.

Within Nepal power struggles continued to shorten the lives of many of its leaders until, in 1846, Jang Bahadur Rana came to the top. He began a dynasty of hereditary prime ministers that lasted until 1951. The kings became royal figureheads without political muscle.

The two regular 8th Gurkha battalions (as opposed to the two war-raised battalions) had a long and proud history, though they were not among the oldest units of the Indian Army. The 1/8th Gurkhas was raised in 1824 under the title 16th Sylhet Local Battalion. The 2/8th was raised in 1835 as the Assam Sebundy Corps. The present titles were fixed during a reorganization of 1907.

The spelling of the word *Gurkha* has varied, and still varies. During the nineteenth century the spelling used was *Goorkha*. In 1901 it was changed to *Gurkha*. After Indian independence (1947) the British army retained *Gurkha*, but the new Indian Army preferred *Gorkha*.

A word on the *kukri* (or *khukri*). The *kukri* is a short, heavy knife with a broad, curved blade. It is a general utility instrument throughout Nepal, carried in a scabbard by most males. In peace it is used for a thousand jobs from chopping wood to paring radishes. In war it is also used for killing. All Gurkha soldiers in the Indian Army were issued one. Contrary to a widespread myth, the *kukri* is never thrown, and the wearer does not have to draw blood every time he removes it from its scabbard.

The ranks within the Indian Army's infantry during the period of my service need explanation. In the Gurkha regiments, privates were called riflemen. The noncommissioned officers (NCOs) were havildars (sergeants), naiks (corporals), and lance naiks (United Kingdom—lance corporals; United States—privates first class). In charge of platoons (about thirty men), and filling certain other responsible jobs within an infantry battalion, was a grade of officer not found in Western armies called Viceroy's Commissioned Officers (VCOs). Responsible to and appointed by the British Parliament, the viceroy of India was the representative of the monarch and was governor general of India.

In Gurkha regiments the VCOs were known as Gurkha officers (GOs). The GOs could be subadars (the more senior) or jemadars. They were full officers, entitled to receive the salutes of their men and to be addressed by them as "Sahib." We British officers (BOs) also called them "Sahib."

Peacetime GOs were experienced veterans, some with twenty or thirty years of service behind them, men who might have been through several campaigns on the North-West Frontier or elsewhere. What they might have lacked in schooling was outweighed by their knowledge of their men and their craft. When too old for battle service, such officers were invaluable for training. Under wartime expansion and because of casualties, plenty of younger men were promoted.

The most senior Gurkha officer in a battalion was the subadar major. He was a man of stature and experience, usually regarded with deep respect, if not awe. He was the colonel's adviser and aide in all matters concerning the men that were not connected with plain soldiering: on caste, religion, and diet, for example; on family welfare; on morale. He was the direct link between a colonel and his seven hundred men. When the colonel and the subadar major were both strong, wise men, a battalion prospered.

In peace, battalions had twelve King's Commissioned Officers (BOs). In war this was raised to eighteen, to include first reinforcements. It was rare for a full complement to be present.

According to the book we junior King's Commissioned Officers were senior to the most senior Gurkha officer. The GOs were adept at supporting the illusion that it was the young lieutenant who made decisions. The young lieutenant, if he was wise, would not fall for this fiction, not in his early months. Naturally some GOs were more experienced than others. The expansions and promotions of wartime had somewhat thinned the supply of grizzled paragons.

Because of this intermediate grade of Gurkha officer, a junior British officer was given considerably more responsibility than was his equivalent in Western armies.

When India became independent in 1947, a new tripartite treaty as to the future of the Gurkha regiments was signed by Nepal, India, and Great Britain. Nepal valued the employment provided for its young men—and the income earned, much of which was sent back to the families in the hills. India and Britain valued the soldiers. Four regiments each of two battalions went to Britain; six regiments of three battalions each went to India. Among the latter was the 8th Gurkhas, my regiment. The British have successively reduced their share until now (1995) there is only one composite regiment, the Royal Gurkha Rifles, plus a handful of support units such as signals and engineers. The Indian government has increased its intake so that its regiments now contain six or seven battalions each.

Back in the 1940s perhaps we underestimated the political awareness of our men. In 1951, only six years after the end of our war, the Nepalese instituted a form of democracy under a constitutional monarch, and chucked out the line of hereditary prime ministers who had ruled the country for over one hundred years.

Perhaps those Gurkhas who had seen Egypt, Libya, Syria and Iraq, Tunisia and Italy, Burma, Thailand, Indonesia and French Indochina, and of course India, perhaps they had absorbed more than we realized of philosophy, politics, and economics.

Whether or not he has become a political person, and whether you meet him in England, India, Hong Kong, Brunei, Nepal, or in the many other parts of the world where his duties have taken him since I knew him, the Gurkha soldier has always been recognized both as a superlative professional and as a delightful human being. It was a privilege to be allowed to command such men.

CHAPTER VII

—

Mountain Interlude

We slept in shelters made from juniper boughs, perched on the rare level clearings that dotted the forested hillside. Groundsheets laced over the roof kept out most of the occasional rain but none of the cold. Nor did the porous army blankets stop the chill from penetrating up through the bough beds. The battered enamel mug of sugared tea shoved into my hand just after dawn provided a lifesaving warmth. Before sluicing cobwebs from the eyes, the skim of ice on the water in my canvas washstand had to be broken. I pulled on starched shorts and an undershirt, then braved the cold mists to trot downhill to join my squad at PT.

Under the direction of a subadar recently returned from PT school and anxious to convey all he had learned, we flayed our arms, bent knees, ran relays, tried cockfights, built human pyramids, and ended with a race up or down the hillside. Then I would join my fellow officers, panting from similar workouts with their platoons, for breakfast.

This was Ziarat, in the forested mountains some fifty miles, as the eagle flies, east northeast of Quetta. Our camp, several miles from the little town, was about 9,000 feet (2,743 meters) above sea level. Here among the juniper woods conditions came a shade closer to the jungle-covered mountains of the Assam-Burma front. Here we could pretend jungle fighting with a little more realism than on the barren plains of Quetta.

> *Jungle Craft.* The term jungle craft implies the ability of a soldier to live and fight in the jungle, to be able to move from point to point and arrive at his objective fit to fight; to use ground and vegetation to the best advantage; and be able to "melt" into the jungle either by freezing or intelligent use of camouflage; to recognise and be able to use native foods; to possess the ability to erect temporary shelters rapidly to ward off tropical downpours. A jungle soldier should be sufficiently well versed in jungle lore to recognise instantly the cry or call of disturbed birds. His ear should be attuned to normal jungle noises in order that he may detect foreign or man-made sounds. He must learn to rely on his observation of broken twigs and branches, of trampled undergrowth and of disturbed mould, to detect the recent presence or proximity of humans. He must use his sense of smell (it is a curious fact, but the Jap soldier possesses a peculiar, unpleasant odour which is most persistent). He must readily recognise the danger of tracks converging at either watering places or gardens, and approach such areas with caution. He must learn to move through the jungle in darkness and be able to retrace his steps. He must learn to move silently, to avoid stepping on rotting logs and twigs and otherwise giving away his presence to the enemy. In short, the jungle is the home of the jungle fighter, and the sooner he learns to feel at home there the better.

That is an extract from *The Jungle Book,* a wartime training pamphlet that was distributed to all officers.[1]

Captain Peter Rawson, in civilian life a teacher, was in charge of this advanced recruit camp. My group of five subalterns, including Jupe Lewis, was expected to assist Peter in the further shaping of several hundred men. On the parade grounds of Quetta these men had been taught the rudiments of the disciplined art of killing with bayonet and bullet. Now they were to absorb more complex skills.

After breakfast we fanned out up the steep mountainsides to spend until late afternoon learning the art of maneuvering groups of men in and out of the glades.

> Infantry is the paramount arm in jungles owing to its comparative mobility, and well-trained infantry can dominate the jungle. . . . Training must inculcate the ability to move quickly and silently; to find the way accurately and with confidence; to shoot straight and quickly at disappearing targets from all positions on the ground, out of trees and from the hip; to carry out tactical operations in the jungle by means of battle drills, known to all, and without waiting for detailed orders. Above all the highest pitch of physical toughness is essential in all ranks, particularly officers, and the leadership of junior commanders must be confident, offensive and inspiring."[2]

Day after day we rehearsed the drill for advancing a section of eight to ten men through the forest against an enemy. Perhaps three men dashed or crawled to the shelter of a hillock, or bolders, or thick brush, under covering fire from the rest of the section. It was a scene often reminiscent of boys on a vacant lot at home. Battle drills for advance and retreat, for setting an ambush and escaping an ambush, for many other situations, were practiced over and over. Soldiers must learn when to remain silent and invisible, when to get up and move with intelligent speed. Then there was patrolling, camouflage, use of map and compass, and always the firing of weapons.

At midday the men would gather in small groups and make a fire with a few twigs to brew tea. They would arrange three stones around the fire as a tripod to support a mess tin full of water, tea, sugar, and tinned milk all sloshed together. With this they wolfed down cold curried *aloo* (potato) and the chapattis that each had carried up from the camp.

By evening, changed into long trousers and bush jacket, we had earned an hour or two of leisure in the rough-hewn mess. Peter Rawson did a creditable job. Not only were the routine and discipline less taut than at the regimental center, the atmosphere of the mess, relieved of the inhibiting presence of the senior regular officers, was considerably more relaxed.

Sitting around the blaze set in the dried mud fireplace at one end of the mess, my companions tended to ignore the war. Except for Rawson, who was nearer my own age, twenty-nine, the rest were young enough not to have formed immutable political positions.

Often the spirited talk was of the role that government would play for a better England after the war. The Beveridge Report, source of so much that was later to be woven into Britain's postwar socialism, had not long been published, and was warmly discussed. The two Scotsmen, Robert Findlay and Russell Fairgrieve, although schooled in England, were united in a half-serious nationalism and were resentful of English domination. The Englishmen, somewhat divided by class, mostly favored a measure of social direction. My own opinions, reflecting my Republican background, favored less governmental interference.

I was to see a good deal of Bob Findlay in Burma, for he was to follow me to the 4th Battalion. Russell Fairgrieve proved that politics was more than a passing interest. After the war he became a Conservative MP in Scotland and a knight.

Excellent whiskey was available in quantities sufficient to dull the monotony of the diet. Somewhat high local goat and lamb, chicken of varying toughness, pilchards from the tin, or the ubiquitous bully beef were served up in rotation by the cook. Shirttails hanging outside his trousers and useful as a towel on which to swab off the grease as he cooked, turban partly unwound, he sat on his haunches before a wood fire just outside the door of the mess. With an assortment of iron pots and an oven made from an oversize biscuit tin, he did well in conjuring up a variety of dishes. Like many of the cooks in India, he had a reasonable competence with the roasts and puddings expected by the British even in the tropics.

Every Indian cook knew how to make caramel custard, usually too sweet. He could handle rice: it has been estimated that there are, or were, ten thousand types of rice grown in India. Usually Europeans ate either Patna or basmati rice. Simple curries, pilafs, and kedgerees were trusted favorites, with a long history behind them.

As for the whiskey, I was to find that having an adequate supply for the officers of the Indian Army was a characteristic of the quartermastering. Much later, during a three-week march through jungle penetrating Japanese territory, Vat 69 and Johnnie Walker, supplied by airdrop, were nearly always with us.

Unfortunately, our diet gave us unsettled stomachs. When it was my turn to be mess officer, I visited the butcher in Ziarat bazaar and the reason for our queasiness became apparent. The lamb hung inadequately protected by torn cheesecloth and black with hundreds of flies.

The Ziarat mess—no more than a large hut made from the local juniper logs, thatched and lined with juniper branches—was one of many in which I ate and drank during four years. It is, however, strong in my memory not only for its beautiful setting—halfway up one of two facing, juniper-clad slopes—but also because it was here in these friendly hills that I first began to know my fellow officers and the Gurkhas we were to command.

Toward the end of my stay in Ziarat the mess burned down. It was soon rebuilt. The cook, however, absconded. Whether he did so from fear of punishment, or because of sick relatives, or because he was unhappy as the only Mohammedan in a Hindu camp, was never established.

We junior officers were theoretically in charge of perhaps a hundred of our grinning men. I say "theoretically" because our knowledge of Gurkhali (Nepali) was still minimal, and we received no instruction. The Urdu we had learned at Belgaum was useful only insofar as most of the Gurkha officers and senior NCOs had also learned some of that language during their years down in India, and because a number of Urdu words had been "borrowed." Not only did we have no formal instruction in Gurkhali, it turned out that many of the men were accustomed to speaking yet another language at home, one peculiar to their tribe. The English-Gurkhali vocabulary still in my possession shows across from each English word not only the *Khas,* or pure Gurkhali, equivalent, but the translation into Magarkura and Gurungkura. There were other less widespread languages spoken in the more remote valleys. There still are.

Thus both new officer and recruit might be equally tongue-tied in their efforts to communicate in the only language common to them, Gurkhali.

Months later, in Burma, with my Gurkhali by this time fluent if limited, and while inspecting our company position, I became incensed when the rifleman I was questioning responded with a blank stare. My subadar, standing behind, stepped toward the offender and demanded, "You stupid son of Sunday, why don't you answer the sahib? He wants to know where your grenades are." The subadar was met by the same stare of noncomprehension. There was further prodding. Then the subadar turned to me in disgust to say in Gurkhali, "This stupid oaf speaks only Raikura."

In Ziarat, because of the communication difficulty, and because the young recruits had seldom before spoken to a *Gora Sahib,* a white officer, and were probably awed by those pale long noses from another world, it was to their Gurkha officer that they looked for guidance.

At the time I did not give much thought to our lack of language instruction. It seemed to be expected that through daily contact, through unstructured saturation, we would acquire the gift of tongues. And so we did, after a fashion. Simple conversational Gurkhali progressed rapidly. But syntax and vocabulary were not what they could have been; and our understanding of the men's talk was certainly limited.

Later, when we met the British officers of other Gurkha regiments in our division whose language training had been taken seriously, I realized what we had missed, how weak was our command of Gurkhali. When General Bill Slim, who had served many years with the 6th Gurkhas, visited us in Burma during the next year, I was impressed at the fluency of his Gurkhali. He was a big hit with our subadars and jemadars.

My view now is that the most valuable gift the center could have given to us ECOs would have been a thorough schooling in Gurkhali. Accurate communication during battle is a matter of life or death. We should not have been posted to a battalion until we had reached reasonable fluency.

Aitwar ko Chorro ("son of Sunday") was the first of a number of colorful imprecations I learned that were part of the repertoire of every NCO and Gurkha officer. Most required interpretation for the non-Gurkha. "Son of Sunday" carried the suggestion that the object of scorn had been conceived during a casual Sunday afternoon dalliance in the bazaar between a soldier with a free hour and a girl of less than strict virtue. An incessant chatterer was denigrated with the phrase *Bukra ko nak men nok nok nok bhanne ho,* which translates: "Yack, yack, yack, you talk like a goat with a leech in its nose." Many of these insults were localisms and in dialect. To follow them required a keen ear and some knowledge of village life.

The basic language was relatively simple. Just one example: "to eat," "to smoke," and "to drink" were all the same word—*khanu.* *Khanu* covered all forms of ingestion.

Much meaning was conveyed by inflection. *Mathi* could mean "top" as in the top of a table. It could also mean "up." *Ooh mathi* might indicate three feet up; *oooh mathi* a half mile up a hill; and *ooooh mathi* at the top of a mountain. With such an inexact language, where tone, emphasis, and context meant so much, it was sometimes difficult to pin down exactly where a patrol had spotted the enemy.

On the rare free days at Ziarat the sport most looked forward to by some of our Gurkha officers was *shikar* (hunting). At dawn on a Sunday two or three cronies would set off for the highest, most inaccessible peaks where dwelt the rare and elusive markhor, the spiral-horned wild goat. After a day of climbing and stalking, they always returned empty-handed and with a story of the one just missed. No doubt these longhaired beasts existed, but the only ones I saw were drawings in books.

A severe test of my resistance to the elements came with the first night exercises. After the evening meal Rawson sent half of us out as "enemy," and later the other half to locate and annihilate the enemy.

We spent much of the night crawling about through the trees, slipping and sliding on the steep pitch, stopping frequently to listen for the other platoons. It was all good practice at moving silently in the dark over rough country.

By two or three in the morning, having taken up positions, we would set a guard and try for some sleep. Even in August, the temperature at a thousand feet over our camp, and perhaps ten thousand feet above sea level, had by this time descended to freezing. Over our jungle-green battledress we had only green pullovers to keep out the cold. Shaking uncontrollably, I waited sleepless for the dawn and the warming rays of the sun.

Later, on real ambushes carried out under a warmer Burma night, I would still get fits of the shakes. And I still prefer to think that these were a result of chill from the long wait for Japanese to stumble into our trap rather than a consequence of nerves.

Toward the end of August we left our comfortable camp for a three-day interplatoon war game in the hills. Some platoons simulated Japs, some Indians or British, and one Naga irregulars, all to roam the slopes in mock battles. The mules carrying our rations and ammunition clattered and skidded and occasionally fell as they climbed and descended the rocky pitches in the dark. Without blankets, the little sleep one grabbed through the penetrating chill was far from restful.

At the end my platoon, which had a generous umpire, tied for first in the most battles won. Our reward was a fat goat on the hoof to be eaten the following night at a *bara khana,* a feast. Rawson and I dined sitting uncomfortably cross-legged on the ground. The curried goat was washed down with generous quantities of fiery issue rum. We made our polite belch. Then a procession of men filed by, one to pour water on our eating hands, one to offer soap, and a third a towel.

The *nach* (dance) that followed in the firelight combined Javanese hand motions and Savoy Ballroom footwork with songs much in Trinidad calypso style telling stories of Inglistanis, the regiment, and hunting. If the song was about a girl back in Nepal, it would be invariably quite crude. The platoon drum banged away. By this time the British sahibs, well stoked, unwound cramped legs and did their little dance, to shouts of encouragement.

Halfway through the time at Ziarat an invitation arrived by runner for Jupe Lewis and myself to be the guests of Major F.G.C. and Mrs. Macartney at one of the regiment's rondavals on the outskirts of the town. We were to arrive at midday on Saturday and return to camp after tea on Sunday. The Macartneys were enjoying a short break from the dust and heat of Quetta.

Fergus Macartney, second-in-command throughout the war to Willasey-Wilsey in Quetta, was easygoing and pleasant. He must also have been efficient, for much of the administration of the center, a large and complicated organism, devolved on him. His wife, Binia Macartney, was a charming lady born and bred on the Channel Island of Guernsey. She is still (1994) alive and well, and still living in her family home.

The distinctive feature setting the rondaval apart from the neighboring wood, stone, and mud houses was the conical thatched roof flowing deep down over the circular whitewashed wall to provide shade. The inside was airy and comfortable. There was a fireplace and there were grass mats over the cement floor.

That evening the Macartneys had been invited to dinner with the deputy district commissioner and General Hind and their wives, and had arranged for Jupe and me to be included. General Hind, area commander and a 2nd Gurkha, was up from the torrid heat of his headquarters in Karachi for a bit of shooting.

Also in the party was the doctor responsible for the administration of the civilian hospitals throughout Baluchistan. The hospital and surgery in Ziarat, which he was inspecting, hardly deserved the name. The building was a two-room bungalow with a few beds and with equipment for only the most minor surgery. The Indian in charge lacked full medical certification. Mostly his time was taken up with doling out potions to Baluchi herdsmen.

We had a late afternoon swim in the icy pool just outside the rondaval. Then we sat with whiskies gazing at the distant mountains while the sun set. Despite dissimilar ages and backgrounds, conversation was easy. It was particularly enjoyable for the inclusion, rare for us in recent months, of the ladies. At dinner the ladies appeared in long dresses, the senior officers in perfectly creased mess dress. The doctor and the deputy commissioner wore correct dinner jackets complete with cummerbund. Everything was as I had read about the British keeping up a front in the remote corners of the Empire.

The flickering candles on the trestle table were a welcome change from the smelly, smoking kerosene lamps back at camp. Another change was in the conversation. With ladies and civilian gentlemen present, we were spared the staple talk of the army regulars: "Did you know old . . . ?"; "Class of 'Thirty-five at Sandhurst . . ."; "But surely he was Hodson's Horse . . ." Any senior officer with aspirations had been to the staff college at Quetta or Camberley in the United Kingdom. Conversation always seemed to get around to "When Monty was teaching at staff college . . ." This was shop talk from which we ECOs were excluded. That evening the conversation was less rigid.

When we were down to the dregs of the port, our host suggested that the men might like to stroll outside "to see the stars." Looking up at the stars twinkling toward infinity in the crystal-clear air of midnight, the stillness was broken by the hissing falls of excess liquid landing on the lawn.

One day tragedy struck. During a rest break in one of the training exercises on the steep slopes behind the camp, a mortar bomb exploded in the midst of a group of men. Russell Fairgrieve recalls that apparently the young Gurkhas had been playing with a "dud" to watch it *not* going off. One of the group began banging it against a rock and . . .

The damage was horrific: gushing blood and severed limbs everywhere. Somehow the ten or twelve badly wounded men were gotten over the rough ground, suffering terribly, to the surgery in Ziarat.

During the long night of horror we amateurs stood by to assist the Indian in charge as best we could with chloroform and amputations until more experienced help, summoned from Quetta, arrived next morning. The victims were all from the same platoon. Several did not survive the night.

Two or three days later I was to see how powerfully belief in the occult can influence human behavior. The subadar of the platoon so decimated by the tragedy invited the officers to a *tamasha* that evening. Although the word *tamasha* (meaning "celebration") was used, the occasion was not to be the usual *nautch* with dance, drink, and feasting. It was more a Hindu version of a wake, an exorcism of the evil spirits responsible, an attempt to ease the memory of what had happened.

The drumbeat was slow and the singing somber, even sad. After an hour or so with no letup, all eyes became focused on one of the men in the center of the firelit ring. He was prostrate on the ground, was shaking and twisting as one possessed by spirits. From his actions, the spirits were unhappy. Some of his companions were now trying to bring him out of his trance. He appeared unable to hear their voices. He seemed to be repeating in tortured gasps messages from the outer world, messages from his dead companions.

Perhaps the young men, boys really, sitting cross-legged around the dying embers and chanting mournful Himalayan dirges were not the only celebrants. Certainly the men believed that the spirits of their departed brothers, their *bhais,* were there to say farewell.

Some days later the platoon subadar, a wise old campaigner, came to Peter Rawson with the request that the platoon site be moved. Rawson was puzzled until the subadar explained: *"Bhut ki-naki,* Sahib" ("Because of the ghosts"). The platoon moved to the other side of the ridge, leaving the dell to the departed souls.

Tragedy defused, we were back into the normal routine: early rising assisted by strong tea, then a full day of training among the juniper woods above the camp.

The men in my charge seemed to enjoy the impromptu field events I would improvise for a change of pace: shot-putting with rocks, long jump, horse and rider, arm wrestling. They laughed gleefully, enjoying any competitive games.

In the 1942 retreat through Burma, many of the Gurkhas had not made it back over the rivers simply because the Gurkha, raised in the Himalayas, is generally a nonswimmer. It was a costly lesson. Now, whenever possible, swimming was put on the training program. A six-foot-deep pool had been scooped out in the frigid stream tumbling down through the camp. Here, though none of us was at all qualified as a swimming instructor, we endeavored to teach the rudiments of staying afloat to our fearless little hillmen.

Not infrequently, doing just as he was told, the recruit dog-paddled manfully as he sank straight to the bottom. One of us leaped in to pull him out and a minute later he would try again, and again sink.

Two years later, outside Rangoon and preparing for the expected landings on the Malayan coastline, we were still trying to get the now experienced riflemen to float. Success was so limited that I believe a scientific study would prove the chunky Gurkha to be completely lacking in buoyancy.

Peter Rawson ordered Jupe Lewis and myself out on a special exercise. We were to take a naik and the intelligence section of eight men to the back of two sharp ranges of hills, our goal to locate and map a pond. The pond did not show on the map but was rumored to be just north of the small village of Wahir. We estimated the distance to Wahir to be about ten miles. Judging from the contours on the map, it would be steep going.

The stated purpose for the patrol, in addition to experience, was to establish the existence of the pond, which could then be used as an objective for a company march. Bodies of water were rare in these mountains.

Our patrol, setting out early, trudged up rocky barren slopes, slid down sharp inclines, and crawled along narrow ledges above gorges, mere shelves impossible to stand on because of the overhanging cliff. Across one defile we negotiated a frayed rope bridge swinging over a turbulent stream. In the distance were always the snow-peaked higher mountains.

By early afternoon we were looking down on Wahir from the top of a ridge. The village proved to be a disappointing cluster of four or five stone huts and several black goatskin tents clinging to a tiny plateau. A search revealed no pond, unless you could so dignify the five-foot puddle the goats were drinking from just before a trickling stream disappeared beneath rocks.

Neither the red-pantalooned women of the village ducking out of sight into their tents nor the unfriendly stares of the rifle-carrying Baluchi herdsmen encouraged us to linger.

After making tea to wash down chapattis and cold curried potato, the patrol, exhilarated by the clear air and the pleasure of matching legs against mountain, started back at a fast pace. Except for the cliff ledges and the rope bridge, we moved at a jog, and on the steep rocky descents, almost at a full run.

I had changed into clean trousers and bush jacket after my evening plunge into the pool and was headed toward the mess when I discovered that my revolver was missing. The jarring and bouncing of our swift return must have slipped it from the holster. It would have fallen unnoticed against the clatter of boots and sliding rock.

My civilian mentality did not at first allow the knowledge of this loss to spoil the evening. Peter Rawson, however, was quick to point out that because such a weapon would likely end up in the hands of an unfriendly tribesman, its loss was a serious crime that deserved unswerving pursuit of the facts—and punishment for the offender.

At dawn next morning I took a section out to retrace every step. We were unsuccessful either in finding the revolver or in stopping a report to the center and the stern eye of Colonel Willasey-Wilsey. Shortly thereafter Fergus Macartney arrived to conduct a court of inquiry.

Somehow the affair never got as far as a court-martial. However, this blot on my record no doubt suggested to the colonel that I represented something less than the type of highly organized officer he preferred on his staff. And clearly I was not material for his team of All-India boxing champions. I suspected that my days in the center might be limited.

Jupe left Ziarat on September 3 to go on a Bren carrier course. I think I was at the camp for six weeks, until mid-September. At the end of this time we marched the eighty miles back to Quetta. The march was scheduled over three days. Each morning the cooks went ahead to set up camp and prepare the evening meal. Never having walked so far, my main apprehension—after the possibility of painful foot blisters—was that I might collapse from fatigue and thus disgrace myself in front of the men. No such problem arose. The whole march in the crisp, clean air of the mountains was an exhilarating experience. Even our strict water discipline—no drinking on the march—did not prove a problem. On the third day we marched into the Quetta compound proud of our accomplishment, fit, ready for new challenges.

Until I might be posted to an active battalion, I now found my-self a company officer, a part of life at the center: drilling recruits, sherry in the mess, snooker, Sunday morning band concerts. On October 10 there was Dashera, an orgy of religious excess granted the Gurkhas once a year, an all-night drinking and feasting contest followed next morning by the sacrifice of a bullock and of a good many goats and chickens.

Immediately following Dashera, Willasey-Wilsey sent me on a motor transport (MT) course outside the city of Ahmednagar, not far from Bombay. Here we drove around the countryside lurching dangerously as our Bren carriers and armored cars negotiated the rough village tracks. I struggled to keep awake during the lectures and to fill my notebook with the cures for a faulty carburetor, locked brakes, or electrical failure.

While I was on this course Jupe Lewis was posted to the 2nd Battalion, which had had a rough time during the 1942 retreat to El Alamein, with about half captured, and was now with Paiforce in the Levant. In August 1944 the battalion moved to Italy as part of the renowned 43rd Gurkha Lorried Brigade. Jupe was wounded in September at the Battle of San Savino.

I missed Jupe. He had been a good and steady friend.

I was back in Quetta by mid-November 1943. A week or two later word came that Second Lieutenant Gilmore, now fully able in the art of infantry warfare and leadership, was posted to our 4th Battalion. The 4th Battalion was in the Arakan Peninsula of Burma.

I departed on December 7.

CHAPTER VIII

To the Arakan

At Belgaum, at Quetta, and at Ziarat, it was hard to have acute concern for a war that was two thousand miles distant. As those miles shrank during the train journey east across the breadth of India, interest quickened. Every morning through the compartment window, along with tea and fly-covered buns, came copies of the latest Calcutta *Statesman* and the *Hindustan Times*.

Writing long after the events, it is not easy to recall what we knew at the time and what has come from hindsight. We knew that the war on the frontier with Burma had not been going well, and that what we read was not the complete story. Censors whitewash defeats. Censors love happy soldiers winning battles over a despicable enemy. We hoped that what we read was not too distorted.

When the Japanese invaded Burma in 1942, it was a British colony. It had been acquired in three stages during the nineteenth century. The First Burma War (1824–1826) was a punitive affair undertaken in response to Burmese raids across the frontiers of the

Arakan and Assam into territory controlled by the East India Company (Map 2, p. xx). The Burmese were made to cede the two coastal strips of Arakan and Tenasserim. Pagan Min, the king who inherited the throne in 1846, possessed in overful measure his countrymen's xenophobia. There were more frontier incidents and there was deliberate maltreatment of traders. After the Second Burma War (1852) the British annexed the province of Pegu, which included Rangoon. Now the whole of southern Burma became a province of British India.

In 1879 another weak, inexperienced, and rapacious Burmese king, Thibaw, succeeded to the kingdom. He too stirred up trouble, and he raised fears of French interference from their base to the east in Indochina. The Third Burma War (1885) ended in the annexation of the rest of the country. Burma was then governed from India until 1937, when it became a separate colony with a considerable measure of self-government and the promise of more.

The Japanese invaded Burma on January 20, 1942. Why? Principally, it seems, for two reasons: to safeguard their hold on Thailand, Malaya, and Singapore—all vulnerable to attack through the long Kra Isthmus—and to cut off Nationalist China from one of the few remaining backdoor sources of supply, the Burma Road from Rangoon to Lashio and across the border to Kunming. Japan had invaded China in 1937. She was anxious to complete her conquests and free troops for other fronts.

When the Japanese entered Burma there began one of the longest ever retreats of British arms, some nine hundred miles over four months, from Moulmein, at the mouth of the Salween River, north up to Imphal, in the Indian state of Manipur.

Should the reader of today offer harsh comments on the British of those days who took such a beating, he can be reminded that they had their hands full defending their small island from air and sea attack, with land invasion still threatening. Their expeditionary force to the mainland of Europe had been decimated with the fall of France in 1940. Their attempts to save Norway (1940) and Greece (1941) had been quixotic disasters, with severe losses. The seesaw campaigns in North Africa had swallowed men and munitions on a huge scale. The fight against Hitler in Europe and Africa had to be given preference to the fight in Southeast Asia.

Of other excuses there were plenty. Neither of the two infantry divisions in Burma was at full strength. The First Burma Division was a makeshift formation composed of an Indian Army brigade trained for the Middle East and battalions of recently raised, lightly armed Burma Rifles. There had been no time for collective training, and the division was short of staff, transport, guns, and signals.

The 17th Indian Division had been scratched together that year and earmarked for the Western Desert. It too had had no collective training and no experience of jungle warfare. It arrived in Burma piecemeal during January, with no time to become familiar with the country or to prepare defenses. All of its battalions had been weakened by the need to supply large contingents of men for the new wartime battalions and for the burgeoning training centers. The gaps had been filled with recruits not yet integrated; many had joined only days before embarkation. The majority of officers were ECOs with only a few months' experience of their men and the language.

The 7th Armoured Brigade of the British army, the one experienced formation, had been hurriedly shipped from North Africa, intended for Singapore, and had not landed at Rangoon until late February. It proved invaluable, but was not enough to do more than slow the pace of the retreat.

From general to sepoy, few of the soldiers knew much about the Japanese army, its tactics, strengths, and weaknesses. At first the Japanese were underestimated, then overestimated. By and large, the British units were roadbound, the Japanese were not. The British were ill-equipped in almost every department, vitally so in their lack of wirelesses and transport. They had no means of gathering intelligence, and were operating among a population that for the most part was either neutral or hostile.

Nevertheless, after months of retreat and frequent battles, progress slowed by tens of thousands of refugees, mostly Indians, the remnants marched across the mountains into India just ahead of the monsoon, ragged, gaunt, but still a fighting formation. They had lost thirteen thousand men killed, wounded, and missing. The Japanese had lost four thousand. Of the Armoured Brigade's tanks, all but one (named "The Curse of Scotland") had been destroyed or abandoned. The last group had to be left on the east bank of the mighty Chindwin at Shwegyin as the Japanese forces encircling the perimeter pressed so close that further operation of the steamer ferries was impossible. Six monsoons later the writer Compton Mackenzie revisited Shwegyin and discovered six of those 7th Armoured Brigade tanks, painted the yellow ocher of their desert camouflage, "still there standing stiffly in exact alignment, for the termites which can fell the most powerful tree cannot destroy those tanks, and they will still be standing there when the chronicler's pen has rusted away."[1]

"For eighteen months after the Japanese attack, the British managed the war in Burma to the accompaniment of consistent frustration and disaster, as well as rising American dissatisfaction with presumed British unwillingness, and obvious British inability, to clear their land communications to China, whose importance in American eyes reached its wartime peak during this period."[2]

This account has so far omitted mention of the Chinese and Americans in connection with the Burma campaigns. Perhaps this is natural. Most of us infantry in the army of India came across neither, and heard of their doings at sixth hand, usually after the war.

It seems that from the start British, American, and Chinese leaders were pursuing divergent strategies, seldom acknowledged as such. The Americans were interested in Burma only insofar as it provided a corridor to Generalissimo Chiang Kai-shek and his Nationalist Chinese armies. They took this requirement seriously. The Chinese must be kept in the fight, must continue to tie up a million Japanese soldiers. In those early months America's ultimate strategy of island-hopping across the Pacific was not yet proven. The best road to Tokyo might still lie across mainland China.

In America the China lobby was strong. China was a cornerstone of American policy not only for the defeat of the Japanese in war but also in achieving postwar stability in Asia and the Pacific. During the 1930s America's "self-appointed role as China's disinterested guardian had been the principal factor in the widening gap between the United States and Japan."[3] There were senior Americans who placed the survival of China above the survival of Britain (a philosophy not grasped by most British).

The Chinese—that is, the Nationalist Chinese under Chiang Kai-shek—were interested above all in survival. They had been resisting the Japanese since the latter's invasion of Manchuria in 1931—and, more intensely, since Japan openly attacked China's heartland in 1937. For a long time they had also been fighting the Chinese Communists. Barbara Tuchman, in her biography of Joe Stilwell, wrote: "From first to last Chiang Kai-shek had one purpose: to destroy the Communists and wait for foreign help to defeat the Japanese."[4]

During the 1940s Chiang Kai-shek was always reluctant to commit his armies to battle. He did so only when forced by political necessity. He saw the Americans and the British (the latter he deeply distrusted) as sources of material and combat help: "To use barbarians to fight other barbarians was a traditional principle of Chinese statecraft."[5] Armies destroyed in battle with the Japanese weakened Chiang's position against the Chinese Communists and lost him influence with those warlords who supported him. For the generalissimo's number-one enemy was always Mao Tse-tung and the Communists, not the Japanese, whom he regarded as but a temporary curse.

The primary British objective, or at any rate the objective probably closest to the heart of Prime Minister Churchill, was the recapture of Singapore. To achieve this there was no need to reconquer Burma overland. Given the ships, Burma could be bypassed. The repossession of Singapore would be both a genuine strategic gain and a reassertion of British "face" throughout Asia.

This was not an objective that appealed much to the Americans, who may have been pro-British at this time but were never pro–British Empire. One American historian has put it nicely. He writes of "the ancient ambivalence of Americans confronted with the descendants of those mythical oppressors who stalked the pages of their elementary school primers."[6] Roosevelt and his advisers wanted the land links with China restored. They demanded that the British reconquer Burma. Any diversion from this they saw as malingering.

In any event, a shortage of sea transport kept postponing plans for amphibious action against Singapore and nearer objectives, and condemned the 14th Army to land campaigns. A double frustration for the British command was that they had no faith in Chiang Kai-shek or his soldiers.

At the time of Pearl Harbor the Americans did not have troops to put into Burma. However, early in 1942, after much prevarication, Chiang Kai-shek agreed to send forces south and took on responsibility for the eastern corridor—the Sittang River valley and the Rangoon-Mandalay railway and road. Cooperation between the two armies, the British and the Chinese, was not perfect; each accused the other of retreating without warning and of much else detrimental to happy relations. The Chinese got thrown back as comprehensively as the British. Their chief American adviser, General Joe Stilwell, had only reached Burma in March. In May he walked out across the mountains to Imphal with a small mixed party. Later at a press conference in Delhi he ended with his now well-known statement: "I claim we got a hell of a beating. We got run out of Burma and it is humiliating as hell. I think we ought to find out what caused it, go back and retake it."[7]

Practical help from the United States was via a squadron of the AVG, the American Volunteer Group, the "Flying Tigers" under Major General Claire Chennault. The AVG had been formed earlier to help the Chinese fight the Japs in China. Chiang agreed to release a squadron, which inflicted and suffered heavy losses in the defense of Rangoon. Without the AVG the Japanese air force might have gained undisputed freedom over southern Burma at an early stage, which would have been a further disaster.

So it was China that brought the Americans to Burma, and to take so close an interest in the strategy of what must otherwise have been, and for the most part was, a British campaign fought by British and Indian troops of the army of India. I will mention later the indispensable contribution of American air transport planes and pilots—which enabled entirely new tactics to be carried through and which, in 1945, turned the Burma war from a footslog into something like a cavalry charge. And it was the promise of American supplies through Burma that focused Chinese interest on that land.

Stilwell was the man in charge of all American interests in the CBI (China-Burma-India) theater. He was simultaneously chief of staff to Chiang Kai-shek, commanding general of U.S. army forces in the area (which at this point were minimal), supervisor of Lend-Lease to China, and U.S. representative on any local Allied war councils. Stilwell despised Chiang, called him "Peanut." He despised almost everyone, and particularly the British. His soubriquet of "Vinegar Joe" was earned. Yet he was a very able soldier, knew China well, and could speak Chinese. He had an abiding faith in the fighting ability of the Chinese soldier if properly armed, trained, and freed from Chiang's political yoke.

In India Stilwell set to with great energy to organize the construction of airfields; to improve the capacity of the railways, roads, and ferries in northern Assam; and to collect pilots and transport aircraft. This was so that increased supplies for Chiang Kai-shek could be flown over "The Hump," the mountain barrier in northern Burma that divided India from China. In addition he was instructed by Washington to build a road across north Burma to replace the old Burma Road. And he obtained agreement from both the British and the Chinese to train and arm Chinese troops in India.

The year 1942 had been one of defeats. By its end and through much of 1943, relatively small bodies of troops faced each other along the Indo-Burmese border. Tiny bits of geography were exchanged with the Japanese. Remote villages, jungle-coated hills designated only by numbers, were scrapped over. Behind this screen on the British side and back in India new divisions were training, supply dumps were being stoked, communications were being improved. Who knew what was happening on the Japanese side?

As in every war, communications were king. On the British side the lines of communication to all parts of the front were unbelievably primitive and extended. Nothing on a large scale could be attempted until the roads, railways, airfields, and ports had been improved. Through the monsoon, May to October, conditions were miserable and communications deteriorated further.

As important, it was recognized early on that soldiers would perform with success in this strange environment only after suitable training. The unlucky troops flung into those early battles had received no training in jungle warfare and knew nothing of the underrated Japanese fighting machine.

The "front line" stretched north-south for six hundred miles; most of it was mountain country, sparsely inhabited, thickly forested, and rather beautiful. Much of it was never held or occupied in the conventional sense. It could be covered only by patrolling. In this, jungle warfare resembled desert warfare: troops occupied smallish boxes and were surrounded by many square miles of space through which either side could move.

At certain times of year some areas were disease ridden: malaria and scrub typhus were rife; such minor irritations as leeches, skin rashes, and dysentery were common. During 1942 and 1943 disease was a more deadly foe than the enemy: "During the monsoon of 1943 for every wounded man of the Eastern Army admitted to hospital there were 120 sick."[8] During 1944 strict health precautions and the introduction of mepacrine cut the numbers of sick dramatically.

In the north, Joe Stilwell was building up his Chinese preparatory to reentry into Burma down the Hukawang Valley in late 1943. On the central front around Imphal there was not much more than patrolling until Wingate's first foray deep into Burma in the early months of 1943 (see pages 83–85). Down south, however, in the Arakan, December and January 1942–1943 saw an attempt at offensive action. The fighting was fierce and bloody. But the objectives of the British—the southern port of Akyab and the airfields on Akyab Island—were never in danger. This first Arakan campaign has been called "perhaps the worst managed British military effort of the war."[9] A much smaller body of Japanese had defeated nine brigades of fresh troops and sent many of them retreating in disorder. Morale slumped.

For lack of troops no other major operation could be attempted before the monsoon of 1943. But there were plans for the 1943–1944 dry season.

Rolling across the continent on India's vast railroad network past millions of fields and several hundred villages, from time to time one did get a sense of the depth of the civil and military machinery deployed in support of the Burma front. We passed huge railyards, steelworks fed by strings of rail cars piled with coal, troops of every description waiting on platforms and crowded into trains.

From the snowy Himalayas to the island of Ceylon the plains and jungles were alive with the thud of boots in the dust and the bawling of commands. There were camps of every description and schools for the teaching of every conceivable skill: small arms (rifle, Bren gun, tommy gun, sten, and others), mortar, signals (especially the upstart wireless, still a relatively new toy), cooking, intelligence, vehicle driving and maintenance, artillery, tanks (in very short supply), and much else.

Within the Gurkha Brigade, specialist post-recruit training battalions had been formed. In August 1943 the 3rd and 8th Gurkha regiments jointly opened the 38th Gurkha Rifles in an area of the United Provinces well suited for the practice of jungle warfare. Ziarat was displaced. I must have been one of the last officers to be sent to an active battalion directly from the center at Quetta.

On this long trip (was it four days, five days, more? Memory fails) across the subcontinent from Baluchistan in the west to Calcutta in east Bengal, I mentally prepared for the transition from backwater military life to the perils of the real war. However, more waiting intervened. First, our progress was interrupted by a missed connection at Allahabad, the "City of God." I had to spend the night in the first-class waiting room of the station. I spread my bedroll on the floor, surrounded by other stranded passengers. In the middle of the night something awoke me. I rose on one elbow to shine a flashlight. Large rats were scurrying over the bodies and bedding around me. Allah would not have been proud of his station.

Then there were three days in the Grand Hotel, Calcutta. What can I recall of Calcutta, second city of the Empire, founded by the British East India Company in 1690 in a malarial swamp? What I remember does not penetrate its cultural world of writers, painters, dancers, and moviemakers, nor the worlds of provincial and city governments, of law and order, of military high command, nor its vast and spreading slums. The Grand Hotel at this time was a superior transit camp for officers passing to and from the Burma front. Superior? Certainly better than tents, but by now run-down, grubby, depressing.

Escaping from my airless, steamy room, which I shared with three others, their beds, bedding rolls, and mosquito nets, I remember the sidewalk of Chowringhee thronged with British troops and American flyers. At the curb Sikh taxi drivers with open touring cars offered to take you where the girls were: "Very clean, very young, virgins, sisters. You have jig-jig." In the street were clanging streetcars (which the British called "trams") loaded with dark-skinned, white-clothed, thin little Bengalis, who not only packed the interior but clung to every possible handhold along the sides and back. Two-wheeled tongas drawn by ponies were the alternative to taxis, cheaper and surprisingly maneuverable. Each had its warning bell that jingled continuously. The streets were alive with bells, horns, the clanging of streetcars, and human calls. Even in the center of a great city, human muscle was in action for the transport of many goods: shoeless coolies clad only in loincloths carried huge baskets of goods from each end of a pole balanced across their shoulders.

I learned that I was to be dispatched to a reinforcement camp at Chittagong to await summons to the battalion, and I was not sorry to go.

Chittagong was now the main port and supply base for the Arakan front, a major target for the stalled Japanese advance. Until a year back hardly anyone had heard of the place, so unimportant was it to the main thrust of man's activity on planet Earth. But then, few had heard of El Alamein or Guam or Wake Island.

We reached Chittagong only after another forty-eight hours of complicated travel, with more rail trips and with an intervening body of water that required a voyage on an ancient river steamer. Rumer and Jon Godden, in their book *Two Under the Indian Sun*,[10] tell how as children they loved the riverboat journeys with their father up and down the many diversions of the Ganges delta. He was an agent for the steamships that plied those myriad waterways. We too now experienced the pleasure of a leisurely side-wheeler trip up a branch of the holy Ganges, an experience perhaps comparable to the early days on the Mississippi.

That the port of Chittagong was an important staging point was evidenced by the cranes and derricks creaking around the clock, loading and unloading mounds of ammunition cases, sacks and boxes of food, drums of petrol, and much else, and by the clouds of dust kicked up by the marching boots of embarking and disembarking men.

The vintage army lorries that carried us to the reinforcement camp plied slowly through the sleepy bazaar, weaving between pedicabs, bicycles, animals, beggars, peddlars, and holy men covered with ashes and not much else. In Chittagong closed carriages similar to those fashionable in London in the 1800s served as taxis. They were drawn by horses so scrawny as to oblige the passengers to alight for any uphill portion of the dusty road.

The camp was like others of its kind. It was a stepping-off place peopled with a constantly changing cast of strangers awaiting transport elsewhere, so it was a place without character, conviviality, or spirit.

Here I found a contingent of our 8th Gurkhas destined for the 4th Battalion, about twenty men, and two fellow officers, young second lieutenants. Brian Irving was large and good-natured, Peter McQueen short and pugnacious. Together we made the best of the drab, dusty site where fate condemned us to spend both Christmas 1943 and the New Year.

Life in the camp was just tolerable. Ignoring the assorted reinforcements for other formations, by day we organized drills and weapon training for our Gurkhas. Late each afternoon we had knock-down-drag-out games of basketball, played on hard, dusty ground. Brought up on the American game in which the player moves the ball by dribbling it, I required considerable adjustment before I could master the rules as applied in India. No dribbling, but some passing and a style of play more closely resembling rugby with the foul rules not strictly observed.

This version of basketball provided an opportunity for the laughing five-foot Gurkhas, usually respectful of rank, to play rough with the officer sahibs. I remember big Brian struggling toward the hoop for a shot with at least three Gurkhas gleefully clinging to his back and shoulders to bring him down by weight of numbers—a veritable Gulliver.

I had first met Brian in Quetta. He could be described as a bon vivant. Many months later while we were both on leave and staying at the Taj Mahal in Bombay, I witnessed his ability to generate a good time despite the handicaps of that humid city.

In the evenings in Chittagong we drifted unhopefully to a large bamboo *basha* identified by a crudely painted sign that said "Officers' Mess." Furnishings were sparse. One rough table carried the same *Men Only* and *Illustrated London News* that we had scanned weeks before in Quetta. Another table was set over a split-bamboo floor mat and was covered with cracked oilcloth on which would be served the bully beef or pilchard concoction of the day. A wireless and canvas camp chairs completed the inventory.

The bar was kept by a small Madrassi in cast-off, too-large shorts and a crumpled bush jacket. Light came from a hissing overhead gas pressure lamp. The floor beneath became covered with the bodies of roasted insects. There was a notice at the bar: "Limit of two chota pegs per officer." This referred to army rum, the only drink available (and *chota* means small). The ration was insufficient to obscure the shabby atmosphere.

Cooks and waiters in such establishments were the rejects from more prestigious units of civil and military life.

Christmas and New Year were undeniably dismal in this desolate spot. Occasionally some excitement was provided by wailing sirens and the arrival far overhead of Japanese bombers. On Christmas Day, a clear bright morning, there was a raid by fifty such planes. The silver casks they dropped reflected the sunlight and could be traced until they disappeared behind the warehouses at the docks. There followed reverberating *crumphs* and rising black smoke. Often the bombs fell harmlessly into the harbor. Nor did our ack-ack score any hits.

On about January 20 we were not unhappy to receive the electrifying news that we were to join the forward troops. Orders were to embark on a boat for a voyage farther south down the Arakan coast to Bawli Bazar. And although I was still a lowly subaltern, hardly six months commissioned, with little knowledge of the ways of war, I was to be officer commanding the boat, a responsibility for which I was eminently unqualified.

My command was a small wheezing steamer overloaded with an assortment of replacements. Bawli Bazar was a hitherto insignificant port well up the Naf River estuary and just behind the front line positions. After a predawn breakfast we marched through the dusty alleys to the port with our medley of gunners, sappers, infantry, pioneers, cooks, sweepers, and even a dozen goats on the hoof—live rations as a treat for the Hindu troops.

My chief responsibility was to look authoritative. I also had to return salutes and approve the suggestions of the ship's capable sergeant major in allotting space as earlier worked out by the Movement Control Officer at the docks. MCOs were often World War I oldsters recalled to duty. Some of them spent years in hot, drab posts working at the unglamorous but vital task of shifting troops from A to B with the least possible delay and waste.

No sooner had everyone crammed on board and we had gotten under way than the smoke of individual cook stoves rose from clusters of men on every corner of the deck. Each unit, with its varying caste and dietary taboos, was cooking up its own thing.

Gurkhas are an inland mountain people. They tend to be apprehensive and distrustful of the great *nun pani* (salt water). Fortunately, when we hit the open Bay of Bengal and headed south, the waves were low. Our ship rolled gently down the coast. Songs of the villages back in Nepal, accompanied by the *bansuli* (bamboo flute), rose from many groups. Boisterous card games which began off Chittagong were still continuing when we sighted Bawli Bazar next morning.

Not much to see. Some bamboo *bashas* clinging to clearings on the jungled hillsides back from the pier; the spire of a pagoda to remind us that we were now in Burma.

Pilings lurched and creaked under the steamer's impact. The muddy waters of the little harbor swirled in diminishing eddies. The engines were cut and we were secured to the dock. On shore under the shade of a tarpaulin were some sick and walking wounded, waiting a return to civilization and safety.

As the throb of the engines subsided, a new sound topped the usual dockside noises, the muffled *vroom* of distant guns.

CHAPTER IX

Cut Off
at the Pass

The sound of the guns grew louder as we footslogged up and over the pass through the Mayu Range. This brought an awareness close to exhilaration. The track had only recently been bulldozed through the red soil and was still being widened. We climbed a continuous succession of twisting hairpins lined by tall jungle, up and along one ridge after another. Some gradients were steeper than one in eight. Vertiginous drops of a thousand feet or more bordered one side, then the other. Wrecked vehicles far below were testimony to the sometimes low order of driving proficiency in the expanding Indian Army. Wheeled traffic, controlled by military police, operated a one-way system.

On this early January morning it was a stimulating march. January is the best month in the Arakan. Cool breezes riffled the bamboo. Shreds of the morning mists rose from the valley.

Once over the highest crest, the track twisted down with equal abruptness. Toward the end we could see through the trees to a valley, patches of open paddy field. In the nearest clearing a Red Cross flag identified the tents of a hospital. Elsewhere there were clusters of lorries, Bren gun carriers, gun pits, and huge stacks of supplies under tarpaulins. The valley floor was crisscrossed with trails churned deep into powdery dust. Clouds of dust rose from vehicles moving between positions. Here and there sharp explosions and puffs of smoke betrayed where the guns lobbed out their shells. All this equipment and lethal hardware was to support our rifle companies, dug in among the forested hills to the south and east.

The booming guns were final proof that after all those months of half-war without an enemy near at hand, a war of parade grounds, classrooms, and transit camps far from the fighting, we were now at the 14th Army's sharp edge. This time, unlike my arrival at war two years earlier in Egypt, I was a combatant.

We were looking down on Sinzweya, administrative and supply center for all the troops in the Kalapanzin Valley and farther east (Map 3, p. xxi). The scene was busy but relatively peaceful. Who could have foreseen that shortly it was to be the stage for weeks of fierce fighting and for the first major defeat of the Japanese armies in Burma? I was to be in the middle of that fighting.

It has been written of the Arakan: "There were few less desirable places in which to fight a campaign."[1] This is due mainly to two factors, communications and climate. When the fighting started in 1942, communications were execrable, virtually nonexistent. They were still not good in January 1944. This earth track over the Ngakyedauk Pass along which we had just marched, so recently a mere footpath, was the main supply route for a whole infantry division, artillery, and many ancillary troops. West of the Mayu Range down the coastal strip there were no all-weather metalled roads, and at first none of the numerous tidal *chaungs* were bridged for motor transport.

As for climate, I was in luck. From mid-November to mid-March the Arakan is dry by day, but not too hot, and cool at night. From about mid-March it gets hot and very humid. From June to early October is the monsoon, when up to two hundred inches of rain can fall, when virulent malaria is rife and leeches flourish. Other torments include prickly heat, ringworm, and in the dry season the jungle tick, which bequeaths the sometimes mortal scrub typhus.

During the wet season large-scale campaigning on land was brought to a halt. On the other hand, boats on the rivers and *chaungs* moved with greater freedom.

The area of northern Arakan where operations were taking place when I donated my services to the Empire was divided into two parts by the Mayu Range. Running near enough north and south down the center of the Mayu Peninsula, the hills rose to over two thousand feet and were covered with thick jungle, mostly bamboo. It was a feature of the Mayus that many of the individual hills culminated in knife-edged ridges leading steeply to small, sharp summits.

To the west of this backbone was the narrow coastal plain running down to the end of the peninsula at Foul Point. This was a land of paddy fields, fishing villages, tidal creeks, mud flats, and mangrove swamps. It was the territory of the 5th Indian Division.

To the east was the broad Mayu River valley and its tributary, the Kalapanzin River, tidal up to Goppe Bazar. The topography of the valley, about 7 to 8 miles wide at this point, is complicated by a series of narrow ridges rising from the paddy fields, from 50 to 150 feet high, and either forested or covered with elephant grass and scrub. This was the territory of the 7th Indian Division. My battalion was part of the division's 89th Brigade.

Still farther east across the Arakan Hill Tracts was the remote Kaladan Valley, and beyond that the Arakan Yomas, thickly forested and sparsely inhabited hill country where dirt tracks petered out into footpaths, and footpaths into elephant trails, and where large-scale operations were scarcely possible. On this lonely eastern flank the British-officered 81st West African Division kept guard, supplied by air and their own porterage. These black giants were so far inland in the deep jungle that we saw little of them. It was rumored that they were terrified of the forest at night, which, if true, must have been a tiresome handicap.

When I joined, both the 5th and 7th divisions were poised to advance on the two towns of Maungdaw and Buthidaung, and the metalled road that connected them through the Mayu Range. Around the towns, and on the steep hills above the road, the Japanese had excavated a series of underground defenses, the Golden Fortress. Both divisions were relatively fresh. Both had been trained for jungle fighting.

The 7th Indian Division was new to battle. It had been disbanded in 1919, and was raised again in 1940. It had arrived in the Arakan four months earlier at the end of the monsoon. After much patrolling and skirmishing, it was now seasoned. I had met the 5th Indian Division in the Western Desert. It had been shifted to Iraq and Persia in late 1942, and to India in June 1943. By November, after a spell of jungle acclimatization, it reached the Arakan. Some of its soldiers were much-traveled veterans.

At the foot of the pass there was a guide to lead us the three or four miles to battalion headquarters. And thus it was that an American found himself slogging down a jungle track in Burma deep in powdery dust, along with Gurkhas from Nepal and a brace of Englishmen, on the last stage of a long trek to reach the fighting tip of one Allied campaign in the war against Japan.

From Quetta the journey had taken some six weeks. Whoever was responsible for the logistics of the Burma War was not sleeping easy. And it was close to a year since Jupe and I had left Cairo. We had not been rushed into battle.

At battalion HQ we were welcomed by the commanding officer and the adjutant, Lieutenant Colonel Billy Twiss and Captain Stanley Ball. HQ was a few hundred yards back from the forward positions dug in astride bamboo-covered hills.

That evening other officers of the battalion came into the mess. Along with the HQ this was located within the protection of a dry streambed. Each had a roof of logs covered with earth, giving headroom of about five feet, and a floor of dirt. There were slit trenches close by.

It seemed a safe place to be. Those who could gathered around a makeshift table for what little conviviality might be had with the assistance of army-issue rum. Forward company commanders got in for only the occasional meal.

Twiss had just taken over as colonel, though he had commanded for a spell in 1943. He was a shortish, rolling-gaited, jovial person, and seemed remarkably unweighed down by his responsibilities and the uncertainties of battle. He obviously looked upon me, his newest officer, less as a pawn to be placed strategically on the military board than as a recruit for the evening game of Monopoly.

As the roll of the dice heightened the chance for a player to gain a monopoly on Mayfair or Park Lane (the British version of Ventnor Avenue or Boardwalk), the *whoosh* of outgoing twenty-five-pounders overhead—or the replying 105-millimeters *crumphing* somewhere outside, or the occasional *snap-snap* of rifle fire—seemed hardly to be noticed by my new companions. I was somewhat more conscious of the sounds and marveled at this detachment.

On the next evening the colonel said, "Gilmore, do you play bridge?"

"Yes, sir."

Apologetically, Twiss continued. "I'm afraid we don't play contract, only auction."

My enthusiasm dimmed. This form of bridge had left New England in about 1925.

We played under the flickering *lal tins* (kerosene lamps). With the limited number of potential players, and some of these apt to be on patrol and picket, how the new officer might fit into the evening game assumed considerable importance.

It was on the first evening that I met Peter Myers and Peter Wickham. I was to see much of both over the next twenty months, and both have remained lifelong friends. Peter W. at that time was intelligence officer, and Peter M. was signals officer, so both were based at HQ.

While the success of a battalion or of any fighting unit depends most of all on the man at the top, both Peters came to play an important part in creating the spirit and cohesion necessary for the esprit de corps our battalion enjoyed. There were sinking moments, times when confidence was shaky, especially as the battalion had already experienced, and was to continue to experience, a series of different commanding officers. But these two young men (of course, with others) accepted tremendous responsibilities. Along with a rugged group of Gurkha officers, they helped to hold the battalion together until in the fall of that year (1944) a strong colonel took over and stayed until the closing weeks of the war.

Like me, the two Peters were emergency commissioned officers, but of an earlier vintage. Peter Myers had joined the 4th Battalion in December 1941, some nine months after it was raised. Peter Wickham arrived early in 1942. They had been with the battalion through its first spell of active service on the North-West Frontier, at the relief of Datta Khel (July to September 1942), and had been with it throughout the subsequent months of jungle training in the teak forests of Chindwara (central India, Kipling country). This long bonding period, when men and officers grew familiar with each other's strengths and weaknesses as well as with their military duties, must have provided an invaluable source of confidence denied to us later arrivals.

Peter Wickham was tall and jovial. Peter Myers was of medium height and handsome. Both were dark haired. Both were very competent. Both accepted, as did so many, responsibilities beyond their years. Aside from the Doc—more about him later—they were two of the officers on hand through most of the Burma fighting. Wickham was absent twice recovering from wounds, and both had spells of leave.

Either because he did not like my bidding during the first evening's bridge game, or did not trust my inexperience in a forward position—or possibly because my record showed that I had spent several weeks dozing through that motor transport course in Ahmadnagar—within a day or two I was dispatched by Colonel Twiss to take over the battalion MT Platoon. Brian Irving and Peter McQueen were sent as seconds in command to forward companies to gain war experience. Brian soon found himself deep in the jungle carrying bags of silver rupees to loosen the tongues of the villagers, and with instructions to penetrate into Buthidaung itself to pinpoint Japanese positions.

As far as I recall, the MT Platoon comprised some twenty or so vehicles and their drivers, including assorted trucks, several jeeps, Bren carriers (tracked, with raised armored sides, open on top), a motorbike, a sweeper, and two Madrassi mechanics (or fitters, as the British called them). In theory my job was simple: to control the allocation and proper use of the vehicles and their drivers, and to insure that night and day all of both were ready for work. This was normally as soft a job as one could enjoy in an infantry battalion. When I took over, the platoon was in a cushy spot well back from the firing. However, there were seldom conventional front lines in the Burma War. The country was too wild and vast, the troops too few. We were in for more excitement than could have been guessed at.

I found our MT grouped with that of the rest of 89th Brigade at Sinzweya, the administrative area and supply dump at the foot of the Ngakyedauk Pass ("Okeydoke," the Tommies called it). We must have been at least a mile from the nearest infantry unit. Our three platoons had been allotted a position on the northwest corner of the thinly defended perimeter. We occupied a low bamboo-covered knoll with three fingers jutting into the open paddy, paddy that isolated the knoll from the surrounding forested hills on three sides. The fourth side was overlooked by a steep escarpment. With the brigade transport officer in command, each platoon—Gurkha, Punjabi, and KOSB (the British King's Own Scottish Borderers)—was dug in around the perimeter with vehicles concealed as well as possible. My bunch of stalwarts was in trenches covering an area of paddy.

On the night of February 4 our ease of mind vanished. We heard that the Japanese were in strength at Taung Bazar, some six miles to the north (that is, at our backs), and were moving south. Near Taung the Kalapanzin River was fordable at low tide in the dry season. By good fortune the 89th Brigade, including the 4/8th Gurkhas, had just been relieved from its advanced position near Buthidaung and was back near Sinzweya. My battalion had been about to train with a squadron of Lee-Grant tanks of the 25th Dragoons which that day had crossed the Okeydoke. The tanks were to provide an unappealing surprise for the Japanese.

89th Brigade was sent north to deal with this infiltration. At first it was thought that the Japanese numbered about one thousand. Estimates were soon revised up to seven thousand. They appeared to be moving in several columns. Undoubtedly their purpose was to cut off and destroy our 7th Division. Within hours my battalion was engaged in fierce fighting, and the administrative area became like a stirred-up hornets' nest as preparations for a seige were improvised. The area was quite unsuitable as a fortress. It was a saucer, a flat area of dried paddy overlooked on all sides by a ring of forested hills, most of which could not be manned.

To summarize the Battle of the Admin Box, the Japanese had launched a bold diversionary offensive. Their purpose was to overrun the 7th and 5th divisions, cause maximum confusion and panic, and thus attract reinforcements from other areas and distract attention from the central Imphal front, some 250 miles to the north, where a month later they were to launch their main attack.

Covered by darkness and the morning mists, they had infiltrated through or around our widely spread defended positions. Our units were spread unusually wide because they were about to launch their own attack. By cutting the division's land supply route over the Ngakyedauk Pass, which they did on the seventh, they expected it to retreat in chaos and be defeated in detail. This tactic had worked well in the past.

They did cause much havoc and confusion. Divisional HQ between Taung Bazar and the Admin Box at Sinzweya was attacked. It hung on for a few hours before General Messervy led the remnants south into the Box and relative safety. The doughty Frank Messervy had a way of falling into predicaments not usually the lot of a general. In May 1942, during my time in North Africa, he had been captured by the Germans while commanding the British 7th Armoured Division. He had passed himself off as an officer's batman, "too old for combat," and had then escaped by jumping out of the back of a moving truck and walking through the night.

Under the initial confusion some rear echelon troops panicked. They tried to make it on foot back over the pass. Others were overrun and those who survived were forced to disperse. Some reached safety. Circling vultures over the jungle told of those who failed.

As was already mentioned, the Admin Box was little but a vast supply dump in a clearing of paddy fields. It was 1,200 yards square and surrounded by steep hills that were covered with thick jungle. In its center was a scrub-covered hill 200 yards long and 150 feet high. Here lay piled much of the ammunition for the coming offensive, ammunition that would now be needed to repel the Japanese attack.

The defenses of the Box were firmed up by slotting in such fighting infantry as were close to hand. Even so, much of the perimeter was held by signalers, engineers, various artillerymen, mortarmen, muleteers, drivers, supply men, veterinary personnel, ordnance people, and salvage and workshop units. Now one of General Messervy's earlier training directives paid off: he had insisted that every soldier in the division, whatever his specialty, must also be able to fight as infantry.

In India six months earlier, when Frank Messervy had first arrived to take command of the 7th Division, he had addressed all officers. He is reported as saying to them: "I foresee one thing above all others that is likely to happen. This is that our Brigades and the Japanese Regiments will become interposed with one another like the layers of a Neapolitan sandwich. Our tactics then will be quite straightforward. We will fight back towards our own people and in doing so will destroy all the Japs between us."[2] This was now the situation that existed. Layers of opposing troops lay sandwiched between one another, the Japanese elements shifting and circling as they probed and attacked, the 7th and 5th Indian divisions closed up in a dozen or so boxes and fighting back while from the north new forces were called in to press and squeeze the life out of the Japs.

The Admin Box was seriously short of infantry (and overendowed with mules!). Reinforcements called in included the 4/8th Gurkhas. They were allocated the "eastern gate" covering the tracks leading to the Kalapanzin River and to the 114th Brigade. Although so close, I saw nothing of them.

For some days my battalion was only at half strength, as two companies had been cut off and had disappeared. These companies crossed the Mayu Range and joined the 5th Division. Eventually they recrossed the Mayu, avoiding the Japanese, and rejoined the battalion in the Box.

The Japanese radio announced the annihilation of the division and reiterated the intention of capturing Chittagong and of marching on Calcutta. They were counting chickens early.

The division's ability to stand and fight was made possible by supply from the air. Now this is commonplace. Then it was new. The techniques were still being evolved and the availability of sufficient transport planes depended on the cooperation of the American air forces and the stamina of the pilots of all nations. For more than two weeks our requirements were dropped into the paddy fields. From our outpost we could see the planes (C-47 Dakotas) and the parachutes opening, and the free-fall bags beginning their plummeting descent, but we could not see the landing zones. Separate drops were made for the other brigade boxes.

At the same time the tenuous supply lines of the Japanese were being strangled. They had planned to dine upon captured British dumps. They failed to do this and hungered. From the north and west other divisions began to press. The attackers were attacked, the encirclers were encircled. But this took a lot of desperate fighting.

The above paragraphs make the battle sound very clear, organized, and certain. To us on the spot it was not so. Especially at the beginning, the fog of war was universal and dense. There was confusion, lack of information, anxiety, fear, bravery, tragedy, and above all, no foreknowledge of the future. Except for the Wingate expedition, the Japanese had beaten hell out of us in every major engagement. Were they supermen? We were not yet sure. By our collective deeds we had to provide the answer.

On the second day of the attacks, our brigade MT group was ordered to establish a standing patrol on the bluff overlooking our position. In turn a section from each of the platoons was to spend three days atop the escarpment to watch for enemy movement.

I drew the first three days and with six Gurkhas climbed to set up a comfortable base. During the day I spent much of the time propped against a shade tree reading a tattered paperback of *The Saint,* a popular mystery series of the era. But at night things became less calm. Down below, our position of a hundred men and assorted vehicles began to be subjected to jitter attacks. With taunts, yells, grenades, and a few shots, the enemy kept our people (and me) on edge. The answer to this tactic should be silence. The inexperienced and highly nervous ordnance-wallas defending the ordnance field park a few hundred yards away fired frantically, tracers lighting up the sky in all directions. For a while they made every night a bedlam.

During the third day, as I was deep in the adventures of the Saint, and happy with the peacefulness of our hilltop by comparison with the chaos below, we heard the clinking of entrenching tools in hard ground. Three men sent to investigate returned with the news: *"China manis khannu"* ("Some Chinese are digging in").

As far as I knew, the nearest Chinese, our allies, were hundreds of miles to the north. I set out to look for myself. Not three hundred yards along the crest was a party of twenty-five or so Japanese. We, being many fewer, did not linger, but after lobbing in our supply of grenades, returned under sparse retaliatory fire to our patrol base. I now felt less comfortable.

Next day it was the turn of the Punjabis to take over the post on the bluff. A young lieutenant was in charge. Just before dawn on their first night a ruckus of shooting and shouts broke out above us, with tracers flying in confusing directions and the muffled explosions of grenades. The whole flare-up was over in a few minutes, followed by an ominous silence. It was not until two survivors who had escaped over the cliff dragged themselves in after daylight that we learned how vicious and successful the Japanese attack had been. No one else lived. One body was found at the base of the cliff.

From that morning our MT perimeter was subjected to constant sniping and sporadic mortar fire from the bluff as well as to night attack from the nearby jungle and across the open paddy. Sniped at by day and vulnerable to sudden attack at night, we spent much of the uncomfortable weeks ahead in the confinement of slit trenches and a good many daylight hours in improving these below-ground protections.

My trench on the edge of the paddy was safe from the sniping

The author (*right*) atop a Royal Armour Corps Valentine tank outside Tobruk in June 1942. (*S. Gilmore*)

The Western Desert, June 1942. The crew of a British truck lies flat as they are bombed. (*Imperial War Museum*)

German prisoners coming in through the minefields at El Alamein, October 1942. (*S. Gilmore*)

TRAINING

Recruits at the 8th Gurkhas' training center in Quetta, India.

After the parade, Quetta.

Jungle training near Ziarat, India, August 1943.

A two-inch mortar crew. Each platoon had one of these weapons, which are light and portable and were effective in close fighting.

Piper, 8th Gurkha Rifles.

THE MEN

Major Scott Gilmore, London, December 1945.

The commanding officer of the 8th Gurkha Rifles, Lt. Colonel Walter Walker, who retired as General Sir Walter Walker, KCB CBE DSO, commander in chief of Allied Forces Northern Europe in 1972. (*W. Walker*)

General Frank Messervy, commander of the 7th Indian Division, July 1943 to December 1944.

Fellow officers of the 4/8th: Peter Myers (*left*) and Peter Wickham, Kohima, India.

Officers of the 4/8th and 4/1st Gurkha Rifles after a basketball game: (*from left*) Peter Myers, Denis Sheil-Small, Runce Rooney, Scott Gilmore, Chris or Cecil Nixon (twins), Peter Wickham, Punch Chedburn, and Dennis Parker.

Officers of the 4th Battalion, 8th Gurkha Rifles, in Kohima, during October 1944: (*back row, from left*) Mike Tidswell, Pat Davis, Howard Marshall, Scott Gilmore, Peter Wickham, Jock Purdon; (*second row*) Toby Wilcox, unidentified, Walter Walker, Lt. Colonel N. D. Wingrove, Subadar Major Chandru Thapa, Peter Myers, Frank Crouchman; (*front row*) Doc Dalton, Denis Sheil-Small.

Geoffrey Bull, Company D commander (*standing hatless behind table*) and Walter Walker (*standing in front of tree*) at the award ceremony of an 8th Gurkhas gymkhana—a sort of social field day on horseback. In this case, mules substituted for horses. Kohima, December 1944. (*S. Gilmore*)

Bill Blenkin, Denis Sheil-Small, and Pat Davis outside a battalion headquarters bunker near Milaungbya, Burma, in March 1945.

The author's company
commander, Mike Tidswell,
killed in action at Taungdaw,
Burma, on May 14, 1945.

Rifleman Lachhiman Gurung, VC, posing for
a portrait by Captain Harry Sheldon, Delhi, 1946.
Lachhiman's Victoria Cross—Britain's highest award
for courage in battle—was the only one awarded
the 8th Gurkhas in World War II. Lachhiman lost
his right hand and the sight in his left eye
in the action.

The author's orderly,
Rifleman Nebilal Rai, during
the 4/8th's service in Malaya
just after the war. (*P. Davis*)

Typical road conditions on the Imphal front during the monsoon.
(*Imperial War Museum*)

Arakan country: steep, jungle-clad ridges divided by valleys with open paddy fields.
(*Imperial War Museum*)

A Gurkha manning a camouflaged foxhole in the Arakan jungle in 1943. He is armed with a Bren gun, the standard light machine gun of the British and British Commonwealth armies during the war. Each infantry section had one. (*Imperial War Museum*)

Gurkhas setting *panjis*—sharpened bamboo stakes—to impede attackers. (*Imperial War Museum*)

Gurkhas on a jungle path in Arakan. (*Imperial War Museum*)

An M-3 Grant tank in the Ngakyedauk Pass during the battle of the Admin Box, February 1944. (*Imperial War Museum*)

Naga tribesmen encountered near Kohima. (*S. Gilmore*)

The author and his troops resting during a route march outside Kohima in October 1944. Doc Dalton is on author's left. (*S. Gilmore*)

The Nyaungu-Pagan bridgehead photographed from the air a day or two after the initial crossing. This view does not show the immense width of the Irrawaddy but does show the barren, broken country beyond those forbidding cliffs. The small town of Nyaungu is about a mile to the right. (*Imperial War Museum*)

An A Company jeep patrol setting out to cut off retreating Japanese below Chauk in late April 1945. (*S. Gilmore*)

A rare prize: a Japanese prisoner, too sick to escape, captured near Mindon in May 1945. He is guarded by Rifleman Sherbahadur Gurung and Lance Naik Narbir Thapa. Note the *kukri* at Sherbahadur's waist. (*S. Gilmore*)

AFTER THE WAR

After two years in the jungle, the author is dazzled by a WAAF in New Delhi, November 1945.

Pagodas at Pagan at sunset in 1982, with the Irrawaddy in the background. (*P. Davis*)

but not from the mortar bombs. I would stare at the forested hills that lined the far side of the paddy. There was no way to tell how many Japanese lurked among them.

During the long string of nights I would hear sounds out there. Was it the wind rustling the bamboo? Was it bodies moving? How close? The Japs would fire a few shots, hoping to draw a response. They would call out in carefully rehearsed English or Urdu: "Give up, Limey, or you will die." "Johnny Gurkha, we are your friends." These voices from the dark were both absurd and unsettling.

Occasionally a Jap would creep really close to lob grenades. The pink arc of the burning fuse hissing through the night might be the only warning. We crouched low, tensed for the explosion. One never knew whether the cautious footsteps, the faint clink of metal on metal, were a prelude to such harassment, or whether, this time, it was to be the onslaught with bayonet and sword. Perhaps a section of Japs would charge the last fifty yards. Then they would be met by a hail of fire. Two or three bodies were left behind. Wounded would crawl back or be dragged off. They were just probing for weak spots.

My orderly and I shared watch, *kukris* and loaded rifles laid out on the edge of our slit trench, one standing in the trench trying to remain alert, receptive to the sounds of the night, the other stretched out under a blanket asleep alongside the trench. Those long hours of darkness brought shivers; the Arakan nights were cool. Or was it stretched nerves that played their part?

Midway through the siege my platoon was subjected to an all-out assault. It was not a soothing experience. In the morning there were sixteen bodies lying neatly in a wedge formation in front of our position. The leading chargers, banzai-yelling shadows with swords outstretched, had penetrated the perimeter trenches. The attack had begun with LMG and mortar fire. During a split-second lull in the firing, the heavy clump of running feet across the paddy had given our Gurkhas enough warning, perhaps ten seconds, to open up on and destroy probably half of the attackers. In addition to the sixteen so neatly laid out in phalanx, there were two bodies just inside our position by the latrines, an ignoble end. Some wounded were dragged away. When dawn came two more were spotted sitting helplessly in the open some seventy yards off. One marvels at the bravery of those men so far from their homes charging desperately and suicidally with sword and bayonet straight into our fire.

Twice during the siege some part of the ammunition dump in the center of the Box was hit, producing loud explosions followed by the crackling of small arms ammunition burning, more explosions, and a great billowing of smoke. We could hear the explosions and see the smoke.

On the first occasion Peter Wickham, who was attached to Brigadier Evans's HQ for the early part of the seige, crouched in a trench only three hundred yards away while red-hot steel fragments zinged and crumped about his ears for several hours. No one near him was hit.

People in our little pocket did not seem too disturbed. Distantly, or close and loud, we could hear most of the battles that flared up around the perimeter. There was nothing to be done but hope that the others too were holding their positions. We learned afterward that the West Yorks (being used as a counterattack force) and the tanks of the 25th Dragoons put in attack after attack on sectors that had been temporarily overrun. The West Yorks lost 50 percent of their strength in the first eight days. My own battalion was deeply embroiled in the battle, at first defensively, then gradually changing to the offensive.

One of the more colorful characters trapped in the Box was our brigade sergeant major of MT, Dickie Bott. Dickie's main job during the seige was the recovery of carrier and other vehicles that broke down. Often the problem was one of thrown tracks on the carriers. Many of these rescue missions took place in exposed positions, perhaps on a bit of no-man's-land in the open, where to linger was certain to bring sniper fire and, quite likely, shells or mortar bombs.

Perhaps the tensions of such dashes into the open were responsible for his other great skill, his adroitness at scrounging rum. Dickie never admitted a need for rum except to cover up "the nasty taste of the water," but it was obvious that it helped in carrying out his perilous duties.

The first order of the day for Dickie was to forage for refreshment. His gaunt frame accoutreed in baggy shorts and standard hobnailed boots, and over his lean and worried face a rakishly sloped Gurkha felt hat, Dickie set out on his BSA motorcycle, his faithful Gurkha assistant, Ranbir, clinging on behind.

Whether his first stop was at brigade HQ or at one of the infantry battalions or at the artillery, ostensibly to inquire of the state of some vehicle, Dickie arrived with a dash. His cycle swung to a skidding halt in a cloud of dust. He would leap from the saddle with a large "Good morning, Sah," a sweeping salute, heels banging together.

On occasion the salute would be performed while mounted. This unique ritual required a sudden stiffening in the saddle to an erect position, a straightening of the arms to a rigid set, and then a sharp eyes right.

Dickie's ability as a scrounger was matched by his popularity, so his dependence on the demon rum was indulged by all. By eleven his spirit and dash were at a peak. He could remember almost with pleasure the challenge of the Bren carrier lying disabled in the open near a KOSB forward company and overlooked by a Jap-held hill position. Carriers were used to bring up both men and supplies, since their armored sides gave some protection against rifle fire and mortar bombs.

Fully conscious of his gallery and center-stage position, bony legs glued to the BSA, Dickie roared across the paddy heedless of bumps, ruts, and deep pools of dust. And locked behind this man who was his bewildering boss, mentor, drinking friend, and responsibility was Ranbir. With a skid and a slide they were up against the lee side of the carrier with a double wall of armor plate between them and any small arms fire.

They were hard at repairing the track with a frenzy of clanking hammers before the Japs woke up and started to range in with a mortar. One of the more unnerving experiences in war is to be beneath a mortar bomb as it drifts down the last few hundred yards and the *sssiiiiiiss* grows louder and louder. It is very hard to judge where it will land. If other noise drowns the flight, the first warning is the last as the bomb explodes.

If Dickie and Ranbir heard the incoming bombs and the resulting *brumphs,* they gave no sign. They did not let up on their hammering. Before the Japs had fired more than half a dozen rounds the KOSB company overlooking the drama had spotted the puffs and was furiously calling for a response from its mortar platoon. A succession of explosions on the enemy position was followed by silence.

Track repaired, the cycle was flung into the carrier, followed by two hurtling forms. Grand as the opening of the scene had been, just as exciting was the close. Accompanied by the cheers of the watchers, the grinding, clanking square steel box withdrew at top speed, two crouched figures glued to the driving slits, ignoring the rifle fire fluffing the dust or ricocheting off the sides, hell-bent for safety.

Dickie would now be thinking of the rum and orange that awaited back at Brigade to cut the dust from his throat and blot out remembrance of the dangers escaped. He was due for leave in a few days. He looked forward to some *serious* drinking in Calcutta.

So the long days and longer nights passed. From beginning to end my platoon and I never left our knoll. We learned that extra rifle companies had been ordered in from outside to reinforce other parts of the perimeter. But at first our small redoubt stayed unchanged. We were a finger pointing out from the central body, unsupported by other positions. We felt isolated.

Each day food and ammunition were brought to us by tank or carrier, and this break in our isolation would raise confidence. As night approached spirits would sag. Between the false and the real alarms, and the Jap jitter parties calling out in English and in Urdu, and the wild firing of our neighbors, sleep was scarce. With first light we stood to yet once more, peering into the thick morning mist. Had anything changed during the night? Were the Japs about to try some new unpleasantness? Nothing could be taken for granted. Those who relaxed too soon paid for it.

The first rays of the sun reached down to warm us. There was a shout from the jungle. It was a patrol returning from a reconnaissance or a night on picket. Soon we were sipping at mugs of strong tea. My driver, who knitted (as did many Gurkhas), took up his needles to continue his sweater and I filled my lungs with sunshine.

With the heat rolled in the stench of the rotting bodies outside the perimeter and odors from the inadequate and neighborly latrines. Never mind. We had survived into another day. But these and other anxieties did affect the nerves.

There were lighter moments, quieter moments: our stoical Gurkhas playing cards, smoking, shaving each other's heads, telling stories, chortling over some joke. If Dickie Bott had conned orange squash and rum out of the brigade HQ mess, we might enjoy a shot or two with which to inspire the lunchtime bully beef, and to assist a postlunch snooze.

Sometime in the second week of the siege there arrived as reinforcement a section of Punjabi Medium Machine Gunners and a forward observation officer (FOO) from the artillery to direct fire from the big guns. With the latter came a telephone line. This was a considerable relief. The FOO could call down heavy fire as close as seventy-five yards to our trenches, and often did so, on enemy lurking in the darkness, perhaps massing for one of those sudden rushes.

The days of the siege wore on and there were signs that the Japanese attack was stalling. More and more our troops were taking the initiative. Hill by hill the enemy was driven off positions that looked down the throats of those in the Box. But constantly on the alert for unfriendly fire, confined in or near a personal trench, sleeping little, with grime accumulating over the body, with water scarce, food adequate but unappetizing, plagued by flies from the all-too-near latrines, sapped by uncertainties, we began to suffer from a perpetual weariness, almost exhaustion. Supplies still came in by airdrop, but there was no way to get the several hundred wounded out to base hospitals.

From time to time news reached us. How? I have forgotten. Telephone? Wireless? Word of mouth via the ration carrier? We heard of the 5th Division's advance over the Ngakyedauk Pass from the west, and of the 26th Indian Division's progress down from Taung Bazar to the north. Now it was the Japanese who were under siege. But they were never a people to give in easily. Until the last day we felt under pressure.

One curious fact should be recorded. Despite the close attention to our perimeter every night and despite many opportunities, not one of our vehicles was harmed. It seems that the Japanese troops had orders to preserve MT for their own intended advance on Chittagong and Calcutta. They are reported to have brought spare drivers with them.

During these last days of the siege there was another small tragedy on our sector. Every other day we sent a water wagon down to a stream at the edge of the jungle several hundred yards from our position. One morning as the wagon stood in the rocky shallows at the side of the stream loading, bursts of fire from the banks above caught our men, causing heavy casualties. Some Gurkhas were killed.

Finally there was a night with no harassing fire, no patrols creeping to the perimeter to toss in sputtering grenades. In the morning the platoon of Japanese on the bluff above no longer sniped. The enemy who had pressed so close about us for two and a half weeks was gone.

We had been cut off on February 7. On the twenty-fourth the first lorries rolled back over the Okeydoke carrying the six hundred to seven hundred wounded. What had seemed sometimes like a nightmare was over. And at once the offensive south was resumed.

Since the long pain of the retreats of 1942 in Malaya and Burma, this was the first large-scale confrontation between British-Indian and Japanese arms. There had been as much fighting outside the Admin Box as around it. Of the eight thousand men now known to have been in the Japanese attack, five thousand were lost.

Air supply had been the foundation for success, as it was to be for the rest of the war in this theater. The Japanese did not have it. We did. When we stayed put to fight, resupplied by air, they ran out of biscuits and bullets. Later, when we attacked, it gave us the freedom to go anywhere. That trusty warhorse of the Burma fighting, the C-47 Dakota, has been called "the new wonder weapon" of those times.[3] So it was. We infantry came to feel great affection for it.

In his account of the Burma War, our General Slim wrote that although the numbers engaged on both sides were not great, the Admin Box battles and the advance that followed were "one of the historic successes of British arms."[4] This was the first occasion when the army in India had defeated a substantial Japanese attack. "It was a victory, a victory about which there could be no argument, and its effect, not only on the troops engaged, but on the whole Fourteenth Army, was immense."[4]

CHAPTER X

——

North to Naga Country

My MT platoon was on its own, camped in a palm grove a few hundred yards from a fine sandy beach. The sea breeze blew sweetly and the gentle roll of surf was balm to the nerves. Shelter from the dew was provided by roofs of thatched palm leaves, run up by the men.

No longer were our daylight hours interrupted by the snap of a sniper bullet or the drawn-out hiss of a mortar shell. No longer was the night pierced by catcalls and taunts. We need not freeze, hearts thumping, at rustles in the darkness. We were free to move across the earth without fear.

The beach stretched for miles. Sometimes I wonder if this paradise at Elephant Point has been found for tourism. Or is it still enjoyed only by a handful of Arakanese fishermen?

Aside from checking over the vehicles our responsibilities were minimal. My football parade on the beach each day was a huge success. Lacking speed and stamina and experience, I was relegated to

146

the protection of the goal. The men dashed up and down the hard sand with inexhaustible élan.

After the game we swam in the blue sea. Presumably it was in these waters that Kipling's "flying fishes played." On the first day I saw that some of the men were reluctant to move down the almost flat beach and into the shallow water. I learned that our old havildar, all of thirty, leaning on one of the many Gurkha superstitions, was reminding the men that *nam pani,* salt water, brought bad luck. Despite his fears, within a day or two the enjoyment of acquatic pleasure had overcome reservations. The standing instruction that our Gurkhas should be given watermanship training whenever possible was a charter for many happy hours of splashing. Moreover, I, who had been raised by the sea, was able to regain some of the prestige tarnished on the football pitch.

Sometimes in this paradise I looked about at my companions, these uncomplicated moonfaced young stoics, calm, smiling now, smoking their *bidis,* slapping down grimy playing cards with a curse and a chuckle, and thought how privileged I had been to be introduced to battle in their company. I, from my background of technological complexity and relative luxury, and they, from their unsophisticated mountain country where the internal combustion engine was unknown and a tap with running water was a rare mystery—together we had survived a tough time with honor.

As a result of total immersion, the secrets of Gurkhali were at least partly revealed. I could now phrase questions on a man's health and well-being and to my amazement be understood, and receive a sensible response, and understand that response. I could sit on the ground with Tokbahadur, Tilbir, Lalbahadur, or Thamansing and discuss elementary world politics or their plans for leave. They told me how from the railhead in India they must first walk through a thirty-mile belt of the flat, malarial Terai and then climb maybe for a week or more over mountain trails to reach their villages. There they would be feted and spoiled by their families. Many of the older men were married. The younger ones were not, and the accumulation of army pay was providing a fine start in the competition for the most desired girls.

When did I and my thirty stalwarts enjoy this elysian ocean holiday? We were certainly on our own far from the rest of the battalion. Was it immediately after the lifting of the Admin Box siege? Was it two months later when the division was airlifted north to the central front and its MT had to follow overland? The fog of war is proverbial, and is compounded by the fog of an ebbing memory.

After the reopening of the Ngakyedauk Pass on February 24 and the retreat back toward Buthidaung of the surviving Japanese, there was no rest for the 7th Division. In early March the battalion was back in action as part of the force surrounding and attacking the Buthidaung fortifications. There was much hard fighting.

Three of our officers were wounded by the persistent shelling (including Peter Wickham, but he soon returned). On March 18, as the battalion was about to move back to Taung Bazar, Billy Twiss and Stanley Ball, the colonel and adjutant, were killed when their carrier ran over a mine. I remember meeting the new CO, who arrived after a couple of weeks—Lieutenant Colonel Wingrove. Of greater significance for the future of the battalion, another prewar regular soldier arrived with him, Major Walter Walker. More of him later.

Toward the end of April we were expecting to move out of the Arakan for a refit and rest. There was talk of a return to India for the monsoon. Most of the men had been in action with few breaks since mid-October. "Soldiers must be trained before they can fight," wrote our General Slim; "fed before they can march, and relieved before they are worn out."[1]

It was not to be. Several weeks earlier, on March 8, and some three hundred miles to the north in Manipur, known as the central front, the Japanese had launched a far more ambitious offensive for which the Arakan had been a bold feint. There were furious assaults by two Japanese divisions aimed initially at destroying the three Indian divisions defending the area and at capturing the immense supply dumps now gathered on the Imphal plain. Imphal was a small town, not much above a village, but capital of Manipur, India's most eastern state. The plain was surrounded by hills. On it were several airstrips of high strategic value.

From Imphal running southeast lay the only all-weather motorable road from India into central Burma. Along this route the defeated British forces had retreated two years earlier when it was no better than a fair-weather track. Back down it we intended to maneuver forces for the recapture of Burma.

From Imphal running north went the only decent road to the nearest railhead, at Dimapur in Assam. The Imphal basin lies at 2,600 feet. The road to Dimapur climbs to 5,000 feet at its highest point. Here lies the village and district center of Kohima. Kohima was the objective of a third Japanese division, moving over minor tracks through the mountains. If this division could take Kohima, it could strangle communications between Assam and the troops in Imphal.

It seemed obvious that Dimapur must be a further objective of the Japanese. Dimapur held a series of even larger dumps, dumps that have been described as "eleven miles long and at least a mile wide."[2] With Dimapur in Japanese hands, the airfields to the northeast up the Brahamaputra valley, from which the Americans were supplying Chiang Kai-shek and his Chinese armies, would be cut off. The progress of the Ledo road across north Burma would be halted, and Chennault's American fighters and bombers in western China would be isolated and starved. It was only forty-six miles from Kohima to Dimapur.

This assault was announced in Tokyo as "The March on Delhi." There was a chance that the appearance of a Japanese army in Assam might spark an uprising throughout India, might cause such chaos that the subcontinent became ungovernable and the British must retreat across the Indian Ocean to Africa.

We know now that the Japanese held no serious expectation of achieving such an outcome. Their primary aim was defensive: to stabilize their positions in Burma and Malaya by shattering the British-Indian forces gathering at Imphal and, if possible, to choke off America's last supply line to the Chinese. They would have known, or guessed, that America's chief interest in the Burma theater was not to help the British regain a lost colony but to keep China in the war against them.

The fighting around Imphal was to continue for many months. Much of it was as fierce and continuous as any fighting anywhere in World War II. At first Allied troops were thin on the ground, particularly at Kohima and Dimapur. Reinforcements were needed quickly. General Slim had our good neighbors the 5th Indian Division flown up from the Arakan in mid-March. It was a battalion from this division, the Royal West Kents, that formed the core of the defending force through the famous siege of Kohima.

Then it was the turn of the 7th Indian Division. With little time to recover from the Arakan struggles, on April 26 the battalion began a move north by road, rail, and air. On May 9 my companions were in action again near Imphal.

My job was to convoy the MT overland up through what is today desperately poor Bangladesh and into Assam. There we were to wait until the tortuous Dimapur–Kohima–Imphal road was cleared of the enemy. Once more I was separated from the battalion.

Our long convoy of brigade MT minus the Bren carriers (which were shipped north by a combination of riverboat and rail) got off to a slow start. Rain had fallen and the road north through the Chittagong hill tracts was so greasy with red mud that one mistake sent a vehicle and its driver sliding off into the jungle. The road was closed entirely during the heaviest downpours. For many miles MPs controlled single-lane traffic, one hour in each direction.

The pleasantest part of the trip was climbing the Khasi hills to Shillong. Along the way we enjoyed a midday swim in a rushing stream running beside the road. Taptabahadur, one of the rare drivers apt to flaunt military discipline, produced a sizable bag of fresh fish for dinner by exploding a grenade in the deepest pool.

Shillong was a delightful hill station, the first bit of real civilization I had seen in four months. For over seventy years it had been "home" for our 1st Battalion, its regimental base. Shillong was where the new regimental center, acting for both the 8th Gurkha battalions, was formed in 1940. It was where the 3rd Battalion and my 4th Battalion were raised in 1940 and 1941. At five thousand feet among rolling hills it was green and cool, and I wished that we could have stayed there.

Down through the hills from Shillong and out onto the Assam plain, we made our way north and then east. On the plain the land was either jungle or tea plantations. Sometimes on the slopes at either side of the road we could see the European planters on their ponies watching over gangs of female pickers with wicker baskets on their backs. By now most of the younger planters were in the army. The older men were hard-pressed to keep the estates in full production.

It took us a week of driving to reach our objective, a spot not far from the mighty Brahmaputra. There we stayed for three months. We camped with our vehicles on a low ridge that was almost surrounded by flooded paddy fields. The monsoon had started. It rained and it rained and then it rained some more. The paddy was under from one to four feet of water. The slippery mud bunds between each field provided pathways of a sort. The men amused themselves by catching small fish using a mosquito net as a trap. The fish, a form of lungfish, were able to survive the dry season in suspended animation buried in the brick-hard mud. With the coming of the rains they wriggled free. More queasy than the men about encountering water snakes and leeches, this sport lacked appeal for me.

I slept in the back of a truck with a tarpaulin canopy. There was a small mess tent along the rise that I shared with the other brigade MT officers. I can recall the lieutenant of the 1/11th Sikhs—a very fine battalion that had now joined the brigade in place of the 7/2nd Punjabis. He was a Sikh, not a Briton, with enlightened (or lax?) views on the enjoyment of tobacco and whiskey, which endeared him to me. Sikhs are forbidden both.

Life was dominated by water. The massive Brahmaputra a mile or two away rolled by carrying uncounted tons of water collected from hundreds of mountain streams back in Tibet and China. It carried oceans of melted snows and torrential Himalayan rains into the Ganges and thence through the intricate delta country to the Bay of Bengal.

When we stood on the riverbank and looked out through the dense rain and haze, the far side was hidden from view. Over the powerful gurgling and rippling of the waters we could hear the drone of the American transport planes taking off from a nearby airfield to fly the Hump with supplies for the Chinese. Not all returned from their crossing of the wild mountain barriers. Weather, mechanical failure, and Japanese fighters took a regular toll.

To appreciate the magnitude of the Indian monsoon in this area, note that the annual rainfall in New York or London is something like thirty-five inches. There are places in Assam where four hundred inches may fall, almost all of it within a period of two and a half months. During these weeks, soggy was a satisfactory condition for clothing. On removing a mildewed green boot, if a guest leech was not enjoying a meal on your ankle, luck was with you.

Outings included a visit to the Chinese restaurant in town (which may have been Jorhat) or an evening at the Planters Club. Having jeeps at my command was an advantage. The tea planters who remained, starved for the company of other exiles, would come from miles around to spend an evening with others who spoke English. They would drink, reminisce, and perhaps flirt with one of the very few women. Rain slanted down outside and dripped from the porch overhang. This and the muggy warmth throughout the evening, the click of billiard balls from a side room, the pad of barefoot bearers, all conjured up a scene from Somerset Maugham. It was good of the planters to let us share their club.

I recall visits to a nearby American radar base, with its very different atmosphere. There we could enjoy a change of diet and, after dinner, a film that had been flown in with the rations.

Perhaps this is the place to bring in a further note on the contribution of my fellow countrymen to the fighting in Burma. Aside from the valiant work of Galahad (the Marauders), a relatively small task force of less than three thousand—more on them follows— there were few American combat troops on the ground. Louis Allen states that by April 1945 the U.S. land forces in SEAC (South East Asia Command) numbered 12,097, but most of these were engaged in rail, road, and airfield construction. Galahad's successor, Mars Force, was of similar strength.[3]

Some of these Americans were training and motivating the three small Chinese divisions (total thirty thousand plus) operating with variable effectiveness in north Burma under the overall direction of General Stilwell. Another handful was in the OSS, the Office of Strategic Services, controlling and leading groups of guerrillas behind the Japanese lines in the north and east. As I have already mentioned, the Americans were interested in Burma only insofar as it was the platform for reconstituting a land link with China. For this large numbers of scarce American infantry were not needed when there were Chinese, British, and Indian forces available.

In the air we have a different story. The war in Burma could not have been won without the assistance of the squadrons of American supply planes and their American pilots. Air supply was the key to victory in Burma. The British and Indian forces fighting around Imphal and Kohima, the Chindits buried deep behind the Japanese lines, the many and various guerrilla groups, all were sustained only because Lord Mountbatten, the Supreme Commander SEAC, "borrowed" aircraft from the American supply squadrons flying the Hump to China. The fly-in of the 5th Indian Division from the Arakan to the central front in March 1944—"a fast and brilliant piece of management"[4]—which required 758 sorties, was done in twenty such borrowed aircraft. Back in Washington, the American High Command did not like these interruptions to its buildup of bases in China, but agreed on them. American leaders knew that if Imphal and Dimapur fell, both their air and their land operations in northern Burma and China would end. In April it was agreed to transfer seventy-five transport planes from the Italian theater to the 14th Army.

To the grossly overworked pilots of the C-47 Dakotas and C-46 Commandos—American, Indian, and British—all of us on the ground owed an immense debt; and so also to the fighter pilots who overwhelmed the Japanese air force so comprehensively that in effect we had freedom of the skies.

Galahad, or 5307th Composite Unit (Provisional)—Merrill's Marauders, comprised nearly three thousand American infantry soldiers, mostly volunteers, about one third with Pacific combat experience. After training in India along the lines pioneered by Orde Wingate's Chindits, and divided into three battalion columns, they set off on February 7, 1944, along the newly constructed stretches of the Ledo road to begin their sentence as Stilwell's shock troops. This occurred just as the Battle of the Admin Box was cranking up down south in the Arakan.

Someone has worked out that enough earth was moved during

the construction of the Ledo road to build a solid dirt wall three feet wide and ten feet high from New York to San Francisco—a useless but hypnotic statistic.[5] It was a great feat of engineering. The British had declared it to be impossible.

Stilwell used the Marauders to make a series of long, sweeping envelopments through extravagantly rough country to cut in behind the Japanese 18th Division. This was the experienced force that was blocking the advance of his Chinese. Then he used their sick, exhausted, and battle-drunk remnants to help in the capture of Myitkyina.

As is now widely acknowledged, Stilwell kept the Marauders in action for far longer than was either humane or wise. They had been told that their assignment was for three months, and this was the period generally reckoned by both British and American experts to be the limit over which lightly armed, long-range penetration units can operate and remain recoverable. The Marauders were in action for almost twice that time.

Even at the end, when the doctors were insisting that most of the men be evacuated, Stilwell and his staff let it be known that in their view the men were malingering. "I had him in my rifle sights," said an enlisted man regretfully, speaking of a time at Myitkyina when Stilwell had withdrawn to relieve himself during an inspection. "I coulda squeezed one off and no one would have known it wasn't a Jap that got the son-of-a-bitch."[6]

Wingate's second Chindit expedition was flown deep into Burma that March. In May two of the brigades came under Stilwell's control. He used them in the same heartless, unsparing manner. In July a medical inspection of 111th Brigade found only 6 officers and 120 other ranks out of a total strength of some 2,500 fit for further duty.[7] Vinegar Joe demanded (this time unsuccessfully) that those 126 survivors be pushed into the battle somewhere. Wingate had been killed early on when his plane crashed, or this situation might never have developed.

The story of the Marauders is a heroic one, and I recommend that anyone interested read Charlton Ogburn's fine book *The Marauders*. But in Ogburn's own words: "In the full picture of the ground war in Burma, extending over three years and some

150,000 square miles, the American part made up only a small fragment."[8]

What is the verdict on Vinegar Joe Stilwell? He did not long outlast the final capture of Myitkyina on August 3. In mid-October he was recalled, never to return.

He was no diplomat. He managed to antagonize Chiang Kai-shek and almost all the British generals with whom he came in contact, except Bill Slim. Most of his fellow American soldiers at all levels disliked him intensely. He was abrasive and opinionated and sometimes plain wrong. And yet he comes through as a man of talent, much courage, and immense willpower.

We in the plodding mainstream of the 14th Army's infantry knew nothing of such activities. But down in my watery camp I had one amenity that would probably have caused Stilwell to write a particularly sarcastic entry in his famous diary. Under my charge were three fine Arabian horses. It seems that some of the ways of the Indian Army had not changed much since Winston Churchill maintained a string of polo ponies as a subaltern in the Hussars.

Presumably these horses were originally kept so that prewar battalion commanders could enjoy a morning canter over the plains of the Punjab. To my recollection no one during the Arakan campaign had been foolish enough to patrol hostile territory on horseback, and I cannot remember seeing the horses down there. However, Peter Wickham has recorded that when the division first came to the Arakan, he and the Intelligence Havildar, Sete Gurung, conducted several day-long patrols on horseback through back areas of the Mayu foothills. Their purpose was to fill in detail missing from the maps and to mark down promising areas where vehicles or armor or dumps could easily be concealed.

The weather was intensely hot. We used to set off clad only in Gurkha hats, shorts, boots and socks; apart from a "packed lunch" I carried only a Tommy gun and a mapcase. Although my knees were extremely sore for the first day or so, they soon hardened and I

rather fancied my bareback prowess. We would find
some shady spot, preferably by a stream, for our picnic
lunch and I know Sete enjoyed our outings as much as
I did.[9]

One day when the rain had let up somewhat, an American warrant officer from the radar station showed interest in riding one of
the chargers. In gratitude for American hospitality, I readily agreed.

Unfortunately, the rain started in again before he had ridden
far. Returning in haste he and the horse plunged through the bamboo floor of a rickety bridge crossing a stream. The horse was quite
seriously cut up. The Syce who looked after him was upset, and I
had visions not only of a dead horse on my conscience but also,
when reports of my unauthorized loan of government property got
to the colonel, of a court-martial.

After much searching by jeep in nearby villages we found a
surly, barefoot veterinarian clad in a *longyi* and operating his practice from a *basha* one step above a hovel. Only after great persua-
sion in my faulty Urdu would this unwilling doctor return to camp
with us. I cannot remember and perhaps never understood the di-
agnosis and prescription. However, the horse soon returned to
normal health and I was saved much embarrassment. Shortly after
this the horses were moved back into India.

Recovering from the near loss of a horse under my command, I
was not pleased a few days later to be told that one of the Bren carriers was resting at the bottom of an algae-infested pond. This
pond now merged into the flooded paddy. The Gurkha driver had
surprised himself by mistakenly releasing the brake. The carrier had
rolled straight into the water, completely submerging the engine.
There being no roof on a carrier, the driver popped to the surface.

Through May, June, and early July I was camped with the MT
on these paddy fields of Assam, damp, bored but safe. What did we
do during this protracted halt? The army abhors a vacuum. We
would not have been allowed to slide into complete idleness. How
did we combat tedium and endure that terrible climate of high humidity and endless rain? I can no longer remember. The whole
episode has become hopelessly obscured, perhaps blanked out because nothing happened and the mind has put up blocks.

The reason we had been unable to join the battalion sooner, why we were mothballed for so long in the steaming, soaking valley of the Brahmaputra, was of course that our friends the Japanese were extraordinarily stubborn in their continued efforts to capture Imphal and Kohima. The road between Dimapur and Imphal, the only road of substance, was cut on April 5. It was not cleared until June 22, and the 4/8th Gurkhas continued fighting along trails to the east for another month.

The Japanese had planned a three-week campaign. They had relied on the capture of dumps for subsequent provisioning. They never did capture any major dumps, but it was nearly three months before retreat was grudgingly permitted. It seems that their commanders had courage for everything except the recognition of defeat.

Sometimes stubborn persistence paid off, especially in small local actions. At Imphal and Kohima, a major campaign, the refusal to acknowledge reality insured a major disaster for Japanese arms.

They were short of food and ammunition, much reduced in numbers, exhausted, often sick, and their effort collapsed. The survivors dragged themselves back along the mountain tracks leading into Burma. Hundreds of dead and dying lay in the mud at the sides of the trails. Disease and starvation and suicide now killed more than bullets and shells. "Naga tribesmen started bringing in Japanese prisoners too sick to move, filthy skeletons, raving, weeping and gibbering in their madness, the ultimate resistance of their minds broken by the unspeakable hardships to which their bodies had been subjected." That is Lieutenant Colonel L.H.O. Pugh writing in the history of our 7th Indian Division.[10] He was commander of the 25th Mountain Regiment, which accompanied one of the other brigades moving on Ukhrul.

Three Japanese divisions were destroyed as fighting units. Sixty thousand men were killed or wounded, or died from disease and starvation. For the Allied side the equivalent figure was seventeen thousand.[11] The 14th Army had some hope of replacing these losses; the Japanese had none.

This defeat inside India's easternmost state was the foundation for the decisive British victory a year later when the Japanese were driven from Burma.

During the whole of this time the battalion was involved in fighting north of Imphal in the Kanglatongbi area, and then in a grueling march eastward to assist in the recapture of Ukhrul.

It was no picnic for them either. The weather was atrocious. The tracks up and down the mountains were washed out, became mud slides. Early on in the Imphal fighting rations had been reduced by a third to ease the problems of air supply. All were suffering from some degree of malnutrition. Then there were days without rations because the planes could not locate the columns when monsoon clouds blanketed the mountains. Some were worn out, exhausted mentally and physically after close to ten months in action with so few breaks. Sickness rates were accelerating rapidly. "Many men and officers were internally too weak to digest or retain their food, and very many suffered from chronic diarrhoea, a legacy of the Arakan increased by the severe exertions of these operations. Rum was fortunately ample and for days on end officers and men whose religion permitted, lived on a diet of rum and hot milk, all they could manage."[12]

My own discomforts paled before these, and when I heard of what had been happening, I was thankful to have been allotted another itinerary.

Toward the end of July the MT and I were at last ordered to rejoin the battalion. To be on the move, motoring up the twisting, climbing road from Dimapur to the cool air of Kohima, was a joy. We found the men settling into a tented camp a few miles out of Kohima for what we all hoped would be a prolonged period of rest, recuperation, and retraining.

CHAPTER XI

At Kohima

The battalion was encamped outside Kohima on the spurs of a ridge. Around the camp blue-green hills stretched as far as and farther than our eyes could see, north toward Tibet and China, east toward Burma and the empire of the Japanese, south toward the Arakan and the Bay of Bengal. The crest of our ridge blocked a view westward. Kohima lay at five thousand feet. Some of the nearby peaks and ridges rose to eight thousand and ten thousand feet. The land here revealed nature at her most generous.

Jungle-covered slopes dropped two thousand feet from the tented clearings. A few Naga paths, invisible through much of their length, led to isolated patches of paddy. At the bottom of the valley wound a small stream, and here blue smoke drifted from a remote hamlet.

The entire 7th Indian Division was to stay in the Kohima area from July 22 until late December. In the ten months since the division had arrived in the Arakan, it had been almost continuously in action. The men were worn, exhausted, undernourished, plagued with minor sickness. They were in need of a rest. The battalion had lost 91 killed or died of wounds, 7 missing, 182 wounded.

Four of the dead and nine of the wounded were British officers. Since the total number of British officers present at one time was seldom more than twelve, the risks of being a tall, white Anglo-Saxon among short, dark Mongolians seemed clear. Proportionately many fewer Gurkha officers became casualties. I was marginally relieved to recall that several of the officer casualties were caused by shell fire or mines, neither of which are size or color conscious.

At Kohima the division would rest, refit, absorb reinforcements, retrain, and thus recover the fighting spirit essential for the task ahead—the retaking of Burma. In peace the little town of Kohima had been a district headquarters for a remote area of the Naga hills, mountains that formed this sector of India's eastern border. Few outsiders were familiar with the area. Among those who had once known it well were my predecessors in the 8th Gurkhas.

The 1st Battalion was raised in Sylhet, Assam, in 1824; the 2nd Battalion at Gauhati in 1835. This was in the days of the old British East India Company. Both battalions started life under different names, and in both cases it was some years before they were enrolling exclusively from Gurkhas. Both campaigned repeatedly in Assam and Manipur. The 2/8th had even been beseiged in Kohima for two weeks in 1879. Both took part in the Third Burmese War of 1885–1889.

As I have said, in and around Kohima there had been two months of the fiercest fighting, fighting critical to the future of our share of the war against Japanese expansion. For two months death had stalked these mountain peaks and valleys. We could see the evidence. Hillsides that had once been covered with forest were stripped bare by shell fire and were honeycombed with foxholes and bunkers. Parachutes still dangled from shattered trees. The smell of death had yet to disperse. Our camp was several miles from this charnel house.

The relentless rains of the monsoon were subsiding. The air in these Naga hills was invigoratingly clear and dry after the stifling humidity of the Brahmaputra valley. We wore sweaters morning and evening and slept under two blankets.

The EPIP tents set out by company areas, each on its own spur, looked across at the stupendous views and down hundreds of feet into the lush green valley. (EPIP stands for "English Pattern Indian Produced," so I am informed by Peter Myers. After the war he became a regular soldier, so he must be right.) These tents, perhaps thirty feet a side, had four-foot vertical walls before slanting to a peak. The walls could be rolled up during the heat of the day to allow the breezes through and dropped again for the cool of the evening. Chairs, tables, and beds had been slapped together using the handy bamboo. Light came from smoky kerosene lanterns or in a few cases from the more modern pressure lamps.

Our officers' mess sat on the edge of a spur. Two EPIP tents were joined, one for anteroom and bar, and one for the dining room. On the cliff side the tents were opened at midday for the view across the valley.

The track through our camp was a main route into Kohima for the local Nagas from their hilltop villages to the north, stockaded clusters of huts overrun with dogs, pigs, and chickens, and usually sited on a defensible ridge. Sometimes a panting, grunting file of men jogged through en route for the bazaar in Kohima, which seemed to have reasserted itself without much delay. Trading completed, the handsome men could be seen standing stalwartly aloof surveying the jeeps and trucks and troops milling about in their normally backwater town. In appearance and style they reminded me of Native Americans. Wrapped in a colorful blanket, each sported a jaunty lone feather jutting from a knot of black hair tied in a bun. Muscular legs protruded below the blanket.

These inhabitants of the Naga hills pose something of a racial mystery. Together with the other hill tribes of Assam and Manipur, they are unlike any peoples in surrounding India or Burma. They are Polynesian in features and coloring, and it is thought by some experts that they originally arrived by canoe on the Arakan peninsula and then made their way inland.

Until recent times the Nagas were animists who, for sport, warred on their neighbors, banqueting on the losers. Baptist missionaries were supposed to have dissuaded most of them from this diet, but we suspected that in the mayhem of war there had been relaxations. Why turn up a rich source of protein? It was rumored that there were huts in the more remote villages where heads were on display again, as in the old days. Fortunately for us, who had to train among these formidable people, the Nagas remained staunch supporters of the British and opponents of the Japanese. If once more there were Naga dogs worrying at human bones, there was no evidence that the bones belonged to friends.

Since 1947 the Nagas, with no fondness for India, have fought underground for independence.

One of our neighbors, the quartermaster of the KOSBs, was so taken with the charm of these tribesmen that when his turn for local leave came up he chose to spend the time visiting one of the Baptist-converted villages rather than take a week's carousing in India.

For the first weeks in Kohima the pace of training was easy, to allow the men to rebuild from their run-down condition. There was a large batch of reinforcements, officers and men, to integrate. And it became possible to send some men on overdue leave. This was a lengthy business, for they had to cross half of India and then walk for a week or more.

The rains tailed off and the air became dry, cool, clear, and breezy. With regular sleep, stress-free exercise, and extra rations, the men regained health and strength. One example: to build up weight, English-style rice pudding made with plenty of sugar and canned milk was dished out with the early morning tea.

As strength returned, discipline and the work schedule tightened. The easy days were over. Ahead, on some as yet unknown date, lay the march into Burma.

This toughening of life was accelerated by a change of command. Major Walter Walker, the career officer who had joined us in the Arakan in April, moved up from second in command to take over as colonel. The departing CO had not been well liked. We had found him supercilious, insincere, and selfish. We suspected that he was more eager to climb the military ladder than to do his best for us. Naturally he was being promoted. The men lining the track cheered as he jeeped off into the distance, and perhaps he thought that these cheers revealed affection, or at least respect. In reality the good humor was surely inspired by relief.

From this moment the pride, confidence, and spirit of the battalion soared. While Walker could be a cold, aloof, and unreasonable person, he was also an outstanding commander. The pace and caliber of the training immediately stepped up: all day and often by night we practiced weapons training, battle drills, digging, patrols, and section, platoon, and company exercises. Discipline became strict, fitness was compulsory. It was a time for absorbing the lessons learned from the battalion's first ten months in action, for practicing those lessons and teaching them to the new arrivals.

In camp there was PT first thing every morning. This often finished with a grueling two thousand–foot sliding descent into the valley and the exhausting slog back up to our tents. Without the advantage of a mountain upbringing, and competing with young men in their teens, I usually dragged in last—to the amusement of my fellow officers and a critical observation from the colonel.

I was instructed to turn over the MT platoon and to move in as second in command of a rifle company, A Company, under the charge of Frank Crouchman, who had been my instructor on the small arms cadre back in Quetta. There were four rifle companies in an infantry battalion. B Company was under Toby Willcox, who was succeeded by the ebullient Denis Sheil-Small before we left Kohima. Peter Myers commanded C Company. Geoffrey Bull, a recently joined regular from the 19th Lancers, commanded D.

Not every rifle company had a British officer as second in command. We did not have enough officers. My job was to learn as much as I could about the skills of running a company of about a hundred infantrymen so that in the case of sickness, wounds, or death I could replace any of the current four commanders.

Pat Davis, who had joined in July with Bill Blenkin and Mike Tidswell, looked after Intelligence. Mike became another company officer. Peter Wickham was adjutant, Tony Brand-Crombie was quartermaster. Bob Findlay and Jimmy Henderson arrived later as reinforcements. Bob had been with me up in Ziarat, but had proved a far more efficient instructor than I was likely to be, and so had been retained at Quetta by Willasey-Wilsey. He had been "rescued" by Walter Walker. This is not a total roll call of the British officers. It is the best I can do at this distance.

The firm hand of Walker's discipline did not spare the officers. To acquire the colonel's displeasure would often result in instant demotion. On the other hand, new responsibilities immediately brought the rank for the job. We learned to keep a supply of pips and crowns so that we could switch rank as fast as our orderlies could sew.

When we got command of a company, which carried the rank of major, the trick was to avoid the CO's wrath for six months. Under wartime regulations, holding the rank of major for six months insured that an officer could not under any circumstances (other than a court-martial) again sink below the rank of captain. All these regulations were for the duration of the war only. Many a colonel, even some brigadiers, returned to major or captain when back in the clutches of peace.

Higher rank meant higher pay, something like 1,400 rupees ($350 at that time) per month for a major. On active service there was no way to spend the money. It simply accumulated in a bank in India. I would carry around the same wad of notes for weeks at a time. And the money could be left anywhere without concern for theft. The Gurkhas were 100 percent honest. Nebilal, my new orderly, would count my money each day. If I had spent five rupees for cigarettes without his knowledge, he would be quite upset and want to be told what extravagance I had been indulging.

Nebilal was a member of the Rai tribe whose people lived mostly in eastern Nepal. He was short even for a Gurkha, with a rounder face than most. His face showed some of the scars of smallpox, a disease quite common at that time in the villages of Nepal. He had been selected by the company subadar as a reliable rifleman who would diligently tend the wants of the lieutenant sahib, accompany him everywhere, keep his equipment in order, bring him tea, protect him in battle, and most important, be strong enough to dig trenches for both.

When on the march it was Nebilal's job each evening to find for me a smooth piece of earth to sleep on. If rain or heavy dew was expected, and if no enemy was near, he would knock up a canopy of boughs. At Kohima in the morning, much the way the dresser checks out his actor before trusting him to go on stage, Nebilal would eye me up and down to make sure I was properly accoutered before I met the inspecting eye of the CO. I sure hope that in due time tough, grinning little Nebilal retired back to his village as a senior NCO and raised a family of happy Rais.

To return to Colonel Walker, he often worked late in his office tent. We could see the kerosene lamp glowing through the canvas. Sometimes he went through until dawn and reveille. This was a deliberate part of his own self-training. He told Peter Wickham, now adjutant, that in case the time might come when he would not be able to get any sleep, he needed to know that he could remain alert even when totally exhausted. We were permitted to sleep, but by day he demanded hard work from all of us, and got it. Very soon we knew that we had a most able leader and a well-organized and confident battalion.

Walter Walker was later to be recognized as an outstanding soldier. He became the general commanding the entire Southeast Asia forces during the 1964 confrontation with Indonesia over Borneo. Then in Europe he was to become the general commanding NATO's northern forces at a critical time in the Cold War confrontation with the U.S.S.R. He was knighted in 1968.

Our mess provided a comfortable refuge from training duties. Gradually the furniture improved. We acquired canvas chairs, built a bar, and installed Gurkha-made bamboo tables. Soldiers grow adept at making themselves comfortable.

Evenings in the mess were at times roisterous. When the whiskey ran low, issue rum was usually available. Bill Blenkin and Peter Wickham were given to reciting from a wide repertoire of racy stories, bawdy limericks, and lubricious songs. Blenkin was a lanky northerner from Durham with a skeptical eye toward the serious side of military life and an endless flow of off-color humorous anecdotes. My favorite story, however, was Peter Wickham's, and ended:

> *Oysters is amorous,*
> *Lobsters is lecherous,*
> *But shyrimps, Ker-ryst!!*

To maintain discipline and respect, Walker held himself aloof. His only chance to relax came with the occasional visit from one equal in rank—for example, his friend Derek Horsford, who had become CO of the 4/1st Gurkhas. The 4/1st were in a sister brigade of 7th Division and were encamped not too far away.

Quite often Walker would invite the subadar major, Chandru Thapa, for a drink and a chat, and perhaps a briefing on the attitudes and morale of the men. Chandru could ill disguise his scorn for us junior wartime officers, or so it seemed to us. He was one of the very few Gurkhas for whom I felt no personal warmth.

Although Chandru was the only overweight Gurkha I ever saw and was a bit slow on his feet, he was a deadly shot with a basketball. Toward the end of each afternoon, games would be under way with the rough-and-tumble style suited to the irregular pitches cut out of the hillsides. We would play platoon against platoon, NCOs against officers, and occasionally an invitation match against another battalion, often the 4/1st. An officers and a GOs team would visit and the games would be followed by drinks and dinner. We enjoyed the chance to get outside our own group and to talk to our counterparts in another battalion.

One day early on, General Messervy, our divisional commander, visited the battalion. He was sitting in our mess gazing across the valley when he noticed the speed with which some Nagas covered the distances up and down their winding tracks. He began to ruminate on the relatively slow pace of his troops on these same paths.

As a result of this rumination a three-page divisional order was delivered down to brigades and battalions for immediate observance. Henceforth companies, platoons, and sections would not walk from point to point but would employ the "Crimean Trot." This unique means of locomotion, apparently forgotten since the fall of Sevastopol in 1855, would "enable the average soldier, if properly schooled, to cover fifty miles a day easily compared with the twenty at the present time."

As outlined in the next paragraphs of General Messervy's order, the Crimean method of self-propulsion required that the soldier take alternately three running steps and two walking steps. The document went on to state that with practice the proper rhythm would be attained, a smooth even gait resulting in speed without fatigue.

Somewhere, sometime, an army may find the Crimean Trot a

benefit to the foot soldier. Practice we did, and as good, obedient soldiers we hid our skepticism. Section after section of Gurkhas counted "One, two, one, two, three; one, two, one, two, three" as they loped in a lilting, uneven fashion on every minor journey. Perhaps there was a small lance-naik in the rear calling out the cadence like a coxswain. Yes, heroic efforts were made to comply with the general's order. But in the rough terrain the men could not keep up the pace and rhythm for fifty yards, let alone fifty miles, without a breakdown. Soon we heard no more of the Crimean Trot.

I had found difficulty with this method for covering ground, as I did with the runs down to the valley bottom and back, but the slower-paced, day-long conditioning marches into the hills were often pleasurable, even exhilarating. A mug of tea before dawn, boots on, the clink of mules being loaded, then into the march before the sun broke up the morning mists; this made one feel very much alive.

Only once did I see Gurkhas drop out from a march. It was later, in central Burma. We were moving down a narrow track of soft sand lined with seven-foot reeds that created a stale, windless corridor. With a burning hot-weather noonday sun overhead and dead air on all sides, one by one a dozen men keeled over with heat exhaustion. We commandeered a passing oxcart to carry them and so reached the village that was the target for that day.

On several occasions when I was left in charge of the company for a day of marching through the hills, the Doc (Doc Dalton) abandoned his dispensary to his havildar and came with us. Like so many Englishmen, he walked for pleasure. But at times for lack of conditioning he had to struggle to keep up. He was, and is, of a cheerful disposition. I always enjoyed his company.

During the midday break the men would throw a tripod of stones together, light up a few twigs, and brew thick strong tea laced with sugar and tinned milk in their mess tins. The Doc and I would sit at the side of the path and share the cold chapatti and curry carried out in the same mess tins.

On occasion a party of Nagas grunted up the trail. They would stop and offer us swigs of *zoo* (rice beer) from the gourds slung around their necks. Our Gurkhas would offer them cigarettes. It was on one of these encounters that I was offered—and accepted, out of politeness—my first toasted grasshopper. It had a passable nutty flavor.

Returning to camp, one could look forward to the evening bath, readied by Nebilal. This was accomplished with a meager amount of water in a small canvas bucket. The water had been heated in a kerosene tin over a fire. There was a mug to pour water over the head for soaping, and two or three more mugsfull would be sloshed over the body to rinse. Refreshed, we could enjoy a drink in the mess and, if we were lucky, a dinner of the New Zealand lamb that had begun to arrive by air. Usually the main course was bully beef, pilchards (a species of herring thankfully unknown in America), or a tinned atrocity combining meat and vegetables known as M&V but tasting mainly of tin.

These monotonous meals were offered up by a staff of two. Asaram, an ancient bad-tempered Muslim, was the cook. The other was the mess waiter, a meek, easily intimidated Hindu Madrassi called Dhanu Khan. There was mutual dislike and constant quarreling between them.

The CO insisted on efficiency and cleanliness throughout the battalion. Occasionally he would order punishment for the mess staff for some infraction. More than once he would demand to know where his breakfast was, only to be reminded that the entire mess staff was at that moment performing pack drill. The wretched Dhanu and Asaram, loaded with ill-fitting equipment and full packs, were doubling back and forth on our tiny parade ground under stern commands from the police havildar. Perhaps this harsh punishment had its reward in that during the hard long marches ahead even the mess staff kept up.

Another pastime shared by myself and the Doc was listening to the news from the outside world. Every noon we borrowed one of the wireless sets from the signalers and set it up on the ridge near the mess, where it seemed to work best. With earphones clamped on we strained to pick up All India Radio's rebroadcast of the BBC news. Then we repaired to the mess to tell the others what we had heard.

The Doc was—and is, for he has changed very little over the years—a short, spare, perpetually good-humored person, looking behind his horned rims a little like Groucho Marx. He was not only cheerful and good-natured but fearless. He was with the battalion for the whole of the Burma experience, and on a number of occasions his RAP was under heavy fire. He had been wounded once in Imphal, and was wounded again toward the end of the war.

Soon after arriving at Kohima I was assigned to sit on my first court-martial. I had not judged my fellow man since serving on a federal jury back in Foley Square, New York.

A short way farther along our Kohima ridge was the camp of the KOSBs (King's Own Scottish Borderers). They had been a fine battalion, but had suffered heavy casualties along the way. Many were now in their third and fourth year away from Britain in a miserable climate, with no end to the war in sight. Perhaps their letters from Britain reminded them of the Yanks now on their island enjoying their tea, their pubs, and their girls. More important, their reinforcements were seldom men trained in their own depot, steeped in their own traditions. Replacements tended to be a ragtag bunch of men from units surplus to requirements, such as antiaircraft batteries. Also by mid-1944 the British battalions with the Indian Army were beginning to lose their remaining experienced men either on long overdue leave or through repatriation.

It seemed that a few of the British soldiers were fed up to the point of despair. While on local leave in Calcutta two of them had "gone over the hill" rather than return to more months of hide-and-seek in the jungle. In Calcutta the better hotels, restaurants, even the better brothels, were reserved for officers. Conspicuous among the dark masses, the two miscreants were soon picked up by one of the numerous MP patrols.

Spiritless and hangdog, they were marched before us to be tried. We were a lieutenant colonel in charge, rigid and ready to throw the book, a young British lieutenant from the Sikhs, and myself. Prosecuting and defending officers came from the accuseds' battalion.

Remembering the drawn-out trial back in Foley Square, which went on for days, my first impression was one of admiration for the speed with which witnesses were wheeled into the tent where we sat hearing the evidence. From the start the Sikh and myself, conscious of the miserable existence these men had endured, were for leniency; the colonel was for stiff jail sentences. In the end, despite his efforts to persuade us, we overruled his stern recommendations and gave the men light sentences, just enough to keep them out of the dangers of the next few months.

Life was not without its gentler entertainments. The hospital at Kohima had been reopened. It was revealed that Denis Sheil-Small already knew the matron and had warm feelings for Sally, one of the nurses. He was our Trojan horse. With the matron's permission we organized a dinner party and dance. A tarpaulin was spread on the ground of the mess anteroom and everything was spruced up as best we could.

Our guests could have been fetched from Kohima in one truck. That was unthinkable. We would use all five of the battalion's jeeps, and lots were drawn for the privilege of chauffeuring the ladies.

On the afternoon of the party the stones lining the path to the mess were freshly whitewashed, a powder room was constructed, and the famous frozen New Zealand lamb, specially hoarded, was being prepared. All was ready. At seven o'clock our crisply starched guests arrived piloted by the lottery winners. The rest of us were clustered in greeting outside the mess, attempting to seem cordial yet not overeager.

Many of the women one met overseas during the war took advantage of their minority position to become spoiled, overly demanding, and unduly vain. Moreover, for most of us juniors in the Indian Army the chances of amatory success were so remote and the logistics of carrying out a seduction so complicated that it was not surprising if some chose to visit such refined, if commercial, establishments as Madame Andre's in Bombay. Kohima was some fourteen hundred miles from Bombay, and our Kohima nurses were neither patronizing nor spoiled, but they were versed in a gentle defense of their virtue from rough soldiery. Also they were guarded by a benign dragon, the matron.

The evening started with polite though lyrical rhapsodizing on the beauties of the sunset behind the clouds over the next ridge.

Soon whiskey had thawed nerves, high- and low-pitched voices interweaved, the scratchy gramophone was wound up, and we were set for dancing on the bumpy floor. I recall Mike Tidswell playing his banjo to our singing. I guess that even through the whiskey, self-censorship operated. Probably we did not chant "Balls to Mr. Banglestein." As the cigarette haze thickened, all blended into a confused, formless evening.

When it was time for our guests to leave each of the officers with the right to drive had no doubt planned to elude the rest in order to enjoy at least a few minutes of solitude with feminine company. But it turned out that by then most had eliminated themselves by reason of too much booze. When the sun rose next morning a jeep was observed parked in the parade ground opposite the guardroom with one of our more conservative officers at the wheel sound asleep. What our Gurkhas thought of it all is not recorded. They were never slow to pursue a chance of carnal love.

It only remains to add that after the war Sally and Denis were married.

Toward the end of our time in Kohima another diversion was arranged, a gymkhana. The gymkhana is usually a sort of social field day on horseback. Apparently the word was invented in the mid-nineteenth century by the British in India. We substituted mules for horses. These hybrids resent having anyone on their backs, so most of the races ended in rodeo bucking, throwing, and general confusion, to the glee of the spectators. Other races were of the three-legged and potato sack variety. The Gurkhas took to these games, unknown in Nepal, with enthusiasm.

Our guest spectators sat along the rim edging our plateau, at their backs the drop into the valley, and behind that the green mountains shadowed as always by fast-moving clouds. It was a fine day and a magnificent setting. Guests included the nurses from the hospital and friends from the artillery and from many other units in the brigade.

Then in October there was the great Hindu festival of Dashera, which I had shared a year back in Quetta. We did our best to emulate the peacetime festivities. At least the men got a break.

Every officer is curious to know how he was regarded by his men. It was during this Dashera, while our Gurkhas were performing lampoons of the officers as part of the entertainment, the enjoyment heightened by lavish servings of rum, that I learned that my nickname was *Moto Sahib*. *Moto* translates as "big," or "fat." Since I weighed 165 pounds soaking wet at that time, the *moto* must have referred not to weight but to height. My six-foot-plus frame did tower over the short Gurkhas. By some I was known as "Uncle" in deference to my advanced age. Many of the other officers were nearer twenty.

During the weeks of relative stability at Kohima the eccentricities of some of my companions developed splendidly. One of the more singular new officers was a young lieutenant given to wearing a monocle, a baroque decoration perhaps not seen as affected by his fellow English, but not often sported back in my native Connecticut. He had been put in charge of the three-inch mortar platoon. But he got into the bad graces of the CO when sent to Calcutta to buy liquor for the mess. He was supposed to return within a day or two. After several days we had messages pleading a lack of transport, though other officers in the brigade returned without difficulty. When our monocled companion did reappear, he was unable to explain his movements satisfactorily. Although he was forbidden hard liquor in the mess as part of his penance, it was noticed that he managed to get quite high on the orange squash, which was being spiked by an understanding mess waiter. This officer was killed later on in Burma.

Another not destined to stay long with the battalion was a regular army officer who had attained the rank of lieutenant only after several years of service. This officer seemed competent except that he would fall into a deep sleep during the CO's conferences. This inattention was not appreciated. Soon he was back in a safe line of communication posting. It was believed that everyone slept on the LOC.

Sunshine Lanham, originally from South Africa, and our brigade liaison officer, was often in the mess. He was likable, efficient, and normal in all respects except that his passion for tomato ketchup became a fixation, a drug. He was unwilling to eat anything, so it seemed to us, without first bathing it in heavy dollops of the red sauce. Ketchup with cornflakes, toast, bully beef; ketchup poured over rice pudding. Now when I think back on the dreadful food, the sameness of it, I wonder if Sunshine did not have the answer.

Aside from the occasional breaks, all our days and many nights were filled with increasingly tough training organized to schedules worked out by the CO. Seldom now could we lie abed until well after sunrise enjoying that first mug of tea. We were out on schemes, standing to before the dawn, staring into the jungle and shivering in the bone-chilling mists. It seemed a long time since the night exercises in the juniper woods of Ziarat. Through the day we sweated up and down the hills, sited and dug foxholes and bunkers for defensive perimeters, and cleared fields of fire, camouflaging the spoil.

Platoons were sent to act as enemy, laying ambushes, circling through the night, crying out, firing flares, shooting blanks, now from this side, now from that, simulating attacks.

We practiced the dangerous art of busting bunkers as well as building them, of patrolling, of laying ambushes and escaping from them.

We studied on the ground some of the battles fought at Kohima, conducted by the men who had fought them. The 4/1st Gurkhas had been heavily engaged for weeks and had since quartered the battlefields, looking at them from the Japanese point of view as well as their own. It is rare that soldiers are able to appraise and rate their own actions from "the other side of the hill" while memories are sharp.

Once we drilled the men for hours on emplaning. Section by section they pretended to climb into a C-47 Dakota, the outline of which had been scratched into the dust. One wag with a good imagination feigned airsickness.

We read the manuals, which by now were thick on the table, packed with advice won from two years of campaigning in Burma and the Pacific. As I write I am browsing in *The Jungle Book*. "Do not carry mangoes, pawpaws or other fruit in the shirt next to the skin," I read in Appendix H, "Living on the Country." "The juice is often irritating and will cause inflammation of the skin."[1] Invaluable.

Ill health was still a serious problem: "In SEAC during the first six months of 1944 some 40,000 men had been killed or wounded or were missing, but wastage from sickness and disease had amounted to about 282,000."[2]

Malaria had been the worst scourge. However, the routine issue of mepacrine tablets began early in 1944. The evening mepacrine parade became mandatory. The little tablets turned us yellow but had a miraculous effect in almost eliminating casualties from malaria.

And throughout these months, so it seems in retrospect, we inspected and were inspected. We checked and rechecked each man's equipment and all the other multitude of items that make a battalion into an efficient fighting unit. We were always inspecting something, always preparing for inspections.

By this time I was no longer the new boy on the block. Those months of training at Kohima, of comradeship on the march, in the mess, and in our company lines, had put me in good health and confident of our commander, Walter Walker.

When Frank Crouchman, my company commander, was elsewhere, I was taking parades and inspections—and enjoying my newfound status. I had been Frank's company officer for some four months now. I think he had been (and he certainly looked the part) an NCO in a Guards regiment: he was a powerfully built, square-shouldered man with a full flowing mustache and an upright bearing. He was very familiar with military customs and regulations, which gave me the opportunity to observe how command was exercised and orders went back and forth from the company commander to the subadars, jemadars, and the company havildar major down to the men. My duties were seldom onerous.

Frank had a bluff heartiness that became more pronounced over drinks. On one occasion at the mess bar just after the arrival of a generous ration of beer, he punched me in the lower chest and said jovially, "How you doing, Scott?" I did not resent this, for I supposed it to be an amicable gesture; but the blow left me with a fractured rib that needed to be taped for a couple of weeks.

The final test of endurance and skill—but mainly endurance—was a three-day brigade exercise. The first night was very dark. We chased an imaginary enemy up and down mountain trails so steep and tortuous that many of the mules collapsed in slithering heaps, spilling ammunition and other supplies down the pitch-black hillside never to be found. There was some barely contained chaos. From the peaks the plan plunged us down Naga paths into densely jungled valleys, through rocky streams, and up the far sides to establish a position on a small promontory covered with elephant grass, sharp edged and taller than most of the men. In Burma, mercifully, the mules were never called upon to scale anything so dense and steep as the tracks on that exercise.

It was the colonel's job to allocate a position to each company. It was the company commander's job to place each of his platoons on the most advantageous piece of ground, carefully studying every knob and fold, anticipating how an enemy might attack. The platoon commanders then sited each section, each Bren gun, to command every likely approach with interlocking fire. Then came the digging of the slit trenches. Sharpened stakes of bamboo, or *panjis,* were fixed in the ground around our positions, preferably in grass or undergrowth. These were to impale a charging enemy. Beyond the *panjis* we strung barbed wire, often hung with tins to rattle if disturbed. While positions were preparing, patrols went out to pin down the location of the enemy.

All this was in rehearsal for what would soon be the real thing. About a third of the men had not been in action.

In mid-December the routine and the mood of the camp suddenly changed. Firm orders came for a move. Now the few remaining days were spent dividing and packing equipment. Tents, ammunition, blankets, stores, all the battalion's paraphernalia down to the bagpipes were sorted into three lots, for we had to remove five months' accumulation of fat, we had to strip for action. Nonessentials were to be stored for the next "rest." Most of the battle kit that remained would accompany the men in the first leg of the move, which was to be by lorry. A light third would follow with the mules, who were destined to walk the entire road toward our final destination.

The battalion had to be able to move quickly and at short notice with what could be carried on the back, on our mules, and in a handful of four-wheel-drive jeeps. If lucky, the carriers and trucks might accompany us part of the way.

We left Kohima on December 23. It was late afternoon. A line of Studebaker six-by-sixes fringed the track above the camp, enough for seven hundred men and their battle kit. Good-bye comfortable tents; we'd be sleeping in the open now. Good-bye beautiful hills, good-bye settled routine, good-bye nurses.

CHAPTER XII

———

March to the Irrawaddy

Christmas Day 1944. On the afternoon of Christmas Eve the lorries had dumped us in a teak forest near Tamu, a burned-out village just inside Burma. The international boundary was of no military significance: in 1944 both Burma and India were dependencies of Britain. But somehow it was of psychological consequence. Burma! An unknown country, a romantic land of pagodas, priests, and pretty girls. There was an absence of pretty girls in Tamu. Mandalay: just the sound of the name was pleasing to the ear. The Irrawaddy: one of the world's great rivers, winding down for hundreds of miles from the snow mountains on the Chinese border to its enormous delta in the Bay of Bengal. And Burma was our gateway to China, Indochina, and Siam, strange lands of threat and promise.

They told us that we would stay a few days at Tamu while Toby Willcox shepherded the mules to catch up and while the lorries went back for other battalions. So Christmas Day was spent clearing for and building bough and leaf *bashas,* not for shelter against your ordinary rain, but against the rain of enormous dewdrops that through the early hours of every morning crashed down from the teak leaves high above, and against the thick and penetrating morning mist. Sometimes it was midday before the sun sucked this mist up through the trees and away.

There was a clear stream close by and we managed a refreshing swim before celebrating Christmas night as best we could in a cobbled-up mess. There were no special rations but there was just enough alcohol to keep us from getting too wistful of past Christmases in other preferred locations. This was my fourth Christmas away from my own people.

At Tamu we learned something of our forthcoming role in the recapture of Burma. There had been a change of strategy. Unexpectedly, the Japanese seemed to be retreating behind the Irrawaddy, a hundred-plus miles away by whatever route. This was unexpected because until now the Japanese had never surrendered territory without a do-or-die fight. It was discovered later that after their Imphal-Kohima debacle, the Japanese commander in Burma (and most of the divisional commanders) had been sacked. It was a new man who decided, wisely, to fight with the Irrawaddy as a bastion to his front instead of in the open Shwebo plain with the river at his back.

General Bill Slim switched his plan. He would make a surprise crossing of the Irrawaddy near the ancient capital of Pagan, way south of Mandalay. He would trick the Japanese into thinking that Mandalay was still his main objective by sending in several separate and strong divisional groups to cross the Irrawaddy above and below the city. Meanwhile the southern crossing, *our* crossing, to be completed by February 15, would be the springboard for an eighty-mile race east across the open central plain of the country to capture the key communication and supply centers of Meiktila and Thazi. Here were airfields, railways, and good tar-surfaced roads.

The loss of Meiktila and Thazi would be fatal to the Japanese armies in central and northern Burma. To strike this blow, the 17th and 5th Indian divisions, which had also been resting and retraining, were to pass through our bridgehead. Both were now mechanized. They would be accompanied by the 255th Tank Brigade.

If the action went well, there would follow a scamper thrust south for Rangoon, down both the rail and road corridor via Pyinmana and Toungoo, and down the Irrawaddy valley via the Yenangyaung oil fields and Prome. The seaport of Rangoon had to be reached before May, when the monsoon would make land and air supply for so many formations an impossibility. This gave us four to five months. Enough? The distances were vast, the opposition still formidable, resources limited.

I cannot remember how much of this we were told at the time; sufficient to make our immediate future sound interesting.

In early January of the new year we left our camp in the teak forest to move south down the Kabaw valley rather than east to the Chindwin River, the Shwebo plain, and Mandalay. The 7th Division was to make the bridgehead across the Irrawaddy at Pagan. The move was secret: no wireless; a web of false signals from the area we vacated; other calculated indiscretions. It was hoped that no Japanese reconnaissance planes would overfly; their air force had been more or less shot out.

After the war it was learned that one sortie had filmed a trail of our lorries moving south, but in the absence of confirmation, the Japanese staff discounted this evidence. Lack of reliable intelligence plagued both sides and distinguished the Burma theater from the European.

First we traveled 125 miles by lorry and camped for a few days by the Manipur River. The trucks lurched slowly over a dirt track. Churned and rechurned red laterite dust billowed over us for hour after hour. When the mules had caught up, we marched the next 42 miles to Kan. This took three days. Beyond Kan the 28th East African and the Lushai brigades pushed farther down the valley to Gangaw, masking our approach.

The Lushais, with their British officers, were a colorful lot. They were hill tribesmen from the Assam side of the border with Burma, tall and lean, hair in a bun at the nape of the neck. I met one of their columns as it emerged from a streambed. The men were well dispersed and in good humor, splashing in and out of pools of water. Their heavy gear was carried on oxcarts that came lurching and creaking into view laden with machine guns, ammunition, and other impedimenta. Cooking pots and lanterns swung wildly from the sides of the carts. They looked most like a gang of brigands in a rollicking comic opera.

The Lushais were accustomed to long-range missions in remote areas. They had been at it for a year. They could talk to the related hill peoples on the Burmese side of the border. The peoples who occupied the mountainous rim of the Burmese polity, the Shans, Nagas, Kachins, Karens, and others, mostly supported the British in the war. At worst they were neutral. On the other hand, the Burmese, who occupied the rich central Irrawaddy valley and its offshoots, and who held economic power, were divided.

The Burmese had never taken kindly to their conquest by the British in Queen Victoria's reign. Their wish for independence was as great as, perhaps greater than, that of the Indians, though they did not yet have a Gandhi or a Nehru. Some were for the British. Some were political activists who saw the Japanese as liberators, believed their promises, and welcomed them. Most must have wished both sides to the devil and tried to keep out of trouble.

By 1945 the political activists were disillusioned. The Japanese were not winning the war and were not keeping their promises to set up an independent Burmese government. Being realists, they offered to change sides. Bill Slim was also a realist and accepted their offer. Late in March 1945 the Burma National Army, under Aung San, rose against the Japanese. They were reported to number some eight thousand.

But this is to anticipate. As we marched into Burma in January, what concerned us ordinary soldiers was that we never knew whom to trust, so we trusted no one.

When the 28th East African Brigade took over from the Lushais as advance guard, our divisional artillery that was supporting them experienced some interesting moments. "They proved to be fast movers: it could be said in almost any direction! Their standards of training and of discipline were wholly at variance with those of our own Indian Divisions, mixed as we were. They seemed to lack any idea of field-craft or jungle-craft and appeared to advertise their presence to the Japs by lighting fires, and making a noise when our own approach was one of stealth and silence."[1] That is Geoffrey Armstrong, colonel of the artillery regiment that was ordered to supply the guns.

At Kan we learned that our brigade was to do a sweep east and south through hill country, a hook of perhaps one hundred miles. This was an attempt to cut off at least some of the Japanese between Gangaw and the Irrawaddy. No one was sure how numerous these rearguard forces were. Communication was to be by wireless, strictly rationed. It was fortunate that we were given a section of divisional signalers to insure that our airdropped supplies found us; our signals officer, Tommy Login, struggled to make the short-range, temperamental battalion wireless sets and his homespun Gurkha operators combine to function passably.

A rear party and most of our remaining kit—groundsheets, mosquito nets, spare boots, and so on—were left in a divisional dump at Kan. On January 17 we set off with only what could be carried on our backs, on the mules, and in our few four-wheel-drive jeeps. Each man's pack was weighed down with extra grenades, an additional bandolier of fifty rounds, emergency rations, and a blanket. All were warned that should they fall out for any reason whatsoever, there would be no jeep to take them back. Three mules, larger and meaner than most, were identified as riding mules. A man unable to walk could be put aboard one of these ornery beasts. Or he could be left on his own.

The 4/8th Gurkhas was the lead battalion. We set off with some excitement. For large numbers of the men this was their first experience of moving into territory where live enemy might be met. Those of us who had been in action before had been fattened and relaxed over the five months at Kohima, despite the hard training.

This is how our Battalion News Chronicle No. 2 described the march. These letters were sent back to the center every few months to form a kind of brief, unofficial war diary for the rest of the regiment, though I wonder now who saw them apart from Willasey-Willsey. Generally the prose is plodding. One can see the writer cursing his luck that it is he who has to sweat through the evening under a hurricane lamp when he could have been catching desperately needed sleep. But just here the writer's thoughts become almost lyrical.

> Much has been written on the horrors of Burma warfare, of rains and leeches, of diseases and snakes, of unseen enemies and deadly ambushes. This time we experienced none of these things. The Burma hills in January are cool and fresh, and when in the sunset the hillsides turn to all the greens and browns of an English woodland in autumn, their beauty is unsurpassed. Between them lie the valleys of paddy stubble, and nearby nestle the villages of picturesque little stilt-raised dwellings, hedged in by high thorn, with entrances guarded by large double doors. If the population is large, one will find a *ponjeechaung*, or priest's house, a solid two-storey affair of wood, forming the cultural centre of village life.
>
> Who can convey on paper the charm of the little pagodas, standing in clusters large and small, guarded on their hill tops by the chinthes, and with their tinkling, silver-voiced wind bells that never stay silent? How clean the villages are, so unlike those of India, where the sanitary arrangements are nil and a circus of hawks wheels above. The livestock seemed in first-class condition, small sleek cattle and poultry that would rival the pride of English farmyards. It was indeed a delightful country to trek through in those January days.
>
> On the whole the villagers were reserved. Some luckier ones had never seen a Jap. Some had been forced to do coolie labour and most had been called on for food supplies. And so the greetings we received were mixed. Sometimes a village seemed empty and dead as we marched through, for the Burmans were hiding, suspicious. Others, who may have heard favourably of us, turned out en masse with fruit and smiles.[2]

Before dawn the cooks were busy working over fires screened by branches cut and interlaced to disperse the smoke and hide the flames. While still dark the lead company, which usually moved an hour ahead, was gulping down strong tea. Each company, each platoon and section, had been given its order of march the night before. We could be on our way within minutes.

Every hour during the day's march included a ten-minute rest. Lookouts were posted off each side of the trail. The men unslung their packs and lay on the ground with legs elevated to let the blood run from their feet. During this break the mules, too, were unloaded. This meant that the poor muleteer got little rest.

There would just be time for an army-issue Victory "V" cigarette. Unaware of the dangers of lung cancer, most of the men lit up and gasped in lungfuls of smoke. My own Camels, sent by my parents back in Connecticut, were much in demand, preferred over the milder English cigarettes. The worldly Peter Myers had tins of Turkish sent from his tobacconist in Calcutta.

In addition to our own seven hundred riflemen strung out along the track, we had with us a platoon of Indian engineers for bridge building and track improvement, and a battery of mountain artillery. The fierce-looking, mustached Punjabi artillerymen were equipped with shiny brass mountain guns. On the march each gun moved in pieces slung over the sides of big artillery mules. But wheels, breeches, barrels, and other parts could be, as they had been many times before on the North-West Frontier, set up and firing in minutes.

After a couple or three hours of marching we stopped for a full half hour, long enough for the men in twos and threes to light small fires and to brew up more tea in their mess tins. They would eat a cold snack of chapatti or whatever. When drinking Gurkha tea, one learned to sieve out most of the leaves through the teeth. There would be a few minutes to lie back and enjoy the rustle of the breeze in the swaying bamboo, or to stare into the heights of a lone giant teak tree. By now there was enough warmth from the dappled sunlight for the pullover to be handed to Nebilal for stowing until evening. This was the pleasantest part of the day. Invigorated by the clear atmosphere, one took in big gobs of morning air and felt exhilarated as we swung once more onto the trail.

By one-thirty or two in the afternoon, after a march of twelve to fifteen miles, we had reached our objective, picked out from the map the day before as having water and a flat space for a drop zone. The drop zone was surrounded and markers were put out for the pilots.

The first time the low-flying planes came floating in, I had not realized that the sacks of mule feed, rice, and other soft stores would plunge in free fall. I was in the drop zone and watched with surprise as the sacks were pushed out of the Dakota's doors and hurtled down three hundred feet to *whumph* into the ground around me. The plane would be traveling at, say, 75 miles per hour, as slow as it could go without stalling. In three hundred feet or more of free fall a sack would accelerate fast, perhaps to 150 miles per hour. The last entry in the record of my earthly span might well have read "Flattened by a bag of mule feed."

We came to love the sight of those overworked Dakotas laboring in across the hills. In the fine weather of a Burmese winter they always found us. They were a military version of the DC-3 airliner with a strengthened floor and a large cargo door cut into the port side. They could carry 9,028 pounds of goods or up to twenty-four bodies. It is said that more than ten thousand were produced during the war. Many were still in use around the world decades later. A few are flying even now.

Each day was much the same: marching at dawn, arriving by early afternoon, laying out the drop area, laying out positions and digging in against possible attack. Though a surprise attack was unlikely, the misfortunes of earlier campaigns dictated that now we always laid out and dug our one-night foxholes and trenches, camouflaged and with interlocking fields of fire. The sweat had hardly dried from a rifleman's back before he began digging. March, dig, eat, and sleep. A simple life, perhaps.

My personal amenities were the responsibility of my orderly, Nebilal. He was always able to usher me proudly toward my en suite washroom, a space set aside and perhaps screened by a few cut branches where he laid out the soap, enamel cup, and a modest amount of water. If the nearby stream was deep enough, we enjoyed a swim.

Freshened up, we gathered for the CO's conference. The latest information and the next day's plan were given out. We in turn would return to company areas to give out orders to platoon commanders, orders for patrolling, the night's sentries, stand-to time in the morning, the next day's march and objective, and passwords.

As second in command of A Company, it became one of my duties to inspect the feet of the men at the end of each day's march. Despite some heavy blistering that might have qualified a good number for a mule ride, not a man fell out during the entire march. In battalion headquarters our older cooks and sweepers, though they might lag behind carrying their boots to ease their blisters, all managed to make the distance.

The colonel decreed that officers would eat together. By early evening we could relax quietly over a whiskey; and perched on rocks, on fallen tree trunks, or reclining on the ground, we enjoyed a surprisingly civilized meal.

Near our slit trench, Nebilal would have spread my blanket on a piece of reasonably flat and soft ground, with a hole scooped out for the hip. Frank Crouchman's orderly would have done the same close by. After only a few minutes to admire the stars through the leaf canopy, I slept the sleep of those conditioned by much physical effort. Fatigue also kept me from too much concern about the sudden ambush that might await us down the track ahead.

No matter how difficult the circumstances or how remote from civilization, the colonel believed in keeping up appearances. To insure a decent turnout, his mule carried starch and an iron. His mustache well trimmed, Walter Walker strode through the jungle and the dust in freshly pressed green battle dress, cap at a jaunty angle. His studied nonchalance was, for sure, part of an act of savoir faire, right down to the imperious wave of his cigarette holder to point out an objective or suggest an emplacement. It was an act that said to the men "Look how calm I am. Nothing to worry about!"

The American officer taught to rough it with his soldiers might consider such style supercilious or at least selfish. To the contrary, Walker's panache was highly admired. Our Gurkhas expected their commander to behave like a commander. Had Colonel Walker's performance been all theater and no substance, they would soon have caught on. But he was first-class at his job, demanding yet efficient, cool and precise. He never showed fear or worry. He was able both to intimate genuine interest in the welfare of the men and to remain sufficiently aloof to keep respect. With his junior officers he seldom unbent.

The American officer would certainly have carried his own pack. Most British officers in other units did so. We were ordered to put our packs on one of the mules. At the end of a march this gave each of us a bit more energy to think, a bit more strength to climb about the hillsides reconnoitering and siting company positions.

Thus we moved deeper into Burma. Crossing the Pondaung range of hills, rocky and steep, we had a struggle with the mules and were forced to send back the jeeps. On the far side, dropping down into the considerable valley of the Yaw Chaung, trees thinned, the country opened up. We had reached the fringe of the dry zone of central Burma, emerging at last from what had seemed like a life sentence in the jungle.

Now leading platoons advanced in wide formation, scouts well ahead, men far to either flank sweeping the countryside. Even the most dim soldier could see that this new land would be a release for our tanks, and for the artillery and the fighters and bombers. We might be able to see our enemy.

We had with us a Burmese Intelligence Corps naik who was able to question at least some of the villagers encountered. Pat Davis and his intelligence section were always busy. The story we heard was the same: the last Japanese seen had left the area one day, two days, a week earlier. It seemed that they really were fading back to the Irrawaddy.

On January 24, the seventh day of our hook, and two days ahead of schedule, we reached and blocked the main track from Gangaw and Tillin to Pakokku on the river. Ambushes failed to catch a soul. We moved on to Sinthe, a village on the lower reaches of the Yaw Chaung. Here for a week we patrolled far and wide. No enemy. We helped to level and defend a new airfield, created out of flat paddy, dry at this season. This airfield was a major construction. It had to be fit to service three divisions. Meanwhile other units closed up on the Irrawaddy and Pakokku.

It was near the half-constructed airfield at Sinthe that I met our army commander, General Slim, for the second time. I had first seen him at Kohima when he talked to a gathering of the officers of the division. His bulldog face and his no-nonsense delivery had been impressive. In some mysterious way he communicated trust: he trusted us and we trusted him. This was a rare achievement. British and American soldiers tended to view their generals with considerable skepticism.

At Sinthe we of the 4/8th Gurkhas alone were the target of Bill Slim's visit. He arrived accompanied by the corps commander (Frank Messervy, formerly our divisional commander), our newish divisional commander (Geof Evans), and Brigadier Crowther, a towering giant of a man who was said to collect stamps, indulging his hobby by hurricane lamp at night even in the remotest parts of distant Burma. Perhaps this story is apocryphal. This time we and the Gurkha officers got to shake hands with Slim. I remember most how he chatted amiably with the GOs in fluent Gurkhali. After World War I, in which he had been severely wounded at Gallipoli and wounded again in Mesopotamia in 1917, he transferred to the Indian Army and served for many years with the 6th Gurkhas.

On February 10 and 11 we marched the twenty-six miles from Sinthe to Myitche on the Irrawaddy. For most of us it was a night march to escape detection. On this march we finally left the forested hills and moved onto the open, undulating plains. Even so early in the year it was hot through the day.

Upstream from Myitche was the town and small port of Pakokku, where the 114th Brigade was fighting a Japanese rear guard that had at last been ordered to resist. We could hear our guns firing in support, the first guns I had heard since a year back in the Arakan. Myitche was a conveniently well-treed large village in which troops could lie concealed close to the selected crossing place. It had been decided to breach the Irrawaddy here and to land on the other bank near Nyaungu, a few miles from Pagan.

We had covered 450 miles since leaving Kohima, over half on foot. We had not met a single Jap. From the north bank—for the river just here flowed east to west—we could look over the water and its dividing sandbanks at one of the world's great sights. Here is our News Chronicle again:

> . . . On the opposite shore in the bend of the river lies
> the old capital and religious centre of Burma, the city

of Pagan, often called the Pagoda City. It seems that
no house could squeeze between the serried ranks of
pagodas, which for lack of space have filled the country for miles around. Little pagodas, big ones, square
ones, round ones, pagodas of mellow brick, huge
white and gold masses, a fairyland of towers and pin-
nacles, dancing in the magic of the warm evening
sun.[3]

The Irrawaddy was wide, sliding silently past, blue and silver in
the sun. It is one of the great rivers of the world. The first Englishman, probably the first Westerner, to sail and row the river from
Rangoon up to Amarpoora, near Mandalay, was Captain Michael
Symes of His Britannic Majesty's 7th Regiment, in 1795. He and his
small staff and escort were on a diplomatic mission to King Bodaw-
paya. They covered the six hundred miles between May 30 and July
17. At that season the river is high but the southwest monsoon blows
a sailing vessel upstream faster than the current carries it down.

The Irrawaddy is born in the northern mountains where the
frontiers of China, India, and Burma meet. From the same water-
shed come the Yangtse, the Mekong, and the Salween, three other
great rivers. After some 1,300 miles of flowing south, the Irrawaddy enters the Andaman Sea through a massive delta, a delta
that is said to be galloping seaward at three miles per century.

The river dominates the country. It has always been the main
artery for the passage of commerce and armies. Our invasion over
the mountains from India was against the grain of the land and
against historical precedent. We paid for this in sweat and tears as
well as blood.

Of course, there were no boats on the river. In 1941, prior to
the Japanese invasion, the Irrawaddy Flotilla Company's fleet of
650 units—powered vessels, flats, and barges—was probably the
greatest inland water transport enterprise under one commercial
operator ever seen (no single company monopolizes traffic on the
Mississippi). The Irrawaddy Flotilla Company had been founded in
1865, and one of the founding directors was T. D. Findlay, a great-
grandfather of the Bob Findlay in our battalion. From beginning to
end Scotsmen took a leading part in the company's affairs.

Come you back to Mandalay,
Where the old Flotilla lay:
Can't you 'ear their paddles chunkin'
From Rangoon to Mandalay?

As so often, Kipling evokes a mood with few words.

During the 1942 retreat to India the flotilla gave invaluable service, transporting ammunition, arms, food, and other essential supplies upcountry from Rangoon. The paddles were "chunkin' " day and night in a last heroic burst of effort, and the army did not starve or run out of bullets. At the end those vessels not already sunk by the Japanese bombers were scuttled. All the handsome, comfortable paddle streamers with their teak decks and cabins, their brass fittings, their bright paintwork, all the flats and barges that had carried the trade of Burma, all had been sunk, soon to be silted up and irrecoverable.

Few Burmese country boats had survived the subsequent years of Japanese requisitioning and Allied bombing. We had to provide our own boats.

For us, and for our seniors plotting ways and means to cross this formidable obstacle, it was water levels, currents, and sandbanks on the river that mattered. The melting snows in the north do not send the water rising in central Burma until sometime in April, the driest season. The monsoon does not add its weight of water till mid-May in lower Burma, and not until June in the north.

So in February the river was low, about forty feet below its full flood level. Sandbanks were everywhere, some visible, many below the surface. These sandbanks shifted from year to year, even from day to day. In peacetime their movements had been mapped by patrolling buoying launches. Elaborate precautions were taken to keep pilots and captains primed with up-to-the-minute information. For night sailings the ships had powerful searchlights that could pick out the river's banks for miles ahead, and whose light was reflected from the tin disks attached to the buoys marking the sandbanks.

Now there were none of these. Our engineers had to discover for themselves a crossing that was safe and reasonably short. The longer the crossing, the slower the turnaround.

Despite the low level of the river, the water was moving at speed. At the time of the crossing there was a three-knot current at Nyaungu and the surface was choppy.

A slanting passage was picked between two vast sandbanks. On the outward journey, heavily laden, boats would go with the current. We must take off from a low, sandy shoreline on the north bank and land among the coves and cliffs of the south shore about a mile upstream from Nyaungu. In a straight line the route was a mile long, and was later described as the most extended opposed river crossing of the war.

Was there a lethal enemy sitting quietly on that far bank? It was thought not. Not yet. But information was a bit thin. Overflying by aircraft, and patrols across the river, had been restricted. It must not appear to the Japanese that we were interested in this area. On the contrary, as was already mentioned, quite elaborate deceptions had been devised at army, corps, and divisional levels to persuade the Japanese that we were fixed on other targets.

Two crossings in divisional strength had now taken place upstream north and south of Mandalay. These were attracting most of the strategic reinforcements the Japanese could muster. Ten days after our crossing there would be a fourth breaching of the river wall at Myittha, still closer to Mandalay, which was planned to convince the enemy commanders that the former capital was the main objective.

Locally our 114th Brigade was assaulting Pakokku, twenty miles upstream. Twenty-five miles downstream the East Africans had reached Seikpyu, opposite Chauk, and had attracted such fierce counteraction that they had been driven back. Around the corner, the 1/11th Sikhs of our brigade were infiltrating into mythical Pagan, using local boats.

At Nyaungu, in the center of things, we relied on surprise to give us a clear field for a few hours. The Japanese could not defend every mile of the shoreline, and it would take time for them to react in strength.

CHAPTER XIII

Across the Great River

February 14, 1945, dawn. It was the sudden gunfire, close and startling, that destroyed illusions. The guns were ours. But the firing spelled opposition. It meant that we had not slipped across unnoticed and would not build up the bridgehead undisturbed.

The lead battalion was from the 2nd South Lancashire Regiment of 114th Brigade. It had been selected because of its experience in the seaborne landing against the Vichy French on the island of Madagascar. That had been back in 1942. How many of the same men served now?

The plan this time was to send an advance company across the river under cover of the dark early hours. These men, rowing silently, were to land and occupy a headland overlooking the most easterly of the four small coves chosen for the bridgehead. This was done.

Then the plan went wrong. Cranky outboard engines and leaking boats delayed and muddled the main embarkation. Due to the

191

need for secrecy, and the last-minute arrival of the boats down the long twisting road from India, no rehearsals with them had been possible. Dawn came too soon, to reveal the South Lancs scattered over the river in disorder, some boats circling to regain their correct places, others with engines silent and drifting rapidly downstream.

This handsome target came under rifle and machine gun fire at close range. The Japanese were attending the operation. Casualties mounted. Two company commanders were killed. Boats began to sink. More engines failed. Bullets splashing on every side, men floundered in the water, struggling to off-load heavy equipment, to swim back to the home shore. Those who made it found themselves a mile or more below the embarkation point. Some were rescued from sandbanks.

Despite the impressions given in the histories, which suggest that all the boats returned or were sunk, some did land their cargoes on one of the more easterly beaches. Among those who landed in the dawn light as planned were Peter Myers and Toby Willcox. Toby had shipped as observer and liaison contact for our 89th Brigade, and Peter was with a small unit of signalers detailed to act as beachmaster on the far side. So now there was an infantry company plus some miscellaneous troops sharing the barren cliffs with an unknown number of Japanese. For a couple of hours the former must have had a nervous time.

The South Lancs were out of the war for a while. Beneath a deluge of covering fire, the 4/15th Punjabis set off and slowly chugged their diagonal way across the water. This time there was a liberating anticlimax. Not a shot was fired. We learned that the initial opposition was from a visiting Japanese patrol. Under the bombardment it withdrew into some caves—and was trapped in them forever when engineers blew in the entrances.

February 14, 1945, afternoon. Indian engineers standing knee-deep in the swirling water struggled to hold the boats alongside a sandbar as the men climbed aboard. The organized confusion was enlivened by the nearby mules, who were putting up vigorous resistance to the idea of mounting pontoon rafts reminiscent of the one

Huck Finn used on the Mississippi. At last each boat was loaded with two rows of crouching Gurkhas. We were released into the current.

The men were probably glad to be still. Many of them had spent the night sweating back and forth through six hundred yards of soft sand to the river's edge with loads of ammunition, petrol, food, and worst of all, with the awkward collapsible boats in which we were now embarked.

Caught by the current, the boats were swept downstream until the engines gradually nosed them around and propelled them crossways. So we found ourselves on the Irrawaddy, with two thousand yards of gray-blue water ahead and a clear blue afternoon sky above.

Considering that few of the men could swim, they seemed remarkably unconcerned. There was a small plane buzzing overhead, either carrying spotters for the artillery or observers from headquarters. Slowly the laden boats crawled across the rippling water. Empty boats returning made what speed they could against the current, a haze of exhaust smoke tracking their progress. The cliffs of the far shore loomed higher and the white pagoda spires gleamed brighter. A spiral of smoke rose from behind the cliffs where shelling that morning had set buildings on fire, a reminder that this was not a picnic jaunt, not a training exercise, that beneath our keels the dead were settling into the sand.

Despite the dawn mayhem, the Japanese had been successfully deceived. They had concluded, as they were meant to, that our southern threats were diversions from the Mandalay battles, that we were not present in strength. Our landing was opposed only by a chance patrol and by an ineffective force of some 160 INA (Indian National Army) whom the 1/11th Sikhs found in occupation of the pagodas of Pagan. The INA had promptly surrendered.

It is worth diverting to explain the INA, for during our advance into Burma in 1945 they surfaced at frequent intervals, and they were the object of much discussion. The Indian National Army was formed from the troops captured by the Japanese in Malaya, Singapore, and Burma during 1941 and 1942. Their commander in chief was the radical Indian politician Subhas Chandra Bose. Some members of the INA were moved by a genuine wish to overthrow British rule in India, though this meant breaking their oath of allegiance to the King Emperor. Others, under physical pressures, saw the INA as a preferable alternative to the miseries of a Jap prison camp, indeed as their only chance of returning to their homes and relatives. Very few Gurkhas joined.

The Japanese commanders appear never to have set much faith in these turncoat soldiers, and in practice the majority surrendered as the opportunity arose. Some units in the 1st Division fought bravely during the Imphal battles of 1944, but they were so badly mauled, and subsequently so weakened by disease and hunger, that the division virtually disintegrated.

Subhas Chandra Bose died in an air crash as the war was ending and has become a hero to many Indians. He was surely a man of stature who believed passionately in the fight for his country's freedom.

The greatest impact of the INA was made after the war. As they surrendered they had been sent back to India, where they were interrogated and sorted. There were about twelve thousand of them. The "white" minority were to be reinstated in the army. The "gray," the majority, men who had surrendered to the Allies at the first opportunity but who were legally guilty of desertion, were to be dismissed from the service and released. Only the "black," the leaders and those accused of atrocities, were to be tried.

Soon after the war ended it was announced that initially three officers would be put on trial in the Red Fort in Delhi. These trials raised a frenzy of protest and public sympathy through India. There was massive rioting. Leading Congress politicians fronted the challenge. Jawaharlal Nehru, the future first prime minister, was one of several distinguished lawyers who worked for the defense. Despite the danger of undermining the morale of the loyal Indian Army, the same army on which an independent India must rely, the discharged INA were greeted as heroes, their negligible military achievements magnified into triumphs of skill and courage, the ignoble surrender of most forgotten. Emotions had overruled common sense.

Only those first three men were ever brought to trial. They were found guilty of waging war against the king and of complicity in acts of murder and brutality. They were sentenced to death, but the commander in chief, Field Marshal Auchinleck, commuted the sentences to imprisonment. Gradually the rioting subsided.

Ironically, when India gained independence on August 15, 1947, only two years after the Japanese surrender, the soldiers who had fought on behalf of King George VI transferred their loyalty without too much fuss to India and Pakistan, but few of the INA men were reemployed.

So on the afternoon of February 14, we chugged slowly over the pretty water and I fear gave little thought to the dead. It was good to be crossing the fabled river. What had happened had happened and could not be altered.

That first night was spent within the beachhead perimeter. Next morning we moved southwest through Nyaungu to the village of Wetkyin on the riverbank. Our fierce warriors were bristling with weapons, and for the benefit of some army cameramen who were following at this point they tossed phosphorous grenades into any trench that looked the least suspicious. But they found no enemy. I think this was our only contact with the press that year.

Next day we moved three miles inland into the undulating semidesert country south of Nyaungu. Prominent on our left was an abrupt ridge more than ten miles long, rising in places to fourteen hundred feet, and running near enough north and south. It overlooked every move we made. From across the river we had viewed it with distaste. The closer we got, the more it menaced.

On the most northern peak of this ridge, five hundred feet above us, were a pagoda and a small monastery. I was dispatched to this pagoda with a platoon of A Company. Our orders were to deny the heights to any opposition and to observe the scene, both westward toward the river six miles off and eastward to Meiktila, sixty miles across the broken plains and the ultimate objective of all this hassle.

We set off early in the morning, spread out in a loose phalanx, sometimes tramping over sand, sometimes over stony ground.

With each of the three sections of eight to ten men there was a light machine gun, the redoubtable Bren gun. The section commander carried a tommy gun or the gimcrack sten gun (which was apt to shoot itself off at any incautious jar to the butt). The rest were armed with the reliable short Lee-Enfield rifle, a precision weapon. We all carried kukris, bayonets, and grenades. Platoon HQ included a two-inch mortar crew. And each man carried a blanket, a groundsheet, and a day's rations in his pack. More rations would come up later by mule.

As we climbed the ridge the going got rockier. The few scrub trees and low bushes gave no protection from the sun, now high and blazing hot, and little protection from view. We found a narrow trail leading to the monastery, and the scouts moved up this cautiously, live bait as always. We were in luck. The summit greeted us with nothing more lethal than gusts of cooling wind coming over the crest from the east.

The two saffron-robed monks must have been as nervous as we but did not show it. They greeted us affably enough and kept to their quarters in the enclosed far end of the wooden structure. We enjoyed the shade and breeze of the open veranda. We dug our trenches under the veranda and in the scrub jungle on the slopes below. One could see for miles, and there was often plenty to watch.

One morning we saw the long lines of a 17th Indian Division motorized column, trucks and armor, raise clouds of dust as it set off on its historic advance to Meiktila. Not only could I see the column in its early start, but later I overheard on our wireless the tank commanders talking to each other and to the infantry and gunners when they got held up at Oyin, some fourteen miles out. Single Jap suicide soldiers were concealed in holes dug into the main track, each waiting to explode a bomb when a tank passed over him. We could hear frantic tank commanders in the heat of battle warning of these maniacs/heroes.

From this front-row observation post we also watched through binoculars an attack made by the KOSBs on February 24 against Japanese entrenched in a small village on the plain between our ridge and the Irrawaddy. It was like looking down on a movie production as hundreds of men spread out and advanced through the open country. Puffs could be seen coming from under the cactus hedges dividing the fields in front of the village. Here the Japanese had hidden the first of their bunkers and foxholes.

The KOSBs were taking casualties. The tanks in support (116th Regiment, RAC, the Gordon Highlanders) seemed to have difficulty spotting their targets. Several times as the infantry was held up we could see officers approach the rear of a tank to use the telephone mounted there. Anyone standing at the rear of a tank holding the telephone made a conspicuous target. Four were killed and five wounded that day. The lead company lost all its officers. In return some 130 dead Japanese were counted. When later we were to do attacks with the same Highlander tanks, we profited by the lesson and kept clear of their telephones. We indicated targets either by tracer bullets, Verey pistol, or by radio.

The battalion's first set-to with the Japanese in the 1945 campaign came on the night of February 25–26. Bob Findlay took a fighting patrol to a village called Kinka, on the Irrawaddy bank. He called in by telephone to say that they had located an enemy position in the village and were about to attack. Communication then ceased. On their triumphant return at dawn we learned that they had killed eleven enemy. Bob and several of his men sustained minor grenade wounds, which, in the elation of their success, they hardly noticed. Nevertheless Bob was evacuated to India.

I came down from my monastic retreat that same morning, in time to enjoy some of the enthusiasm for Bob's experience. The battalion was moving across to the Irrawaddy and a mile or two forward. I found that Mike Tidswell was now in command of A Company. Mike was a very different character from Frank Crouchman. In his early twenties, he was handsome, quiet, amusing, softspoken, calm, a most congenial companion.

Our brigade was still holding the right flank of the bridgehead and was not permitted to advance too far. We occupied Kinka and patrolled forward to establish that the Japanese were now dug in six miles south at the northern edge of the village of Milaungbya (Map 4, p. xxii), protecting the oil field town of Chauk. It is not sound tactics to allow an enemy to develop his affairs in peace. An attack was arranged. On March 2 the suave, ever-cool Peter Myers and C Company made the attack.

The objective was an outpost code-named Bastion, a tree-covered rise several hundred yards short of the main village and overlooking the Mu Chaung to the south and the Yaw Chaung to the north. Cliffs dropping to the Irrawaddy flood plain protected the west. Both chaungs were dry. Peter was supported by medium machine guns of the Frontier Force Rifles and a battery of 136th Field Regiment's twenty-five-pounders.

In bright sunlight those watching from the comparative safety of the CO's command post had a clear view of C Company's right-hand platoon about six hundred yards away as it advanced with fixed bayonets through thin scrub and infrequent palm trees. They were moving from left to right above the far bank of the Yaw Chaung. The Japs were in the tree-covered rise. When the Frontier Force guns stopped firing, the onlookers could hear distant shouts and shots, the sharp grenade explosions.

Although I could not see the action, I could follow Peter's steady reports on my company wireless. His observations and cool commands as he advanced into enemy fire were electrifying to the rest of us. His account went something like this: "Enemy LMG straight ahead, I have a section flanking him. . . . We've knocked out the LMG . . . a few grenades coming at us from the left, am putting our mortars onto some bushes. . . . Now we're crossing the road. . . ." All this was said as matter-of-factly as if he had been broadcasting a cricket game.

Eleven enemy dead were counted. C Company had a few wounded. A minor battle, but another lift to the battalion's morale. The company remained in occupation of Bastion, which became a key prop in the operations around Milaungbya throughout March. We were not permitted to advance south, but our presence invited the enemy to attack; and we in turn, as will be seen, carried out a series of strong raids.

Two days after C Company's attack, B Company and Denis Sheil-Small were ordered to occupy some high ground astride the Mu Chaung, to the east of Bastion. It was open, barren, stony ground, but it overlooked both the Japanese in Milaungbya and C

Company in Bastion. Apparently this worried our opponents, for they attacked even before Denis had finished his recce and before a spadeful of defensive earth had been dug. A tense, knockdown, catch-as-catch-can scrap seesawed back and forth for several hours. Early on, Denis's wireless set had been destroyed by a mortar burst. He sent a runner back asking for help.

My company was called up. By the time we came on the scene, the Japs had retired, but Denis was delighted to see us as he knew now that he did not have enough men to form a sound all-around defense, particularly at night. Moreover, we brought with us machine gunners from the Frontier Force Rifles, an OP party from the gunners of 136th Field Regiment, wire, and a telephone link. With two companies and all that firepower, there were few problems with repelling the next attack, which came in that night.

Both Denis and Jemadar Jitbahadur Ale were awarded the MC (the Military Cross) for this fight. Among other commendable deeds, Denis had rescued a wounded man under close fire.

The new position was code-named Fort. Because of its strategic elevation, it became the key to holding the defenses around Milaungbya, and was the focus of the Japanese attempts to drive us off.

Night after night the Japs would crawl to our trenches with small but daring patrols, trying with grenade launchers, LMGs, and hand grenades to find weak spots in our position. Occasionally as few as four or five, or as many as a platoon, would make a suicidal charge, leaving no doubt as to their bravery.

Our Colonel Walker, too, was not one to sit still and wait. It would have been preferable to roll up in one's blanket and sleep under the brilliant stars, but Walker ordered patrols out every night. And over the next few weeks we made a number of punishing attacks designed to keep the Japanese off balance, kill as many as possible, and return with prisoners and captured weapons. We were scrapping over rolling, scrubby, sandy terrain, often quite bare except where the villages were sheltered by dense groves of toddy palms. At this season the Irrawaddy plain was dry (except for the main channels of the river and some wells) and close to desert. It was getting hotter by the day. In Fort temperatures of more than

100 degrees Fahrenheit in the shade became routine, and shade was scarce. The rains were not expected until May. When they came they would cool the air but mess up all the tracks.

Battalion HQ was set up some one thousand yards to the north of Bastion and Fort around a toppling old brick pagoda and above the riverside cliffs. The mess took over the *hypoongyi chaung,* the living quarters for the monks (who were not present), beside the pagoda. Trees gave the pagoda area some shade and made it a minor oasis of comfort for the HQ people and the reserve company.

Our mess cook, Asaram, lodged his pots and pans in the courtyard of the pagoda. There was no danger of rain. He frequently aroused the colonel's wrath for not producing more interesting food, though this was hardly within his capabilities considering the limited rations. No doubt to compensate for this censure from on high, Asaram continued his running feud with the timorous Dhannu, our mess waiter. Hostilities erupted suddenly one day when four or five of us were eating lunch. Our serenity was disturbed by the shouting outside. Investigating, we found Asaram, an upraised ax in his bony hand, pursuing the terrified mess waiter, shirttails flying, around and around the pagoda. The circle was broken by the whistle of incoming shells. Kitchen staff and officers, rudely reminded of the real enemy, scrambled for slit trenches, from where they could hear Asaram's shouts of wrath gradually subside. In a later bout of shelling Asaram was wounded in the rump and was absent for a month.

During the morning and again in the evening the 75-millimeter and 105-millimeter guns of the Japanese would lob from fifty to a hundred shells on our positions, usually on Fort. A good number fell harmlessly in the open or in the middle of the sandy Mu Chaung, which divided the position.

These dry riverbeds, some small and narrow, some wide, cut back at right angles from the Irrawaddy every few hundred yards. They made excellent defensive positions. At Fort, dug into the bank nearest the enemy, our company headquarters, aid post, and kitchens were virtually proof against artillery fire. Unfortunately, shelter from fire was also shelter from breeze. It was always broiling hot in Fort during the day. Down in the sandy bed of the chaung it was hotter.

The afternoon temperatures made even the Jap gunners somnolent. It was toward dusk that the shelling increased, as if to disturb whatever small pleasures we could obtain from the evening meal, the rum ration, and the off-river evening breeze.

This regular Jap artillery hate caused little damage. A trench had to be occupied and hit directly for a shell to inflict casualties. A well-constructed bunker, roofed with several layers of thick palm trunks and packed with earth, was safe even against a direct hit. But the shelling did wear at the nerves. When battalion HQ back at the Kya-O pagoda was shaken up, it was with the bigger 105-millimeter guns from Singu, farther south. There were several near misses, and one hit on the bunker of the new second in command, Watson-Smythe, when he was not in residence. The Japanese down the road were entrenched in the same way, and probably most of the rounds poured out by our gunners did little damage.

On March 8 Geoffrey Bull led his D Company in an attack on Milaungbya north and south (the village was in two parts). They were accompanied by a squadron of the Gordon Highlander tanks. It was the first time most of the men had worked with tanks. There were rehearsals around a sand model, and signaling arrangements were carefully devised. On the day of the attack the men swept through the village areas eliminating the Japs with tank fire, grenade, bullet, and bayonet. I can find no figures for the casualties on either side, but I do recall that the colonel was greatly pleased with the results. The commander of the tanks insisted that Geoffrey Bull be put in for an MC, which he got. All on our side returned to previous positions and the Japanese were soon back in the Milaungbyas.

For eight miles east of us, as far as the long ridge I have mentioned, and for four or five miles south toward Singu and Chauk, the open land rolled gently. Sandy soil supported scattered scrubby growth and an occasional palm. Distant bells on the pagodas of the riverside villages tinkled in the parching breeze. The Irrawaddy on our right, swirling between islands and sandbanks, and swinging from one side to the other of its flood plain, was deserted of traffic.

The RAF had long since sunk or driven under cover any remaining boats. This was the landscape we looked out over from Fort. Mostly it was too devoid of cover for us to patrol close to the enemy by day.

Sometimes one met Burmese villagers driving creaking oxcarts along tracks in the open country inland. They regarded us apprehensively. Nor could we be sure that they were not informers to the Japanese. The older women, sitting on their haunches smoking large cheroots, neither veiled their faces nor scurried out of sight, as would have been the case in rural India. One did not blame the village maidens for showing some shy unease in the presence of our fierce, slant-eyed Mongolians bristling with arms.

If patrolling by day was limited, every night some of us were out. With Bob Findlay in the hospital being patched up, Pat Davis, our intelligence officer, and I were at this time the only spare officers not either commanding companies or in a vital battalion HQ job. Consequently we drew most of the officer patrol assignments. Pat, spare of frame and quietly peering from behind his spectacles, was an unlikely looking soldier. Intelligent and somewhat introverted, he proved one of the best, a pillar of the battalion. In his book, *A Child at Arms,* he tells us what it was like for a young man just out of school to accept a responsibility far beyond his years.

One felt alone and vulnerable under the stars with a handful of men, groping and stumbling about in this vast no-man's-land, never sure when you might run into enemy waiting in the dark void. As the night wore on and the chill got more penetrating and one's adrenaline thinner, shivers would set in both from anxiety and cold.

Straggling back into our lines after dawn, we reported whatever sparse information we had uncovered on enemy positions. One supposed that this was eventually plotted on the maps at Brigade, then Division, and possibly even back to play some small part in Bill Slim's planning. Tired but happy to return unscathed, the men were on their haunches over steaming mugs of tea in clusters of three or four buddies, chattering over the night's adventure, and in turn hearing of whatever enemy harassment had taken place against the company position during their absence.

This was the best part of the day. We had survived the real and imagined perils of darkness. The sun had not yet blazed up the temperature. The uncertainty of the night ahead was not yet in our thoughts.

Whichever companies were in Fort, the colonel would often swing into the dividing chaung by jeep for an evening visit. With him on occasion he brought a supply of whiskey. Also on the jeep there might be assorted officers' rations, and perhaps bouncing in the back the mess waiter, Dhannu, who had some rudimentary knowledge of cooking for *sahib log*. On other visits the CO would have with him one of the HQ officers, perhaps Bill Blenkin, or Tony Brand-Crombie, the quartermaster, to "keep you company for the night" and to give him an "opportunity to visit the front."

Tony BC had been with the battalion for a long time, looking after our permanently voracious appetites for the most esoteric pieces of equipment. He was not one of your skinflint quartermasters, suspicious and begrudging of each request, bitter at the loss from his stores of every .303 bullet. He had always done his best to get us what we needed.

One afternoon when the colonel arrived, dressed as usual in crisp, freshly ironed greens, he removed his cigarette holder from even white teeth and said, "Guide me around the position again. We're going to do another attack and I need to pick the spot for the battalion observation post. The brigadier is coming up. He wants to see the show."

This time A Company was selected to play the lead. Mike Tidswell was now running the company with unflappable maturity. The Gurkha platoon commanders and the NCOs and riflemen under them trusted him. Already he knew most of them by name, knew their strengths and their weaknesses. He was unassuming yet decisive, giving the company confidence and spirit.

On the day before the raid the CO held a briefing around a sand table. The "table" was a patch of natural sand under a palm tree. Walter Walker brimmed with enthusiasm as he drew diagrams with his stick and efficiently put into operation so many staff college lessons and his battle experience from the North-West Frontier and elsewhere. He had to integrate our Gurkha infantry, the attached machine gunners, the Gordon Highlander tanks of 116th Regiment, and Royal Armoured Corps, together with a bombardment by Hurricane fighter bombers, by our own three-inch mortars, and by the faithful supporting artillery of 136th Field Regiment. This collection of arms and armor had no common language.

Shortly after dawn on March 18 the jeeps of the dignitaries who were to observe the battle from tactical HQ arrived in the Mu Chaung and took cover under the lee of the south bank. Runners led the colonel and his guests along a narrow trench to the elaborate observation post dug into the rising ground that faced the Milaungbyas. Over the past few days various indicators had suggested that the Japanese were also preparing an attack. There was anxiety that they might start first. Documents captured later revealed that indeed they did have an attack timed for 0900 hours that same morning. Our kickoff was an hour earlier.

Before that, to drown the noise of the approaching Sherman tanks, artillery fire began on the Milaungbyas. Then we watched a flight of three Hurricanes circle the village, alternately straffing with cannon fire and dropping high-explosive bombs. The silver bombs glittered as they rotated in the sun, then disappeared into the smoking village. There came a series of deep explosions and fast rising columns of black smoke.

The men downed the all-important last mug of tea. We strapped on extra bandoliers of ammunition and hung additional grenades from our belts. Final pep talks were given by the platoon commanders. The experienced rifleman was supporting his *bhai* who was on the attack line for the first time.

The tanks were now in position, hidden in the chaung. Each was paired up with sections of Gurkhas. The tank-infantry communication drill was now well established: we, the English-speaking white officers, could talk to the tank commanders by 48 set radio, but in the heat of the skirmishing for ground in the village our men would indicate targets by firing Verey lights or tracer bullets from our LMGs.

With all this display of power on our side it was hardly possible to give much thought to the danger in the part we were about to play. The men who stood watching the planes, laughing and cheering the performance, certainly showed no sign of nerves.

At 0800, as the planes turned back with a farewell roll, the lead riflemen and the tanks emerged from the chaung and set out at a steady pace across the barren ground between Fort and Milaung-bya North. Shells were still hitting the edge of the village. We could hear the crackling of the burning houses. Walls and floors were often of tinder-dry bamboo, which exploded as it burned.

Overhead there was now an air OP from 136th Regiment, flying in a tiny L-5 plane piloted by an American from the USAAF. He was there to spot any targets, but especially the flashes of the Japanese guns. Several were knocked out by counterbattery fire during the day.

Now the staccato rattle of the machine guns supporting us across the last few hundred yards increased to a crescendo. Well spread out in open order, each man kicking up his own small cloud of dust, we trudged toward the trees. We were not to be distracted by the occasional Jap shell burst. In our midst the tanks clanked and lurched. The tanks were our life insurance. We must guard them like the gold in Fort Knox. Far out on each flank were platoons from our brother companies.

Two hundred yards short of the village we ran into a Japanese forward screen, a thin platoon, perhaps fifteen men with rifles and a couple of machine guns. Pretty much cowed, they stayed low while our men yelled excitedly for covering fire and dropped their grenades one by one into the scattering of foxholes. Three or four of the Japs made a break for the village, to be shot dead as they ran.

The excitement of this, our first big-scale battle, was intense, yet I felt strangely detached. Was this really happening to me? What I saw around me was more a giant pageant, a Cecil B. De Mille film set out of Hollywood.

Soon we were at the edge of the village. The artillery support had lifted. There were flashes on either side, more Japanese shells exploding on the hard ground. Bits of hot metal flew by but nobody seemed to be hit.

Then we were inside, green shadows, dappled sunlight. We paused in a gully that should have given shelter. I was busy with the signaler establishing communication on the 48 set. There was a great deal of noise. Then my orderly touched my arm and pointed out that the spurts of sand a foot or so away were a consequence of unfriendly rifle fire. It was coming from a clump of bushes ahead. We got a tank to deal with that.

The area was a labyrinth of defenses, bunkers and foxholes packed in among the burning houses, the palms, the thick cactus clumps. There were far more Japs than had been expected, brought up for their own attack. Among the steep reentrants that honeycombed the riverside cliffs, there were bunkers sited most cunningly on the reverse slopes, inaccessible to tank fire.

There was small arms fire on all sides. One of the Sherman tanks moving down the hard sand of the flood plain to the right was being shot at by a 75-millimeter gun dug into the bank. From two or three hundred yards the shells were hitting the tank, but they were not penetrating. One orange ball after another bounced off harmlessly. The Japanese gunners must have been in despair.

The other tanks were with us in the village. Section commanders were firing tracers to pinpoint targets. The tank would deliver a blast, and with much shouted advice from the rest of the section, one or two of the gutsy Gurkhas would make the final assault with grenade and bayonet.

Mike was the center of the action. From what he could see and from assimilating reports of progress from the platoons, he kept control. There were many small confabs about what to do next with Subadar Thamansing, with me, with the platoon commanders. Runners came and went. He could report back to the colonel on the telephone the signalers had strung in behind us, as well as on the wireless.

I took shots at movement in front with the light Japanese carbine I had acquired. There was the snap and crackle of bullets over our heads. The machine guns on the tanks were yammering. Men were crawling and signaling. There was shouting across open ground. So it went on.

After six hours of fighting in the hot sun and through burning houses and smoldering vegetation, the Japanese were eliminated from Base, the northern section of Milaungbya. The village was strewn with the debris of battle. There were Japanese bodies everywhere blackening in the sun. Ahead lay the rest of the village, the areas known to us as Pagodas and Bottom. But our Gurkhas and the tank crews were tiring and short of ammunition. The tanks needed petrol. It was decided to close down the action for the day. I could not believe that we had been engaged for so long.

It had never been the intention to occupy Base, so the order came to return to Fort. The colonel, our fellow officers, and the visiting dignitaries lined the side of the track to welcome us as we streamed in, exhausted and much like winning football players straggling off the field to the applause of fans. Even an army psychiatrist was on hand to study the effect of battle on morale.

Some of the men were grinning down from their perches on top of the tanks; others, covered with sweat-caked dust, laughed as they filed past the welcoming committee dragging Japanese rifles, LMGs, flags, and assorted booty.

I have been asked whether I was scared during this battle. I do not recall that I was. For me fear was more apt to be a problem when facing the unknown: when out on a night patrol groping over strange terrain, or guarding a thinly held perimeter during a long black night. There were plenty of nights when I was scared to death imagining that noises "out there" were a prelude to a banzai attack. But this battle was in daylight, we had trained hard for it, we had the upper hand, and I was surrounded by power and by men who valiantly followed commands. I was too keyed up and too busy to feel the same fear that one feels when the initiative is with the enemy.

No, there was no cause for the psychiatrist to report concern. These dirty, grinning riflemen were flushed and triumphant, still full of enthusiasm and pep. Probably the battalion was at the peak of its effectiveness on that day.

The BRO (battalion routine order) next day summing up the battle read in part:

> The Commanding Officer heartily congratulates Major M. Tidswell, Lt. S. Gilmore, the Gurkha Officers, NCOs and all ranks of A Company on the overwhelming and crushing defeat which they inflicted on the enemy yesterday, 18 March 45. . . . The Brigade Commander has sent his personal congratulations to all ranks of A Company who have killed more Japs in

one battle than any other Company or Battalion in the
Brigade. . . . Killed (actually counted)—94.

The above casualties do NOT include enemy
wounded nor those enemy who were buried in
bunkers or blown up by artillery and tank fire. The
Brigade Commander considers that the total of casualties inflicted on the enemy was between 150 and
200.

Our own casualties including No 11 Platoon of D
Company who co-operated in the attack were: killed
6, wounded 13.

In addition to bodies, three 75-millimeter and two 37-millime-
ter guns were destroyed or captured, a significant total in our war.

Two days later the battalion made a final attack on the Milaungbyas. Two companies were used, B and C, and they came in
from the southeast, sweeping northward to our fixed frontier at
Bastion. But on hearing the tanks, most of the enemy escaped
south toward Singu (and got caught in the open by the artillery).
Few remained to allow themselves to be killed.

So for the third time we returned to Fort, Bastion, and the
other familiar haunts. The Japs harassed us at night as usual. But
we, too, had our patrols out searching and probing. Most such patrols were uneventful. They proved little beyond the capacity for
the same men who broiled by day to walk long miles by starlight,
enduring the shivering cold of the predawn hours. It was a relief
when the light grew strong enough to allow a safe return into Fort
for a mug of sweet, strong tea and, if we were lucky, a snooze in the
shade of a scraggly cactus.

During the heat of the day, except for a few shells whistling
overhead, probably aimed at an incautious truck somewhere to the
rear, and except for the occasional sniper, the Japs were quiet. On
one of these days through the shimmering haze we spotted with
the binoculars a Japanese officer astride a horse of sorts. He sat ob-
serving from a rise and we discussed the chances of hitting him at
such extreme range with our Lee-Enfields. As we debated, the
horse, more of a shaggy pony, ambled out of sight together with
his Nipponese passenger. Perhaps some grandfatherly character in
Tokyo owes his existence to our hesitation.

During this period we were sent a platoon from one of the many far-out Special Forces units that imaginative souls had dreamed up to harass the Japs. Irregular intelligence units like V Force and Force 136 operated throughout the war behind the Japanese front lines with imagination and daring on many dangerous missions. They inspired some, but greatly irritated others of us sloggers cast in less exotic roles.

Our D Force platoon was something else, a bearded, tousled, piratical bunch, eccentric in dress and armament. Lounging around Fort during the day, they created an interesting diversion for the highly disciplined Gurkhas.

They were armed with fireworks, explosives, and assorted gadgets with which they could simulate anything from a full-scale company attack to a river crossing. During our A Company attack on Milaungbya, they were used to create a diversion on one flank while we moved in from the other. On another occasion, escorted by Pat Davis and some of our men, they marched through the night to set up a simulated attack on the cliffs to the south of Singu, six or seven miles behind the Japanese in Milaungbya. It was thought that these cliffs must be occupied, and the idea was to draw fire and spot positions, and to ambush any Japanese who might come out from Singu to investigate. But the cliffs were uninterested in the grand firework display; no one in Singu was foolish enough to leave his billet.

It was men from another specialist group who, on several evenings at dusk, took off from the riverbank in Burmese dress and, paddling dugout canoes with mounted machine guns, lurked midstream about twelve miles below our forward positions hoping to intercept and shoot up the Japanese supply ferries crossing from Chauk to Seikpyu on the west bank. The Irrawaddy was not much above half a mile broad at this point. This lot may have been from the Special Boats Section or from the Sea Reconnaissance Unit, both of which, I now read, had been active on the river earlier, selecting a safe route for our crossing and investigating the proposed landing beaches.

V Force units were ubiquitous. This organization sent out small patrols led by officers to collect information and to build up a network of agents in the areas immediately behind the Japanese forward positions. The men in the patrols were usually from the area. V Force aimed to get information of immediate tactical value.

Force 136 existed to provide long-range intelligence of strategic and political use. It operated throughout Burma and in Malaya, Siam (Thailand), and French Indochina. Besides gathering intelligence, its other main function was to organize local resistance groups that could harry Japanese lines of communication and form the basis for an armed uprising when the tactical situation was ripe.

"By early 1945, teams of British officers and nearly 12,000 men under arms—Operation CHARACTER—were waiting in the hills of eastern Burma, from as far north as Maymyo down almost to the edge of Rangoon itself. All were in wireless communication with Force 136 HQ. . . ."[1]

Force 136 was the equivalent in Southeast Asia of Britain's Special Operations Executive in Europe.

Farther north, in Stilwell's area, there operated yet a third group of irregulars, Detachment 101, American led, and organized by the secret Office of Strategic Services (OSS), forerunner of the CIA. Their guerrilla bands provided information on targets for bombers, laid ambushes, blew up bridges and railway lines, and generally caused the Japanese to use up a lot of troops on internal security who could have been fighting in the regular battles. Detachment 101 units, lightly armed and mobile, avoided pitched battles with the Japanese, as did Force 136.

According to Roger Hilsman, who wrote an interesting book about his experiences in command of a guerrilla group of Detachment 101, over several years a total of 1,000 American officers and enlisted men were employed in the detachment. The highest guerrilla strength was 10,800. Known Japanese killed were 5,400, with a further 10,000 estimated killed and wounded. They demolished 57 bridges, derailed 9 trains, destroyed 272 vehicles, rescued 425 Allied airmen, and so on. They were awarded the Presidential Distinguished Unit Citation.[2]

The strength and movements of those Japanese still west of the Irrawaddy were of concern to our general during the weeks we were frozen on the east bank in the Milaungbya area. The Japanese on

the west side had been expected to withdraw across the river to
Chauk, but had not done so. Indeed, they had been reinforced and
were reacting to the attempted advance by another brigade with
uncomfortable vigor. Probably they were moved by the need to
keep open the retreat routes, which any further advance south by us
must threaten, for their men in the Arakan. It was to find out what
they might be up to in the hilly, barren land opposite and below
the Milaungbyas that we ferried over a platoon under Pat Davis to
set up a patrol base.

From March 25 to mid-April, Pat and I took turns running this
base, three days at a time. We each did three tours. Meanwhile, on
March 27 the battalion was pulled back for a rest. The 1/11th
Sikhs took over and occupied the Milaungbyas.

By day at our patrol base it was impossible to move unob-
served. Unlike the flat east bank with its numerous villages and motorable tracks, the west bank presented a continuous barrier of
barren, broken hills rising to as much as a thousand feet. It was oil
well country, but there were few tracks and fewer villages until, five
miles to the south, one came to the small town of Lanywa, an oil-
storage depot and peacetime steamer station. Another six or seven
miles south was Seikpyu, sited where the considerable Yaw Chaung
joined the Irrawaddy. Seikpyu was not much bigger than a large village, but it was the Japanese base for their forces on the west bank.
Patrolling toward these targets would have to be done at night.

The colonel had set up the base on the highest of several small
hills just back from the river's edge. Here, during the blazing heat
of the long day, and protected by outposts and small patrols, we
would laze and doze in what meager shade was provided by a rock
outcrop or the rare stunted tree. Our limited cooking equipment
and few supplies were partially concealed at the base of the hill.
Doing my best to be comfortable hunkered down on haunches, a
position that came naturally to the men, I would join them in their
meal of rice and dhal.

On these outpost assignments, with no English-speaking companions, my Gurkhali improved immeasurably. With one jemadar
in particular I chatted by the hour, often on global politics, a subject on which his interest was high though his grasp was limited.
This was Jitbahadur Ale, one of Denis Sheil-Small's platoon com-

manders. He was the jemadar who had done well in B Company's
battle on March 4. Jitbahadur had learned some English, which
was rare in those days, but not enough to make possible a discussion of Japan's thirst for oil and other basic raw materials, or
Hitler's poor strategy in Russia, or the subtleties of the submarine
war in the Atlantic. My Gurkhali was stretched.

There was a small hamlet upstream, the only one for some way.
From it sometimes there floated on the faint breeze a pleasing
plinking, bonging music that sounded like a Central American
marimba. The resonant tinkling rhythms, played on bamboo keys,
provided a melodious background for the conversation and tea
drinking that broke up the long, torpid days. I learned later that
this instrument is played in villages throughout Southeast Asia. In
Burma it is known as a *patalla*.

One afternoon I got into trouble with the boss. In my youth I
had built a transmitter, passed the Federal Communications test,
and held an amateur broadcast (ham) license. As a ham operator it
was a sort of game to throw out over the ether an invitation to par-
ley. The more distant the responder, the more one would boast
next morning. It must have been boredom and my memories of
those days that led me to raise the adjutant (at that time, I think,
Bill Blenkin, who was no mean mimic) in the lingo of the thirties:
"Roger Dodger give me a call." Our chitchat back and forth over
the river was interrupted by the brigadier, who was visiting the
colonel. I heard a furious "Get that smart-ass American off the air."

As the sun dropped our evening patrols would set off. Patrols
probed east and north, but mostly south. The men were lightly
armed and, to make less clatter over the stony ground, wore
rubber-soled jungle boots. We had blackened our faces, hardly as
necessary for the Gurkhas as for Pat or myself. By darkness we
would be approaching the area of enemy activity.

I spent several long nights tramping around in the dark. One
night I did the round-trip to Seikpyu, a total distance of twenty-
four miles. To reach it and allow time for a couple of hours of in-
vestigation, we had to leave in the late afternoon and thus risk
observation. I was delighted to get back unambushed.

Pat had already located Jap positions around a prominent
European-type red house on the highest hill at Lanywa. He also

saw fresh tank tracks in Seikpyu. I cannot remember uncovering any especially startling information.

I do recall how glad I was when each tour was finished and I could return to the safety and considerable comfort of the battalion's rest area beside the cool Irrawaddy.

CHAPTER XIV

―――

Enemy on the Run

April 15. Dawn was breaking. It always came swiftly. Stand-to was over. I was enjoying the first slug of strong tea. Suddenly the distant sound of cocks crowing, tranquil, comfortable, was drowned by a rapid succession of dull thuds, not unlike rolling thunder, from across the river. The gunfire seemed heavier, more prolonged than usual. I stared across the blue water to the distant, flat shoreline of the far side.

Orders crackled over the signaler's receiver: "Close down the patrol base. Rejoin the battalion. The boats will arrive in an hour's time. We're shifting south."

The heavy shelling was the prelude to an advance by the battalion through the 1/11th Sikhs to capture Singu. Word to move forward had come from Slim. Singu was a large village, the last Japanese strongpoint before the oil field town of Chauk. The first move had been a night infiltration by B Company under Denis

Sheil-Small and Pat Davis. I was not sorry to leave my hot and isolated post.

Our 7th Division had been directed to make what speed it could southward toward Rangoon down the axis of the Irrawaddy valley. Rangoon was not our prime objective. That glamorous assignment was given to the capturers of Meiktila, the 17th and 5th Indian divisions and their accompanying armor.

Meiktila had been secured by March 3, but there was further fighting in the area as the Japanese launched piecemeal attacks from every direction to regain the town. It was not until March 30 that 17th Division could launch the drive south. They were to go for broke down the rail and road corridor of the Sittang River valley, cutting through and destroying the disorganized Japanese 33rd Army, but not allowing themselves to be delayed.

Everything depended on capturing the port and capital, Rangoon, before the monsoon—and on the ability of our tight-stretched supply services to feed the scattered divisions with all their needs for another two months. General Slim has written: "Throughout the battle we were never without acute anxiety on the supply and transport side. . . . Time and again, and just in time, the bare essentials for their operations reached those who so critically needed them. Very rarely had any formation more than its basic needs."[1]

It is as well that we in the front line knew little of these crises. Occasionally our supporting guns were rationed. Otherwise I do not recall that we were seriously limited by shortages.

To the north of Meiktila other divisions were in action. Mandalay had fallen to the 19th Indian Division on March 20. The 20th Indian and 2nd British divisions were across the Irrawaddy, between us and Mandalay. Way up north the British 36th Division had been steadily advancing south from Mytikyina alongside the American-Chinese forces of NCAC (Northern Combat Area Command).

It was in mid-March that Chiang Kai-shek released another startling bombshell: he insisted that the Chinese divisions and the American Mars brigade (successor to Merrill's Marauders) be withdrawn from northern Burma. It was done. They took no further part in the Burma fighting. This soon released substantial Japanese forces just when all formations of the 14th Army were fully committed in central Burma.

Chiang's shaky hold on power was under threat. The Japanese armies in China were moving against him and had already overrun some of the airfields so laboriously constructed and supplied with American help via India. "No one ruled China during the last year of the war; the Japanese held the north-east and and key points in central China, while Mao's communist armies controlled the north-west, without owing any allegiance to Chiang and his government in Chungking."[2]

We in the 7th Division were not interested in territory or ports. Our job was to cut off and take out the Japanese 28th Army, still coming through from the Arakan, and to defeat the Japanese already in the Irrawaddy valley who were holding open the tracks. Nobody knew exactly what numbers we faced, nor what shape they were in. We knew they would fight if caught.

Some days later, on April 25, now twenty-five miles beyond Chauk, the whole of the 89th Brigade moved back to the west side of the Irrawaddy to join the 114th Brigade, advancing from the north. We hoped to slip in below the Japanese line of escape. Our third brigade remained on the east bank, making for the oil center and river port of Yenangyaung.

Through the last days of April and the first week of May, and mostly on foot, we slogged a zigzag course at first southward through the level, green, well-irrigated countryside about Sagu and Minbu, then west into more rugged terrain. Where we marched, the one-inch maps (not available to us at the time) show a thickly contoured land with peaks above a thousand feet, rising to two thousand feet farther west, the entire area colored green to signify jungle. At intervals rivers twist from north to south, like disturbed serpents, through deep, narrow valleys. In these valleys here and there might be space for a few fields and a scattering of hamlets.

We were constantly on the move, racing the Japanese columns through the increasing humidity and continuing heat of premonsoon Burma. The monsoon could be expected around mid-May. Then life would become even rougher.

Once more we were far from supply bases and were provisioned by airdrop. Each afternoon we dug new positions. Constant move-ment, little sleep, and meager diet were beginning to catch up: fa-tigue showed in faces and lean bodies. My own weight, once a hefty 215 pounds, was down to a gaunt 165 in July, when I found a scale on the Chowringee in Calcutta. The same men who had marched and dug by day would be sent out on patrols to search through the black night.

Stealing through the jungle on just such a night, flanked by a small band of Gurkhas with darkened faces, all of us loaded with the paraphernalia of war, I suddenly dropped into a void, clawing helplessly until I landed in a heap on my back. Peering about and up, I lost all sense of where I was. Not until dim outlines of heads loomed above me haloed by stars, and a Gurkha voice inquired *"Sahib tallah cha?"* ("Sahib, are you down there?"), did I take in that I had fallen into a hole. Possibly it was an abandoned well. For-tunately it was dry and the total descent had been only a few feet, but the second or two suspended in space, falling into darkness, had seemed like an eternity. I stood up and grasped the arm grop-ing down to assist me.

By day Walker directed probes over a wide area on both flanks. Much of the search was carried out by patrols mounted in jeeps. Five or six men perched in a noisy jeep were told to motor down a dusty track: "Keep going until you run into something." These jungle tracks wound and twisted up and down endless hills. Visibil-ity was rarely a hundred yards. The strong possibility existed that at any moment the jeep might drive into an ambush.

On one nerve-harrowing patrol my jeep roared right in among the stragglers at the tail end of a sizable column of Japanese. They were apparently too dazed to take advantage of the target. On an-other expedition we drove into the bazaar of a small town and into the midst of a good number of Japanese wandering up and down the dusty main street examining the merchandise spread out on the ground. Our luck held. They were as surprised as we. Amid a good deal of shouting, and a few random shots, our jeep spun around 180 degrees, churning clouds of dust, and raced out of town.

When the next day's newspaper in London carried the line "Enemy forces located at . . ." it would perhaps be based on just such a harum-scarum encounter.

It was an enemy on the run, desperate to cross Burma and escape into Siam. But we were to find this enemy quite capable of ferocious resistance when trapped!

On several nights a handful of suicidal Japanese led by yelling officers with outstretched swords rushed likely soft spots on our perimeters. At dawn their bodies were found sprawled at the edge of the position. Few of our men were lost, yet the need to be constantly on the alert for such last-ditch charges out of the dark tended to keep us from the sleep we longed for and needed. Sometimes exhaustion was so complete that men slept through every interruption. We had to rely on those on watch to rouse us.

Most of these encounters were with small formations trying to slow our advance. The battalion's chronicle records our passing through dozens of forgotten villages, many little more than a cluster of bamboo huts. Every so often the track was blocked until the Japanese in their holes were winkled out.

May 8, 1945: Victory in Europe Day. So in Europe the war was over. Thousands would still die—concentration camp victims too starved and ill to recover; German, Ukrainian, and other prisoners of the Russians; Germans who committed suicide rather than face trial. But at least the guns were silent; the planes no longer carried bombs.

We heard the news. I cannot remember that it made much of an impression. Europe was too remote from our concerns. Ultimately Germany's defeat made Japan's end certain. But there was a lot of fight left in that obstinate people. The Japs lurking down our trails were not going to cease pulling the trigger for a while yet.

In the Pacific, the bloody battle for Okinawa (only 325 miles from Japan) was in full spate and was to continue through most of June. Air raids on the Japanese mainland were now incessant, and the Americans were bombing Japanese installations on mainland China. The bulk of the Philippines was back in American hands, though fighting was not over until June 21. Despite these advances, no one expected the Japanese to surrender.

One evening an hour or so before dark I was with a platoon of A Company climbing along a narrow footpath high on a ridge. With us was a forward observation party from our faithful 136th West Lancs artillery. Suddenly we saw considerable movement in the shadows of the valley a thousand feet below. Fixing binoculars on a clearing in the jungle we watched in amazement as a column of over a hundred marching men emerged from the trees followed by mules, lorries, and a gun or two. Clouds of dust rose as to our further surprise the column churned in a circle right below us to take up what was obviously a nighttime laager. The FOO, a decent, scholarly sort, was hardly able to contain his excitement. Inside a minute he was calling ranges and map references on his wireless.

From our catbird seat we watched transfixed as devastation rained down upon the target. Smoke from the shell bursts was hardly distinguishable from the dust clouds stirred by the madly confused enemy seeking safety back in the jungle.

It was mortal ill luck for the Japs below that the valley sides were not higher and the valley bottom narrower. In hill fighting dead ground is always a problem. Every ridge and peak creates dead ground where men can lie safe from artillery fire. Mortars, with their high lobbing trajectory and vertical descent, can search into such dead ground, but do not have the range of conventional artillery. The maximum range of an infantry battalion's three-inch mortars was 1,600 yards. The twenty-five-pounder field gun could throw a shell for 13,400 yards, but with a relatively shallow trajectory. In our war, so often fought in difficult broken country, thickly forested, the gunners had to find clearings that were accessible to wheels, that gave a 360-degree field of fire, and that allowed them to reach whatever positions the infantry chose to fight in.

Our bombardment stopped as suddenly as it had started. Ammunition was in short supply. No human movement was visible below. Spirals of smoke rose and spread, the reddish dust slowly settled. My initial sense of wild elation began to subside, to be replaced by something like guilt. It seemed somehow unsporting to rain death on surprised and helpless men.

By mid-May, after many days of pushing south and east with intermittent skirmishing in the hilly jungle, B and C companies were in position astride the last remaining escape route, the north-south Mu Chaung valley. They dug in near the village of Taung-daw, B Company under Denis Sheil-Small blocking the track by the ford in the valley, C Company under Peter Myers on the steep commanding forest-covered ridge immediately to the west.

Trapped and desperate, the enemy gathered their harried remnants for a fierce effort to break through. This was their final chance to escape with guns and lorries and bullock carts. There were no more motorable tracks through the high hill country to the west. These two companies were to come under one of the most concentrated and sustained attacks that the battalion was to endure. The battle lasted through four days and four nights.

On the night of May 12–13, the most severe of the repeated attacks focused on the northern point of the ridge overlooking the track. It was defended by Number 9 Platoon of Peter Myers's C Company. During desperate night-long attacks Rifleman Lachhiman Gurung and two companions hung on to the most forward trench. The live grenades lobbed in gave off a fizzing noise and a faint glow from the burning fuse. Lachhiman had six seconds from the time the Japanese soldier out there in the dark had pulled the pin until the explosion would rip their trench. He threw back a grenade that landed on the edge of his trench. It exploded in midair. As mortar fire *whooshed* in and rifles cracked on all sides, another grenade fell inside the trench. Lachhiman reached for it and sent it back. A third grenade landed in front. This time he was not quick enough. The bomb exploded. Bits of tendon and bone were hanging from where a hand had been and he was blinded in one eye. The two riflemen with him were also severely wounded. For the rest of the long night Lachhiman managed to reload and fire his rifle with his left hand. For his bravery in the action Lachhiman received the VC, Britain's highest award for courage in battle. It was the only VC to be given to the regiment in World War II.

Peter Myers played a vital part in this crucial battle. Deservedly, he was awarded a bar to the MC he had won a year earlier at Ukhrul.

It was during one of the many other scraps at this time that my company commander, Mike Tidswell, was killed. The Japs had moved in to block the track between the rest of the battalion and the two companies at Taungdaw. They occupied the pass where the track crossed the steep ridge east of the village. Now B and C companies were cut off. It was impossible to send them fresh supplies of food and ammunition, impossible to evacuate the wounded, of whom there was a growing number. The situation was becoming serious.

On May 14 A Company was ordered to drive the Japanese off the high ground commanding the pass. We attacked from the south and by eleven in the morning were spread out advancing through sparse bamboo groves up a slope toward our enemy. As the jungle thickened the advance platoon was held up by heavy bursts of rifle and LMG fire. Mike went forward to encourage the men of the advance section, perhaps no more than forty yards ahead. Fair-skinned and taller than the Gurkha, the British officer always stood out as a target. Mike drew rifle fire. Hit mortally, with an ugly wound at the side of his neck, he was carried back to the RAP. He died an hour later.

Seconds after Mike was hit his orderly shot the sniper responsible.

Mike Tidswell was one of those many young Englishmen, hardly out of their teens, who in wartime assumed responsibilities much beyond their years. When bravery was called for, they delivered. When the chips were down their upbringing and background did not allow them to flinch.

On the march with A Company I had walked for nearly three months over the plains and through the hills of Burma with Mike, in the evenings had shared countless tins of bully beef with him. Over thick tea or whiskey in warm water, we had had many long talks: about company affairs, about Gurkhas, about women, about what each of us looked forward to after the war. Now, because of a system that selected the best for the most perilous forward assignment, Mike was to be buried in this remote jungle spot.

Ordered by the colonel to take over command of A Company, I asked for support from the lone Hurricane on "cab" call overhead and pushed on toward the pass. Visibility was never more than thirty to forty yards. Rifle and LMG fire came at us from several directions. I glimpsed Japs running across our front in and out of the trees. Left and right, men were shouting to warn of targets. We could have used a tank or two. The fighting was how I imagine the American Civil War fighting in the Wilderness battle to have been, the Wilderness being in Bruce Catton's description, a "scrambled, brambly maze . . . of second growth forest . . . where a soldier might walk into ambush at any moment."[3]

By late afternoon we were still two hundred yards short of the objective and very tired. The colonel ordered us to consolidate for the night. Although depressed and anxious, we did have the satisfaction of learning that B and C companies had passed a relatively easy day. It looked as though their attackers had shifted to stop us.

During the night there were sporadic exchanges of rifle fire with the Japanese out ahead. It rained hard, a prelude to the imminent monsoon. At daylight we were still being resisted. Now the Japs were well dug in. However, when D Company came down at the pass from the heights to the north, our opponents faded away. Suddenly the track to Taungdaw was open. Almost simultaneously the 1/11th Sikhs descending the Mu Chaung reached B and C companies. They had passed many abandoned lorries loaded with stores.

On that day the colonel promoted me to captain.

It was in the middle of this roughhouse that we were delighted to see Peter Wickham's smiling face again. Peter had been on leave in England. Because of the distances involved and the inevitable periods of confinement in transit camps, he had been away for several months. I think he was the only officer to enjoy leave in England during my time with the battalion. Some of the older officers had been away from home four and five years.

So the battle of Taungdaw was over. The Japanese had lost over three hundred men and had left behind quantities of supplies, guns, and vehicles. They would miss those supplies during the coming months. Our own casualties were remarkably light. In the two months from the capture of Singu to the end of the Taungdaw fighting we had nineteen killed and fifty-eight wounded.

Who should we remember when the generals order an attack on some jungle-clad hill? It is the men in that forward section, boys really, many not yet twenty, far from their hill villages in Nepal. To the rear stretches a long chain of support troops; innumerable road, rail, and boat men; hordes of ordnance and supply people; flocks of staff officers and their attendant clerks; a two thousand–mile trail back to New Delhi and Quetta. At the tip of this mighty effort there is always one little rifleman, nothing between him and death but his wits and a few feet of jungle.

There are moments when a key battle may hinge on whether this lone man wavers or plunges on. All the building of bridges, the widening of roads, the air cover, the support from the gunners, will go for naught if this single infantryman with his Lee-Enfield hesitates. Now is the moment when the many months of training, discipline, and pride of regiment pay off. Covered by support fire from his section, he dashes ahead fifty yards and drops to the ground, his *sathi* yelling encouragement like spectators at a game. The rest of the section moves out. Perhaps men fall. The platoons on either flank are weaving through the trees at the same time. Weak spots must be discovered and exploited. There are muffled explosions as grenades are pitched into bunkers. Over the din of fire on all sides comes the battle cry of the men: *"Ayo Gurkhali!"*

The battle at Taungdaw was one of the last major efforts of the Japanese trapped west of the Irrawaddy to get out as an organized body. Badly knocked about, continuously harried, without artillery or transport, these rearguard groups now headed south and east in small parties. Their instructions were to cross the river at a place called Kama, and then to concentrate in the shelter of the Pegu Yoma hills, a vast area of thinly populated and thickly forested country that lay between the Irrawaddy and the Sittang River valleys. Once across the Sittang, they might hope to reach Siam or Malaya.

The fighting around the Kama bridgehead fell to others. We were given one more objective, to occupy Mindon, about twenty miles to the south. Our A Company jeep was the first to enter this pleasant, well-laid-out town, far more civilized than the villages we had seen over the past weeks. The populace gave us a friendly welcome, many speaking English and apparently happy to see us. They reported that only a few Japanese stragglers were left in the area.

It was mid-May. The battalion was now promised a rest. We had been on the move since leaving Kohima on December 23. The nearness of an angry enemy, tension, extreme fatigue, chronic sleep deprivation, the drab food, the humidity of the premonsoon weeks,

all these had sapped our strength. The men were becoming suscep-
tible to various ills: dengue fever, jungle sores that would not heal,
malaria, and one fatal case of typhus. The rest was much needed.

On May 23 we arrived at Thayetmyo on the Irrawaddy. Here
we expected to stay, refit, grow fat, and enjoy shelter during the
monsoon.

CHAPTER XV

The End of the Chase

Prewar Thayetmyo had been a comfortable seat of British colonial authority. Thus, to our delight, we found a row of verandaed bungalows lining the river, some in reasonable condition. Each owned what had once been a trim lawn running down to the heavy swirling water at the riverbank. The bungalows would provide a welcome change from jungle life, a big step up from stony, damp ground. Except for our stay under canvas at Kohima, I had slept in the open for most of the last eighteen months, many of my companions for two years.

Each night Nebilal set up my *machchhardani*, the mosquito net. A homemade table held my library of two Penguin paperbacks. In the bathroom hung a container of water alongside a cake of Sunlight soap and a steel mirror. Back of my bungalow, with suitable screening, was the sahib's private latrine, dug by the company sweeper, a casteless Hindu. This shadowy soul lurked out of the way except when summoned by the shout *"Mehtar,"* sarcastically translated "Prince."

There was a nine-hole golf course. Its fairways, deep in weeds, had been ignored by the Japanese. The golf craze was not to reach Japan until the 1950s. Prewar caddies emerged from the town to present us with carefully hoarded clubs and a few well-hacked and yellowing balls.

The next step to civilized living came with the discovery in the town of an intact soda water bottling plant. The officers were soon enjoying an evening whiskey and soda, the traditional British mix. The elderly bottles were stoppered with wired-on glass beads.

In the evenings, as a diversion from listening to the rain beating on the tin roof, we played cards. One night the others asked me to teach them the American game of Red Dog. This simple game of chance requires each player in turn to fold or bet against all or any part of the pot on the turn of a card. Should the player bet the total pot and lose, the pot doubles. Simple mathematics will suggest how a modest kitty of eight or ten rupees, fed by double-or-nothing bets, could quickly skyrocket to a thousand, a month's pay. Due more to the recklessness of my companions than to my own ability to compute odds, I was a consistent winner.

Poker was equally popular and profitable. One day five of us were playing shortly after breakfast. Perhaps it was a Sunday. Normally a martinet, the colonel made only one comment when walking in on this unmilitary activity, an indulgent "Gentlemen, I don't mind the poker, but you might shave first." My friends were eager to learn all the American versions of the game, from Spit in the Ocean to High Low. They tended to stay in on every hand when prudence should have told them to fold.

None of us was to enjoy these comforts for long. The colonel went on leave to India, richly deserved, and then was appointed GS01 (General Staff Officer Grade 1) to our 7th Division. He was replaced by Bob Watson-Smythe, the second in command, who had joined in January. He had a tough act to follow. Six other officers, including three of the company commanders, also went to India on leave.

This left the battalion with only a handful of officers, enough to supervise refitting and the inevitable program of drills and weapon training.

I was with the leave boys. Returning to India overland the way we had marched would have taken weeks. We were able to fly on returning American supply planes, first over the Arakan Yomas to Chittagong, then on to Calcutta. From Calcutta some of us went by rail across the breadth of India to Bombay.

We embarked on this extra travel, two or three days and nights either way, principally because the Taj Mahal Hotel in Bombay was infinitely more comfortable than the ratty Grand in Calcutta. And the atmosphere in Bombay, 1,000 miles farther from the war, was less military. And we preferred Bombay's salt breezes to monsoon steam: Calcutta was 120 miles from the open sea. Also, our two weeks' leave did not start until we had arrived at our destination. And sitting in an Indian train was not such a terrible fate. The bunks were luxurious after hard ground; the food was marginally better than, certainly different from, 14th Army rations; the heat was no worse; responsibilities nil. Above all, no one was likely to shoot at us.

I shared a spacious, high-ceilinged room at the Taj with Brian Irving. It was with Brian that I had first joined the battalion. He was a most gregarious fellow. Before lunch each day he gathered friends in the Harbour Bar for endless rounds of gin-and-limes. To pick up the tab for even one round would destroy a fifty-rupee note. Incidentally, Brian's baggage always contained bottles of whiskey against the possibility that thirst might strike during an hour when the bars were closed.

By two o'clock, lifted by drink, we would ascend the wide staircase to the lofty dining room where Goanese waiters carrying plates heaped with curry weaved in and out among the tables. Through the clatter of chinaware and the din of conversation rose the valiant sounds of the small string band still sawing out a version of the Warsaw Concerto. It was nearly two years since Jupe and I, freshly commissioned officers, had first sampled these delights.

The heavy food, the drink, the noise, and the warm, soothing breeze off the ocean induced an irresistible somnolence. We slept for an hour or so under the drone of the *punka*.

From the Taj it was a short ride in one of Bombay's Sikh-driven open taxis to the Cricket Club. Here we worked off our noontime indulgences on the squash court, and then took tea on the veranda overlooking the cricket ground. Most of the regular members were rich Parsee businessmen, fanatic bridge players but not given to active sports. We suspected, perhaps wrongly, that they tolerated our intrusion only as a relatively painless contribution to the war effort.

Or we might visit one of the comfortable "air-cooled" cinemas to spend an afternoon with Dinah Shore.

At that time the Taj provided a bearer who sat outside the door ready to shine boots, mend shirts, or summon the *bihishti,* the water carrier. In more primitive surroundings the *bihishti*'s job was both to fetch the water and heat it for the sahib's bath and his shaving. In the Taj Mahal, with hot water running, he expended his energies turning on the taps and spreading the bath mat.

We, of course, were desperate for feminine company. The available Englishwomen in Bombay were so few and so ardently sought as to be hopelessly spoiled. We did arrange an occasional outing with young ladies from Cyphers or the WAAF, but got the feeling that these outnumbered females waited until the last moment, hoping for offers from the higher-ranked big spenders.

Perhaps Brian's most successful achievement was the corralling of two young and acquiescent Burmese girls, recent refugees and as yet unspoiled by the free-spending hordes. Taxis were in short supply, so the evening might find the four of us jammed into one pony-drawn *tonga* setting out through the blackout for either the Bristol Grill to eat steak, a dish not widely available in the land of the sacred cow, or for one of the Chinese restaurants.

Until midnight one could dance at the Taj to a band reminiscent of my high school band swinging it up in Connecticut. Next door at Green's, frequented more by noncommissioned soldiers and sailors and by girls from the Eurasian community, the scene was more raucous: most nights brawls erupted into the street. Squads of tough military police separated the bloody, drunken combatants and hauled them off to the cooler.

Curfew closed the public rooms of the hotels near midnight. A number of officers, driven by lust or simply unwilling to quit, would then transfer to Madame André's establishment. Hers was a bordello with the decorum and class of a girls' finishing school.

Madame André, in evening gown down to the floor, would sweep about her salon checking that her guests were comfortable and making introductions as if at a social function in Belgravia. Drinks were served and there was dancing to the low-keyed jukebox. Officers were free to negotiate quietly for the merchandise and to disappear into one of the surrounding cottages. Should one choose to be less active, to abstain from the pleasures of the back rooms, no pressure was applied. One simply spent the evening drinking in a congenial atmosphere surrounded by a spectrum of young ladies, Chinese, Punjabi, French, English, Lebanese, and many in-between pleasing blends. All were gowned and perfumed as for a hunt ball. One British major, posted to Bombay to be in charge of the docks, found the atmosphere so congenial that he took up permanent residence for the balance of the war.

Enjoying gin-and-limes in the cool of the Harbour Bar of the Taj Mahal, protected from the incessant pleas for *baksheesh* chanted by the beggars on the hot streets, we had no way of knowing that the promised rest for the battalion had been abruptly closed. While we were enjoying the fleshpots of Bombay, our comrades in Burma were having a rough time.

In mid-June the battalion had been rushed by truck convoy south to the flooded paddy fields of the Sittang River valley. Japs from the hills beyond the river were crossing at night and threatening a counterattack. Probably this was intended to relieve pressure on their battered formations cut off in the hills of the Pegu Yomas. The threat centered on an area known as the Sittang Bend and on the village of Nyaungkashe, by the Sittang Bridge (blown in 1942). Here, on June 22, the battalion was again in action.

The monsoon was in spate. The land was only a few feet above sea level. It was intersected by tidal chaungs that had overflowed. The paddy was under water for miles around and the rain was still sheeting down. Only the villages and some of the narrow tracks that joined them were above water.

It was impossible to dig trenches in such country. Breastworks and bunkers were built up, some protection against bullets, but of limited value against shell fire. And from hidden sites in the hills across the river the enemy began throwing in his heaviest shelling of the Burma War. During one fifteen-minute period 143 shells fell

within the perimeter of battalion headquarters. Three shells made direct hits on the regimental aid post, killing some of the already wounded, including Quentin Kennedy, and wounding the Doc, Tony Brand-Crombie, and others. Doc Dalton had been a good and cheerful friend to us from the early Arakan fighting of 1943, through all of 1944, and now through this 1945 campaign. Under very primitive conditions he had ably patched up many a wounded man, providing that first skilled attention that so often made the difference between survival and extinction. Fortunately, his wounds were not too serious.

The Battle of the Bend was a last desperate effort of the Japanese. With half of our officers on leave and several of the rest wounded, much of the burden fell on the tough Gurkha officers. It was largely the subadars and jemadars who held the platoons in position despite furious attacks and many casualties.

At last the battalion was given permission to withdraw from its exposed position. The withdrawal took place on the night of July 6–7, and under horrendous conditions. In total darkness and through water at times armpit-high, they carried all the wounded and much of the equipment, from heavy mortars and wirelesses to the *durzi*'s sewing machine and the more important files. In this deeply flooded land no rest was possible. The stretcher bearers could never put down their loads. Patrols later reported that large bodies of Japanese were moving around the escaping column. By a miracle there were no clashes.

I and the others on leave had indeed been fortunate to miss this nasty round of fighting, which was palpably a defeat.

With traveling time, I had been away five weeks. This included a sea voyage from Calcutta to Rangoon. I found the battalion strung out for miles guarding approaches to the north-south Rangoon-Mandalay road. We of 7th Division and 17th Division to the north had men astride every track and footpath coming from the west. There were still over thirty thousand Japanese gathering in the jungled hills of the Pegu Yomas. Many were sick, all were near starvation, a few were demoralized.

The guard chain had to stretch for 130 miles. But someone had captured the Japanese breakout plan, which allowed us to concentrate on the vital areas. Night after night, through the constant

rain, large and small bodies of our enemy tried to rush the road and then a few miles farther on to cross the swollen Sittang River. It was between road and river that most of the killing took place.

Our 4/8th Gurkhas were at the extreme southern end of this barrier and saw little fighting. No one complained. The men needed a break.

Up north some 17,000 Japanese were killed, died, or went missing. Around 1,400 prisoners were taken, an unheard-of number. Fourteen thousand reached the east bank of the Sittang. We lost 97 killed and 322 wounded. This must have been one of the most comprehensive defeats of Japanese arms in their history.

In 1945, as the Japanese hold on Burma disintegrated, the Burmese turned against the losers. Political factions began to re-emerge, some with armed support. Most were willing to offer their help to the Allies in the hope of gaining a share in the power as the war ended. Most were looking for independence from Britain.

Among the best organized and most intelligently led was the Burma National Army, under Aung San, and its linked civilian arm, the Anti-Facist People's Freedom League (AFPFL). Through the activities of Force 136, our commanders knew a good deal about Aung San, and about other rival Burmese leaders at large in Burma.

Aung San had achieved some prominence in the 1930s as a young student hothead with Communist as well as nationalist views. In August 1940 he fled from Burma to avoid arrest. Along with a small group of like-minded revolutionaries, he received military training from the Japanese. He was prominent in the formation of the Burmese Independence Army under the Japanese in Bangkok on December 31, 1941. Six months later this was disbanded and in August 1942 a new army was formed out of more carefully selected recruits.

In 1945, on March 27 (the day when we were relieved in front of Milaungbya by the 1/11th Sikhs), the Burma National Army (BNA), then numbering perhaps ten thousand men, marched out of Rangoon and into the jungle. It was open rebellion against the Japanese. Naturally there was a degree of mutual suspicion between the Allied authorities, military and civilian, and these turncoat rebels.

There was not unanimity on the Allied side. Back in India, the Burma government-in-waiting wanted no truck with Aung San: they doubted that he had popular support and feared that negotiations with him would present him with an unfair lead in the jockeying for power that was already in progress. On the other hand, the military—both the clandestine organizations within Burma, like Force 136, and commanders, like Lord Louis Mountbatten and General Slim—tended to favor any policy likely to avoid the need for the 14th Army to fight a Burmese rebellion while still engaged with pushing the Japanese out of Burma and organizing the invasion of Malaya. Resources were too strained to contemplate such a future. As important, there were doubts about the wisdom of asking Indian troops to suppress an independence movement in Burma. Public opinion in India would have been extremely hostile.

On May 16, 1945, the day after the ending of our fierce battle at Taungdaw, Aung San came in to Meiktila under safe conduct to meet with Bill Slim. Later Slim was to write: "I was impressed by Aung San. . . . The greatest impression he made on me was one of honesty. He was not free with glib assurances and he hesitated to commit himself, but I had the idea that if he agreed to do something he would keep his word. I could do business with Aung San."[1]

Without granting political promises, Slim absorbed the BNA on the British payroll and was able to achieve some measure of control over them. They followed his orders and proved useful in obtaining intelligence, in speeding up the retreat of the disarranged Japanese, and in eliminating parties of stragglers.

Thus it was that through July and early August we might suddenly encounter some trigger-happy band of brigands walking down a track waving a flag of truce. They were dressed in motley uniform, often Japanese, and armed with weapons scrounged or stolen from both sides. We fingered our rifles nervously as they closed, for some of these groups were little better than dacoits, and others were not supporters of the BNA but of rival political coteries. Even at our small-time level of platoon and company, we were required to be diplomats! On occasion it was a relief to see striding at their head a lone British officer, one of those brave souls dropped in by Force 136.

The situation was complicated by the dislike, even hatred, the hill peoples around Burma's rim felt for the Burmese. The former had no wish to be bulldozed into a union with Burma when the time came for independence. They wanted (and still want) some measure of autonomy, if not complete separation. These antipathies were centuries old.

This is not a history of the Burmese independence movements. I just record that in the elections for a Constituent Assembly of April 7, 1947, Aung San and the AFPFL won an overwhelming majority and that independence was scheduled for January 4, 1948, when Aung San would have become the first prime minister of an independent Burma. However, on July 19, 1947, he and seven of his fellow councillors were assassinated by a rival (who was subsequently tried and executed).

There were not too many able, experienced, and principled Burmese on the political scene at that crucial time. Probably Burma has never recovered. After a few years of indecisive and ineffectual "democratic" government, in 1962 the army under General Ne Win took over, and the military has held power ever since. It has been an incompetent dictatorship, which one observer called "a dotty combination of wholesale nationalisation, chauvinism, Buddhism and rejection of the modern world."[2]

Burma used to be rich in natural resources, an exporter of rice. It is now one of the world's poorest countries.

Aung San had a daughter, born in June of that last year of the war, who was two when her father was killed. Aung San Suu Kyi has proved to be a remarkable woman. When the military junta allowed an election in 1990, the voters overwhelmingly supported her National League for Democracy (392 out of 485 seats). The junta did not shift, and Suu Kyi has been incommunicado under strict house arrest ever since. She was awarded the Nobel Peace Prize in 1991.

Out in the hills the junta is still fighting the Shans, Kachins, Karens, Mons, and Muslim Arakanese, with occasional cease-fires with one or the other.

Back in July of 1945, we of the infantry were not much concerned with Burmese politics. Hounded by incessant rain, with sodden blankets and boots green with mildew, we were unable to forget the dead and numerous wounded from the recent battle, unable to forget that for those in Europe the war had long finished while we faced, at the least, another campaign of hills and jungles and lethal bullets. We had been warned that we were earmarked for Malaya. All this tended to create a general (and temporary) depression.

We knew that my countrymen were making giant leaps from island to island across the Pacific—Okinawa had finally fallen in late June, and the Philippines by late July—but it seemed unlikely that they could reach Japan itself before we got embroiled again. And would the Japanese surrender even then? Many believed that these fanatics would fight on in every outpost and that we might spend endless months winkling out every last suicidal holdout. Ten million Japanese might die. How many from America and the British Commonwealth? A million?

By early August most of us were camped back at Hlegu, just north of Rangoon. We were to refit and prepare for the next move. Malaya was another of Britain's prewar colonies that had fallen to the Japanese in their victorious advance of December 1941 and early 1942. Although Britain's new Labour government under Clement Atlee (elected on July 26) was considerably less solicitous of empire than had been Winston Churchill and his Conservatives, the loss of Singapore still cut deep at the self-esteem of the British High Command.

It was at Hlegu that we received the news that Japan had surrendered on August 15. Atom bombs had been dropped on two Japanese cities. What were atom bombs? No one could say, except that one of them had wiped out a whole city.

The news, hardly believed at first, became firm. Gradually it also became clear that the Japanese armies, so conscientious in their fighting, were to be as conscientious in the laying down of arms. The war really was finished. The deaths of those seventeen thousand Japanese soldiers up north less than a month earlier had been quite futile.

CHAPTER XVI

—

After the Monsoon

VJ Day did not immediately change the daily routine. We were soldiers and must remain ready for war. There was an increase in guard duties, and in spit and polish. The men's ability to shine their boots and present arms crisply had certainly diminished from disuse during the haul down the length of Burma. Then there did come some shift from concern with the techniques for the eradication of human foes toward schooling designed to equip the men for peacetime. Like us younger officers, the men were enrolled for the duration only and must soon revert to a life in the hills.

Beneath the shelter of stretched tarpaulins that warded off the diminishing rains one day, the searing sun the next, they sat cross-legged in small circles. One group chanted arithmetic tables, another was lectured on world affairs by a jemadar, another was practicing the alphabet and writing.

Swimming parades continued. Earlier they would perhaps have

concentrated on how best to survive a river crossing under fire. Now there was emphasis on fun, on water games.

Of course those two props to every soldier's life on days not devoted to killing, drill and physical training, were pursued hungrily.

Whenever time allowed, the Gurkhas, inveterate gamblers, sat around a blanket spread on the ground, slapping down their grimy playing cards with sweeping gusto. Bought at some village bazaar months back, the cards had been carried and crumpled in their packs ever since. In the army the men were not allowed to gamble for money. This did not seem to curb their pleasure in the cards.

As always, another favorite pastime was *shikar* (hunting). There were no elusive horned *markhor* to be stalked in southern Burma, but the Gurkha was happy to wander off into the scrubby jungle with his army rifle to shoot whatever small game crossed his path. We had a problem when one of the men took a shot at an elephant. Elephants in this area were almost certainly not wild. They would likely be escapees from the Burma Forest Department, or from one of the licensed timber extraction firms. Moreover, this beast was female, strictly not for hunting. The elephants of India and Burma are smaller than the great African elephant, and the females are easily distinguished from afar: they are tuskless. Fortunately, the .303 bullet seemed to do little damage. Other illegitimate targets to fall from time to time were chickens that had strayed outside their village compounds. Plucking was taken care of by throwing the whole bird onto a glowing fire.

Out for a ramble with his Lee-Enfield one day, Nebilal bagged a white pelican. Proud of his prize, he presented the bird to me to be cooked and served up at the officers' mess.

The mess was now housed in a good-sized EPIP tent, walls rolled up to allow whatever breezes existed in the flat countryside to filter through. That evening our mouths watered as the dark, turkeylike meat, neatly carved, was presented for dinner. We craved a change from bully beef with mustard pickles, bully beef with Major Gray's Chutney, or bully beef with HP Sauce.

What a letdown! The fishy flavor of the sliced pelican was overpowering. One mouthful explained why nowhere in the civilized world is this fat bird served as a culinary triumph.

The Doc had recovered from his wound of early July. At the first opportunity he and I took a jeep and, with our orderlies and a driver, set off for Rangoon. The city was a disappointment. Aside from the graceful, gold-spired Shwe Dagon Pagoda, which is surely one of the wonders of the world, there seemed little of interest. Life was at a standstill. The city had been repeatedly bombed, had been neglected for nearly four years by its Japanese occupiers, and then had been suddenly abandoned. The British were hardly beyond the stage of getting the docks to work and rubble cleared.

Two or three scruffy Chinese restaurants were open. We sat outside one of these and ordered eggs and chips. For the first time Nebilal was confronted with the need to use a fork. I pretended not to notice as in frustration he gave up on his efforts to spear bits of elusive egg and slipped a spoon from his pocket. Spoons were now commonplace among the more worldly Gurkhas. They could see that foods new to their experience like tinned peaches responded better to spoons than to fingers.

After the meal we ambled through the fly-blown bazaar where *longyi*-clad purveyors stood behind wares that were spread out on bamboo mats: razor blades and matches, rulers and pencils, secondhand novels from the thirties, crude paintings of local scenes, bales of cloth, some silks. These were the remnants of prewar stock. During their sovereignty the Japanese had imported little but military necessities. Such was the excitement of downtown Rangoon.

Soon the battalion found itself living in tents pitched near Mingladon Airport, waiting to be flown into Siam. It was here that most of the officers got caught up in what seemed the investment opportunity of a lifetime. In Rangoon there were many small jewelry factories where artisans bent over worktables wielding miniature blowtorches. We were convinced that these simple people would have no concept of the true value of the rubies and sapphires (mined in northern Burma) they handled. For a modest investment we, who would soon return to the Western world of sharp commerce and bejewelled women, must profit handsomely.

Evening after evening we sat around the mess table after dinner and brought out matchboxes and cigarette tins full of stones. We discussed the merits or demerits of the cracks in a particular ruby with the savvy of lifelong gemologists. We traded stones between ourselves, might even sweeten the deal with ten or twenty rupees.

Alas, the bubble of fortune burst when we discovered that the stones were "French Stones." They were synthetic. We had returned our treasures with the demand for money back when we learned that while synthetic stones indeed did not command the value of the real thing, they did have a value in England that would have shown some profit.

With peace came bureaucracy: forms to fill out, records to be kept at Company and to be channelled to battalion HQ, from where the havildar clerk collected them and passed them back to Brigade or to distant Quetta. Our havildar clerk, at that time one of the few Gurkhas with an education and some English, was also unusual in that he was a high-caste Brahmin. As such he doubled in officiating at religious holidays, blessing the goats and chickens to be sacrificed at Dashira.

Because of my own impatience with record keeping, Bob Findlay, now my second in command, was indispensable at duties like pay parade. On payday the grinning Gurkhas marched up one by one to our makeshift office, a collection of ammo boxes for seats and tables. There sat Bob, the subadar, and I. The men smacked their heels together, saluted smartly, and announced whether they elected to take part in cash—to spend on cigarettes or razor blades with which to trim their shaven skulls—or to have the whole amount recorded in their pay book, already covered with the scrawled cyphers of previous scribes.

Bob's family fortune had been made in teak in Burma. The profits over several generations had gone into Boturich Castle, on a thousand acres of forest and grazing overlooking Loch Lomond. A staff of retainers had made life pleasant for young Bob during the thirties. When not in school—Harrow at war's onset—there was sailing on the lake, fishing, and deer stalking.

Bob's family firm was the smallest of the five major teak firms, with its Burma HQ at Moulmein, at the mouth of the great Salween River. But much of the extracted timber was floated down the Sittang. The firm had a manager's bungalow high upon the bluff on the eastern (Jap) side of the river above the infamous Sittang bridge. It overlooked the battalion's recent battle perimeter at Nyaungkashe. Bob could see it clearly. While he and the men were crouching in their exposed emplacements in and around Nyaung-kashe under heavy shell fire and continuous rain, the RAF bombed Moulmein. Masses of beautifully prepared Findlay teak, stacked on bogies throughout the war, caught fire. The blaze lasted for ten days. The bogies were welded to the rails. Unfortunately the heat did not reach our shivering men eighty miles to the north.

With the Japanese surrender, our orders to invade Malaya by sea were abandoned. Now we were to be flown to Siam. Bob Findlay was part of the advance party that accompanied the brigadier into Bangkok. Reports filtered back, perhaps just a little exaggerated, of a city teeming with beautiful Siamese maidens, all grateful for their release from the Japanese and all anxious to please their saviors. We heard with less pleasure of the social ailments with which many of these girls were infected.

It was rumored that our mess was to be housed in a palace vacated by one of the more affluent Siamese princes. In the royal stables were polo ponies that would be available for those of us interested in that gallant sport. This rumor proved to be an illusion. There was also talk of some resurrected players of Western music who, in return for a modest fee, would provide music for gala evenings in the mess. And the shops were said to be full of goodies not seen in England, India, or along the jungle trails of Burma for many a tumultuous year.

Even better news: despite earlier predictions from some that the Japanese in Siam—undefeated and in strength—might fight on, defying the emperor's edict to surrender, they were cooperating 100 percent.

In due time, when the battalion eventually reached Bangkok, it took over a private house owned by the local Mitsubishi manager, who had a fine collection of 78 rpm records, watercolors, china, and glass. In the garage was a Morgan sports car, which would have been more to my taste than polo ponies. But I was not destined to sample these delights.

The move to Bangkok ran into delay after delay. The long power struggle, which for the French would end with Dien Bien

Phu nine years later, had already started in Vietnam (still called French Indochina at that time). The planes scheduled to take us to Bangkok were diverted to fly more troops into Saigon while we sat around our tents waiting.

Much as I looked forward to seeing for myself the pleasures of Siam promised by Bob Findlay, it would be twenty-five years before I reached Bangkok. By that time I had lost interest in adding polo to my repertoire of sporting accomplishments.

I had now been overseas for more than four years. Continual existence in debilitating tropical and desert climates could be coped with so long as the esprit de corps of myself and my comrades was supported by a compelling cause. With peace, this had gone. The foe was vanquished. The fighting was done.

I began to wonder what was happening back in New York. Did my teeth require the attention of someone more able than the bearded Sikh who, using a foot-powered drill, had recently worked on them? I began to have serious cravings for a real steak and my thoughts returned to the enjoyment of a cool breeze ruffling the waters of Long Island Sound.

At just this time a cable arrived from New York that helped make up my mind. The cable told of the death of my uncle Franklin Johnston, who had so ably headed our family publishing business. "Make every effort to return," it said. Two days later, having conned a pass from the brigade major, I was flying back to New Delhi to file the papers for my release.

The days of waiting for these documents to make their way through the labyrinthian bureaucracy, which had been multiplying like a voracious fungus since the time of Clive, would have been intolerable except that the monotony of an all-male society suddenly changed. In the lounge of the Women's Auxiliary Air Force I found myself confronting a vision of loveliness, a young lady of the WAAF fresh from England. With courage bolstered by months of celibacy, I immediately introduced myself as someone anxious for a game of tennis, a ploy suggested by the fact that she was carrying a tightly strung Slazenger.

My naive approach disguised (I hope) any other intentions I may have nurtured toward this Aphrodite. The next morning found us face-to-face across the nets of the Imperial Gymkhana

Club courts. Ball boys scampered over the well-tended grass to save us the effort of retrieving wide shots. She played a polished game. Afterward we sat in the shade and she crossed her sleek, well-tanned limbs as I ordered *nimbu pani* from the turbanned Punjabi in attendance.

The weather—we were now into November—was clear, dry, warm by day but crisp enough in the evenings for me to sport the barathea uniform made for me two years back by a tailor in the Quetta bazaar and in storage all these many months. After some days of tennis and lemonade our friendship ripened, and my efforts to escape India became less persistent. The suggestion was made that we pay a pilgrimage together to take in the beauty of the Taj Mahal at Agra.

There was one flaw connected with my beautiful companion. This was the resentment that her dog showed me. Although hardly in keeping with a military atmosphere, she led her small dachshund on a leash everywhere we went. Possibly suspicious of my intentions, he showed his ceaseless dislike of me with frequent snarls. I attempted to put him in his place by showing similar disdain. On the train to Agra, in the rickety *tonga* transporting us to the Hotel Cecil, and later as we strolled in the moonlit grounds of the Taj, we were chaperoned by this unpleasant and jealous protector.

The presence of the dog, together with my companion's somewhat soignée appearance, which she accented by flourishes of her ivory cigarette holder, served to disguise any appearance of an illicit tryst. We three gave every outward sign of married respectability.

Not even the spell of Shāh Jāhan's most famous monument by moonlight, nor my own long absence from sophisticated feminine company, were to lead to a long-lasting romantic entanglement. The interlude was cut short, to the certain satisfaction of the dachshund, when a document arrived telling me to report to the transit camp at Deolali. There transportation to England, and eventually to America, would be arranged.

Deolali's vast cantonment lies inland from Bombay. Sooner or later, coming or going, every British soldier in India got stuck in Deolali, sometimes for many weeks of mind-destroying boredom. Jupe Lewis and I and the rest of the original AFS contingent had spent a month there that included Christmas 1941. This time I had better luck. Within a very few days word came to embark on the P & O liner *Strathmore*, even now steaming toward Bombay.

Winding down the Western Ghats, our troop train, of which I, as senior officer aboard, had command, carried a full load of soon-to-be-released Tommies. They were in high spirits, jubilant at the prospect of quitting this miserable heat, of returning to the dank climate of England that now seemed so desirable. Most of them had spent three, four, or more years overseas. They would be leaving this land where the pungent smoke of burning cow dung hung over every village for a world laid over by the smoke of burning coal.

Coming around a bend as we slowly descended I could see out ahead of my compartment car after car jammed with West Kents, East Lancs, KOSBs, Royal Scots, South Wales Borderers, men from the Chindits, crammed together on hard benches of All India Railways' third-class carriages. Unmindful of discomfort, these veterans of the Arakan, Kohima, Imphal, Mandalay, and Meiktila were singing, singing songs they had chorused nostalgically many times before to keep up their spirits. This time spirits needed no lifting.

Above the chugging of our steam locomotive and the slow clacking of wheels over the railbed, the words came reaching back, lusty basses and shaky tenors bellowing "Waltzing Matilda," "I Belong to Glasgow," "Take Me Back to Dear Old Blighty," "She Was Poor but She Was Honest," and, especially appropriate, "They Say There's a Troopship Just Leaving Bombay (Bless 'em all)." There was unaccustomed exuberance to their rendering of the sentimental favorites like "Keep the Home Fires Burning," "Nellie Dean," and "There's a Long, Long Trail," for now they really were headed homeward to Blighty, to sweethearts and mums and home fires.

The *Strathmore* pulled away from the dockside in Bombay and out into the gently rolling Indian Ocean. Ahead lay our voyage up the Red Sea, through the Suez Canal, across a Mediterranean now free of German submarines and German bombers, through the Straits of Gibraltar, and across the Bay of Biscay to England's Southampton.

Looking back, I watched the Gateway to India grow smaller and smaller over the blue waters. This famous landmark was a triumphal arch, the British Empire's nod to the Roman Empire. It was perched on the dockside not far from the Taj Hotel, and it marked the spot where the King Emperor, the bluff and libidinous Edward VII, had landed in 1911. By 1945 empires were out of fashion.

The only occasion that I know of when the Gateway was used was months later, in February 1948, when the last unit of the British army in India trooped the King's and the regimental colors through the arch to the playing of "Auld Lang Syne." The 1st Somerset Light Infantry, who had been chosen for the honor, had a long connection with India. Among many and older campaigns, this battalion had fought with our 7th Indian Division in the Arakan in 1943–1944. But I doubt that any of the 1948 men were survivors of that remote time.

All through the voyage my thoughts were split between the joy of churning slowly toward the world I had known on Madison Avenue and in Connecticut and my experiences of the last four years, immersed in war and in a colonial military atmosphere so strange to my New England background. I was leaving behind the blare of oriental music competing with the traffic noise of the narrow city streets: horse *tongas,* bicycles, cows, taxis, slow-moving rackety lorries, and always multitudinous people, so many people. I was leaving farther and farther astern the family cooking fires on station platforms, the shifting crowds of coolies, merchants, beggars, tea sellers, shrouded women and solemn children, soldiers on leave, dignified clerks in flowing white.

I thought back to my days at the OTS in Belgaum: dawn PT, live ammunition fired over our backsides as we crawled through the obstacle course, the hubbub at the bar each evening before dinner, getting accepted, I think, by the Brits. I remembered the heat and starchy discipline of Quetta, and the exhilarating air of our six weeks in the mountains at Ziarat. I looked back with less enthusiasm to my introduction to life-threatening moments in the Arakan, where one learned quickly to dig deep and to keep to the shadows. I thought then as I often still do of the happy times in the cool

Naga Hills around Kohima, and of our long march down into the plains of central Burma, of the excitement of shaking out into open formation, covered by artillery fire, to attack our enemy, the Japanese dug in among the toddy palms of the Burmese village ahead. I remembered, and I will not forget, Mike Tidswell, my company commander, who would never return to his home.

These thoughts have come back many times over the years. Strangely, and just as well, I am seldom reminded of the times we slept with pools of rainwater seeping through our blankets, and amid the hum of thirsty mosquitoes and the sliding infiltration of leeches.

Many times I have thought of my little sawed-off orderly who, believing me careless with the few rupees I carried, would meticulously count out my change and admonish me: "But Sahib, you had ten rupees, you have only eight here." There was the unspoken suggestion of loose living somewhere along my day. When we came into a new position and I was off reporting to the CO, that same Nebilal would dig both his and my slit trench. It was he who, while we were paused on the edge of a Japanese-held village, suggested that those puffs in the sand at our feet were indeed evidence of bullets and that I would do well to duck. It was he who, on a short trip to Calcutta from Kohima, built a fire for tea in a stone-floored hallway of the Grand Hotel.

I will always remember with affection the young men of my company, who showed no deference to age or rank as we played soccer on the beach at Elephant Point, or basketball on a baked mud pitch at Kohima, but went for a rough-and-tumble, no-holds-barred game.

Some years back I did visit one of the Gurkha battalions on guard at the borders of Hong Kong. But I am not now apt to get to Nepal to visit the survivors of our gallant World War II warriors in their mountain villages. Some of our officers have done so.

Through the Gurkha Welfare Fund (see Epilogue, page 248) the British do much to help many thousands of individual soldiers who in old age are falling into difficulties. My regiment keeps in touch with our battalion's VC winner, Lachhiman Gurung, and following a recent report on his situation, is raising further funds to buy him a more comfortable old age.

All the Gurkha regiments of the old Indian Army have active officers' associations that meet at least once a year and publish their respective journals.

I think that no one who has soldiered with the Gurkhas can forget them, nor can he be unmarked by the experience. Fifty years afterward, the memories remain strong.

But I should be honest. In 1945 I did not spend the entire three-week voyage to England reliving the past. At the start my mind was on the future. Off Hornby Road in Bombay I had bought a Spanish primer. I had the notion that I would study on the ship to increase my linguistic skills. Back at Johnston Publishing I would be better equipped to deal with our Latin American editions.

Fate intervened. A bridge game started, and owing to a shortage of tables in the ship's lounge (a table vacated was a table lost), it had to be continued nonstop from Bombay to Southampton.

I went to London for the process that the British called being "demobbed." Demob involved receiving an official discharge, a farewell bonus (which I thought handsome), and from a large warehouse called Olympia a pair of brown shoes, a raincoat complete with lining, a hat, and an ill-fitting pin-striped suit. By the addition of spikes the shoes were later converted for action at golf. I was also given a letter from the India Office stating my right to suffix my name with "I.A. Rtd"—Indian Army Retired.

When I was released from duties, uniforms, and military discipline, the door was opened to the indulgences of theater, nightclubs, restaurants, and the English pub. It was not long before I met the girl of my dreams. She admitted later that my mass-manufactured, pin-striped demob suit did little for me, but she must have recognized potential. Peggy was a beautiful, effervescent Kentish pearl.

She was also a WAAF, a plotter in the Operations Room at the RAF Fighter Command's HQ at Stanmore, on the outskirts of London. These plotters, real or fictional, have often appeared on film. Buried deep beyond the reach of German bombs, reacting to telephoned messages received from the coastal radar stations and Observer Corps spotters, and armed with long-handled, magnetized rods, they calmly moved arrows across a huge map of England. The colored arrows represented formations of German bombers and fighters converging on their targets. In the gallery overlooking the map, like the dress circle of a theater, the top Fighter Command officers juggled with their limited squadrons of Hurricanes and Spitfires. On occasion Prime Minister Winston Churchill would be watching.

Peggy had joined this exclusive club in 1942. As the bomber raids decreased, she and a few others spent part of their time "reading" the developed film that was now being taken automatically by certain fighter planes, British and American, as the pilots engaged special targets. The small band of women engaged on this for Fighter Command Operational Research were not allowed to talk of their work, and even now are reluctant to disclose details.

I had to leave England and return to New York and my publishing firm. I had started my adventure to escape the world of commerce. Four years later I leaped back into that world with enthusiasm.

My good friend, boss, and mentor, Gerard Kievenaar (Kiev, I called him), was now eighty-seven. He had hung on all through the war. Now he wanted me to take over as New York manager. Because of demand pent up through the war years, exports were booming and so was our *American Exporter*. Soon we would start two new magazines. It was an exciting time.

Wishing to shed the label "One-Man Slum" once attached to me in the Western Desert, and aiming to meet the standards of elegance expected of the Madison Avenue adman, I allowed my uncle Walter, a snappy dresser never without a flower in his hand-stitched lapel, to introduce me to his tailor, Morris Roud, who operated out of a fifth-floor loft on West Forty-fifth Street. For the then stiff price of $120 each, Morris produced three elegant and conservative suits. They were set off by my Borsolino hat from Cavanaughs and correct shoes from Church. Here was a rising young publishing adman; trust him with your business.

No problems arose from this radical change of lifestyle. The only unwanted legacy from my venture into Asia was recurrent malaria, which hung about for a couple of years and gave me spells of sweating, shakes, and shivers.

Through all these excitements and distractions I could not forget Peggy. She was demobilized and had returned to her family, and no doubt felt the world to be at her feet. It took a number of months and many letters to persuade her to marry me. The wedding took place in Greenwich, Connecticut, in May 1946. A smasher then, a smasher now, Peggy can still attract admiring eyes as she enters a room. She has helped me to enjoy life ever since.

Epilogue

When a war ends, a soldier's second life begins. On returning to Johnston Publishing my travels took me to places more comfortable than Tobruk, Aden, or Chittagong—places such as London, Paris, and Berlin; and I enjoyed foods more satisfying than bully beef or powdered whale meat in hotels more luxurious than the transit camp in Deolali.

I soon became responsible for the efforts of our sales offices in five major cities in the United States. As business grew overseas, I set up our people in Europe and Asia. Along the way we expanded from the original general trade magazine *American Exporter* to global magazines, starting with *Industrial World*, read by manufacturers, and *Automotive World*, going to garages and fleets abroad. Both had separate English and Spanish editions.

Our most successful start-up was *Alam Attajarit*, a magazine like *Business Week* in Arabic. Started just before the oil boom, it proved a bonanza and brought me back to Beirut, where we published on a regular basis. Not long after *Alam* was off the ground we launched a similar business magazine for Asia published in Hong Kong. *Modern Asia* also did well. Spellbound by our success with these new ventures we launched *Modern Africa* out of London. We soon found that there was not much that was modern about sub-Saharan Africa. This venture became less than a resounding success.

These interests often took me on a swing to Asia, and from there to the Middle East and Europe to urge our salespeople to book more ad pages.

Acting as a Johnston representative or editor overseas was not without peril. Our man in Tehran, Roger Cooper, whom I had visited before the Shah left the country, was jailed by Ayatollah Khomeini and it was some years before he was released to return to London. Our advertising manager on *Modern Africa* died of fever while traveling in West Africa, once called "the White Man's Grave." Nadim Makdisi, editor of *Alam Attajarit*, was kidnapped off the street in front of his Beirut office, taken at pistol point into a cellar, told he was to be shot, and given his last cigarette. He only just talked his way out. The advertising manager for a Mexican edition of *Industrial World* was kidnapped at the Mexico City airport, stuffed into the trunk of the kidnapper's car, and taken for a bumpy drive around the city. Then he was relieved of his credit cards and released. Our man in Germany, on one of his visits to Moscow, was slipped a knockout pill in his drink. He woke up hours later to find his room and papers had been ransacked for evidence that he might be a spy.

I have put on sales presentations in Osaka, Hong Kong, Beirut, Dubai, Moscow, Warsaw, Belgrade, the English Midlands, and up and down the Ruhr Valley: some successes, some flops. There were few dull moments in my business life.

One day I told myself to quit before anyone said "When is old Scott going to let youth take over?" For some while I did enough consulting to keep off the welfare roll.

Today, on the edge of my ninth decade, I am content typing these recollections, painting an occasional acrylic, attending my grandchildren's graduations in this country, with more to come for my son's children in England. As long as I can lift a racket, I will.

Also, I struggle not to lose too many one-dollar Nassaus on the links.

My three children and four grandchildren have all learned to enjoy steak and kidney pie, kippers, toad in the hole, and treacle tarts. While Peggy has taken over much of the driving and decision making, her efforts to mold my opinion toward the Democrats have failed. I remain the same lifelong, rock-solid Republican.

Somewhat gregarious by nature, I have many good friends in America. None mean quite so much to me as those English and Scots mentioned on these pages. Even now I return to Britain to see them.

Doc Dalton, retired since 1988, was in practice for forty-two years as a family doctor in London. He still carries around in hand and face bits from a Japanese-made grenade and shell. He has three children and five grandchildren.

Pat Davis has worked in book publishing and university administration. He edits the journal of the 8th Gurkha Rifles Regimental Association. His volume of war memoirs, *A Child at Arms,* published in 1970, remains in print. He is married with two children and two grandchildren.

Bob Findlay's family business in Burma (teak and elephants) was nationalized in 1947, so he never returned east. He qualified as a chartered accountant, but has devoted much of his considerable energy to his idyllic estate on the shores of Loch Lomond. I asked him once, "When will you visit America?" and got the reply, "Whatever for, Scott?" He is married with three children.

Brian Irving stayed in the army until 1952. He then sold Rolls-Royce and Bentley cars, and finally joined Manpower, the employment agency. Always good at sports, he played high-level hockey in the army, and later competed at county and regional levels as a civilian. He married in 1961.

Peter Myers also stayed on in the army and retired as a brigadier in 1972. He fought in Malaya and Borneo, was awarded the OBE while serving once more under Walter Walker. He is a founder and trustee of the Gurkha Welfare Trust. His wife, Anne, died in 1991. They have two children and four grandchildren.

Ebullient Denis Sheil-Small rejoined the insurance company he worked for in prewar London. He married Sally, one of the Kohima nurses, who died in 1978. Retired, he now lives in South Africa with a second wife. He has published his own war memoirs, *Green Shadows,* and several other books on Gurkha themes.

General Sir Walter Walker KCB CBE DSO, our colonel in 1945, went on to high command in the British army and NATO. He ended as commander in chief of Allied Forces Northern Europe, retiring in 1972. His wife, Beryl, died in 1990. They have three children and six grandchildren. The last ten years of his life have been grim as a result of a hip operation that went wrong and left him badly handicapped.

Peter Wickham joined the British Broadcasting Corporation (BBC) in 1947 and held a number of appointments until retirement in 1978. He is married with two children and five grandchildren. To everybody's enrichment, he is still the genial and skilled raconteur he was fifty years back.

Of the other five AFS who volunteered with me for the Indian Army in early 1943, three sustained battle wounds and one was wounded in training. So our choice was not without risk.

Jupe Lewis, after being wounded with the 2/8th Gurkhas at the battle of San Savino in Italy, joined the UN Secretariat and was involved in many field missions of inquiry, peacekeeping, and truce supervision. He is married with two children, and is now retired.

Ralph Muller's wartime story is outlined on page 72. In peace his life has been equally adventurous, ranging from time in the U.S. Merchant Marine, to smuggling in the Mediterranean and around Europe, to yacht brokering, skippering, and chartering. He lives on a motor yacht in Cannes.

Bill Nichols joined the 18th Royal Garwhal Rifles. After a bayonet wound in training he was judged unfit for active service, whereupon he joined the American Mars Force in northern Burma. Postwar he worked for American Express, with years in Paris, the Riviera, Germany, and Morocco. He is married and has five children.

Pat Pattullo was posted to the 13th Frontier Force Rifles and became adjutant of one of their battalions operating in Iran. Since the war he has had a distinguished career at Harvard, including time as director of Harvard's Center for Behavioral Sciences, and has written books on what makes people tick. He is married with two children.

Al Wright is the only one of my AFS Indian Army compatriots on whom information is scarce. He was commissioned into the 5th Royal Gurkha Rifles, and was badly wounded in Italy in the autumn of 1944. For many years he lived in Vermont, where he died in 1993.

What happened to my battalion, the 4/8th Gurkhas? It was a war-raised unit and could have expected disbandment soon after the ending of the war.

In mid-October 1945 the battalion flew into Bangkok, Siam, and was fully occupied mounting guards on military property against the ubiquitous and very skillful Thai thieves. In December the battalion moved to Malaya and spent a peaceful Christmas in Gemas, 150 miles north of Singapore. Everyone thought that this would be the last Christmas.

In June 1946 the 4/8th was sent to Java at a week's notice and there was involved in the last months of a sad and often ferocious little war with Indonesian freedom fighters. Java had been a Dutch possession before the war. Many Indonesians did not want the Dutch back.

The 23rd Indian Division had gone to Java in September 1945 to collect and evacuate the many thousand prisoners of war, civil and military, most of whom were in poor shape after four years of confinement under the Japanese; and to collect and disarm the Japanese troops on the island. They were also there to provide some kind of administrative framework and to keep order until the Dutch got themselves organized after their five years of German occupation.

When I tell you that the 23rd Division's casualties in Java at the hands of the Indonesians were 569 killed and missing and 808 wounded; and that we had to instruct our enemies, the Japanese, to keep their weapons and join us in subduing this mayhem; and that they, the Japanese, lost 544 killed in action in Java postwar[1]; and that the 5th Indian Division was flown in to help, you will know that this episode was poisonous. That it took place after the end of a world war when we temporary soldiers might reasonably have expected safety from spear and bullet was an additional irony.

Coming in for the last act, the 4/8th lost only five killed and three wounded. The battalion was back in Malaya during November 1946. It remained there in various quiet stations until December 1947, when it returned to a now independent India. It was never disbanded and is still an active unit of India's army.

Soldiers of the British and Indian armies who served for the duration of the war received only gratuities on demobilization, but of course no pension (unless disabled). To help Gurkhas who are now in difficulties, the British have organized the Gurkha Welfare Fund.

Nepal is a poor country. Many of its inhabitants are subsistence farmers. Population growth, climatic fluctuations, erosion, earthquakes, and limited medical facilities bring hardship to individuals.

The Gurkha Welfare Fund and its constituent charities—the Gurkha Welfare Trust (GWT [U.K.]), the Gurkha Welfare Appeal (Canada), the Kadoorie Agricultural Aid Association, and other smaller trusts—all exist to raise and distribute money for the relief of poverty and distress among Gurkha ex-servicemen of the British Crown. This includes aid to the communities in which ex-servicemen live.

The main priorities for individual aid are providing hardship grants to relieve distress among those who are destitute and too old to work, improving and providing medical care, and maintaining support for education. Community projects include help with the installation of footbridges, drinking water systems, schools, and with advice and training on animal husbandry and on the growing of fruit trees and vegetables.

Needs are increasing, not diminishing. There are still many thousands of Gurkhas alive out of those who served in World War II. More and more of them can no longer work and are pensionless. More and more are turning to the trust for help and a minimum welfare pension; over 9,000 now receive £10 a month from the trust. It is estimated that there are 45,000 ex-servicemen and 200,000 dependents eligible for help.

There is still an urgent need for funds in order to continue and expand this work, to repay in some small part the immense debt the free world owes to the Gurkha soldier. If any reader is interested, contact one of the following:

The Gurkha Welfare Appeal (Canada)
7 Tanager Avenue
Toronto
Ontario M4G 3P9

The Gurkha Welfare Trust (U.K.)
Room 017, Ripley Block
Old Admiralty Building
Spring Gardens
London SW1A 2BE

For readers who wish to expand their knowledge of Gurkhas, a trip to the new and lively Gurkha Museum in Winchester, England, will prove a treat. The museum sets out to commemorate the services of the Gurkhas to the British Crown since 1815. Through tableaux, dioramas, showcases, and visual and voice descriptions, you learn about the long history of the Gurkha soldier and the campaigns in which he took part, and something of the man himself and his homeland.

Appendix:

The Gurkhas in and After World War II

During World War II Gurkhas (and Indians) were in action in Egypt, Libya, Tunisia, Palestine, Lebanon, Syria, Iraq, Persia, Aden, Italy, Greece, Cyprus, India (North-West Frontier and Assam), Burma, and Malaya. In the turbulent aftermath of peace Gurkhas found themselves in French Indochina, Siam, Dutch East Indies (Sumatra, Java, Celebes), North Borneo, and Japan.

Over fifty Gurkha battalions were employed (as against twenty in peacetime), including two Gurkha parachute battalions and the five jungle training battalions. Add in the ten training centers, the units of the Nepalese regular army that were loaned to the British, and the many Gurkhas employed in other Indian Army units and in the police, and we calculate that more than a quarter of a million men served. All were volunteers. They came from a country with a total population that in 1939 was probably under eight million.

Taking Indian and Gurkha together, a significant percentage of

255

the fighting units in the Western Desert, in Italy, throughout the Middle East, and a very great majority of those in Burma, were from the Indian subcontinent. Without the Indian Army it is doubtful whether Britain could have held on to the vital oil of the Middle East or sustained communications across the Indian Ocean to India, Australia, and New Zealand.

Gurkha casualties overall in World War II are reported at twenty thousand dead and wounded.[1] In my regiment, the 8th Gurkha Rifles, according to the regimental history, the four fighting battalions suffered the following casualties through the war and in the peacekeeping operations that immediately followed:

Battalion	1/8th	2/8th	3/8th	4/8th
Killed and died of wounds	45	179	152	165
Died in enemy hands	—	14	—	—
Missing	—	11	3	12
Wounded	179	470	335	376
Total	**224**	**674**	**490**	**553**
British officers killed or died in enemy hands	2	2	7	7
British officers wounded	1	13	10	9
Gurkha officers killed or died in enemy hands	—	5	5	6
Gurkha officers wounded	3	18	7	12

It will be seen that a man was much more likely to get into trouble if posted to the second battalion, which served in North Africa and Italy. This battalion also lost a large number of men as prisoners during Rommel's 1942 summer offensive. Most of these survived the war and are not listed above. There is no mention in the regimental history of prisoners lost by the three battalions fighting in Burma.

For my battalion, the 4/8th, casualties were heaviest in 1944, which is the year when an even larger number went sick. Many of the sick and the wounded returned.

The 4/8th was fortunate, as were all four battalions, in that it was never placed in an impossible situation, never called upon to die in large numbers. Not for us the slaughter of the Civil War in America, or of the western front in World War I. All the same, we paid our dues to Mars and Durga. And once or twice we came close.

It has been calculated that nearly two million men must have fought in Burma during World War II. The historian Louis Allen in his book *Burma, the Longest War, 1941–45* has attempted to total the casualties of the participants. These include Japanese, Chinese, American, African, Gurkha, Indian, Burmese, British, and no doubt men from other British Commonwealth countries. Seldom has such a polyglot army been gathered to fight a major war.

Allen comments: "The casualty figures are often difficult to deduce, to compare, and square with one another."[1]

The Japanese won Burma cheaply: 2,431 killed and wounded against 13,463 British and Commonwealth. Chinese casualties for this 1942 retreat are not given, probably are not known. The 1942–1943 Arakan campaign and the first Wingate expedition of 1943 also saw higher Allied losses than Japanese. From 1944, however, the balance tilted the other way.

The Japanese report having lost 185,149 troops from all causes in Burma, men who never returned to Japan. This includes the many thousands who died of starvation and disease in 1944 and 1945.

British and Commonwealth killed in battle were 14,326. This figure does not include American and Chinese casualties, nor civilian losses, nor the Allied deaths from disease. Large numbers went down with malaria, scrub typhus, dysentery, dengue fever, and other tropical diseases, especially in the early years. But after an initial hiatus there was a good record of recovery, as with the Allied wounded. By comparison the Japanese medical arrangements were primitive.

Total Chinese and American casualties are not given by Allen. For the Battle of Myitkyina, the major engagement of Stilwell's forces, the Chinese lost 972 killed and the Americans 272. Sick and wounded were many times more.

Allen states that Japanese losses in Burma were roughly one twelfth of their losses during the war, which are given as 2,300,000. Of the Allied total, Indians and Gurkhas account for approximately half, and British for one quarter.

For readers interested in such matters, these figures will enable some sort of comparison to be made with campaigns in other places and in other times. The Burma War may be little known and less understood, but for sure it was more than a skirmish.

In the postwar years the British army's Gurkhas have served, in varying numbers, for short or long periods, on operations or on station, in Hong Kong, Singapore, Malaya, Malaysia, Brunei, Indonesia, Nepal, India, Bangladesh (on disaster relief work), the Falkland Islands and South Georgia, Belize, Saudi Arabia, Kuwait and Iraq (the Gulf War), Cyprus, southern Turkey, south Arabia, Bosnia, Germany (British Army of the Rhine), and of course in the United Kingdom. As part of UN forces, they have also been in Cambodia, Cyprus (again), and South Korea.

Over recent years Britain has been cutting her armed forces, and the Gurkhas have not escaped. One by one the eight battalions remaining after World War II have gone, until now only two remain, renamed the Royal Gurkha Rifles, together with some specialist units. There are highly placed officers and politicians in Britain who consider that a Gurkha brigade would be ideal as part of a permanent peacekeeping force for the United Nations.

Notes

1. A Call to Africa

1. Chan Ives, quoted in George Rock, *History of the American Field Service 1920–1955* (New York: Platon Press, 1956), p. 65.

2. With the AFS in the Western Desert

1. Poem composed by unknown AFS hands in Syria in 1942.
2. Barrie Pitt, *The Crucible of War: Year of Alamein 1942* (London: Jonathan Cape, 1982), p. 116.
3. Pitt, *The Crucible*, p. 150.
4. Letter to the author from Bill Nichols, February 5, 1994.
5. Adrian Gilbert, ed., *The Imperial War Museum Book of the Desert War* (London: Sidgwick and Jackson, 1992), p. 17.
6. Barrie Pitt, ed., *History of the Second World War* (London: Purnell, issued in ninety-six weekly parts, 1966–68), p. 1162.
7. Pitt, ed., *Second World War*, quoting George Greenfield, p. 1172.
8. Ronald Walker, *Alam Halfa and Alamein, Official History of New Zealand in the Second World War 1939–45* (Wellington, New Zealand: Historical Publications Branch, Department of Internal Affairs, 1967), p. 225.
9. Evan Thomas, *Ambulance in Africa* (New York: Appleton-Century-Crofts, 1943), pp. 134–35.

3. We Shift Our Talents

1. Philip Mason, *A Matter of Honour: An Account of the Indian Army, Its Officers & Men* (London: Jonathan Cape, 1974), p. 13.

2. F. W. Perry, *The Commonwealth Armies: Manpower and Organisation in Two World Wars* (Manchester: Manchester University Press, 1988), pp. 97–98.
3. T. A. Heathcote, *The Indian Army: the Garrison of British Imperial India 1822–1922* (Newton Abbot, Devon: David and Charles, 1974), p. 94.
4. Perry, *Commonwealth Armies,* p. 115.
5. Perry, *Commonwealth Armies,* p. 115.
6. Mason, *A Matter of Honour,* p. 15.
7. Patrick Davis, *A Child at Arms* (London: Hutchinson, 1970), p. 258.

4. An Officer of the Raj

1. Heathcote, *Indian Army,* p. 28.
2. Geoffrey Moorhouse, *India Britannica* (London: Harvill Press, 1983), p. 257.
3. Moorhouse, *India Britannica,* p. 242.
4. Humphrey Trevelyan, *The India We Left* (London: Macmillan, 1972), p. 114.

5. I Join the Gurkhas

1. F. H. Willasey-Wilsey, *A Brief Outline History of the 8th Gurkha Rifles* (Lahore, India: The Civil and Military Gazette, 1944), p. 1.
2. Willasey-Wilsey, *History of the 8th Gurkha Rifles,* p. 50.
3. Bernard Fergusson, *Beyond the Chindwin* (London: Fontana paperback edition, 1955), p. 237.
4. David Smurthwaite, ed., *The Forgotten War: The British Army in the Far East 1941–45* (London: National Army Museum, 1992), p. 125.
5. Louis Allen, *Burma, the Longest War, 1941–45* (London: Dent, 1984), p. 148.
6. Harold James, *Across the Threshold of Battle* (Lewis, Sussex: The Book Guild, 1993), p. 40.
7. H. J. Huxford, *History of the 8th Gurkha Rifles 1824–1949* (Aldershot: Gale and Polden, 1952), p. 276.

7. Mountain Interlude

1. *The Jungle Book* (Military Training Pamphlet No. 9, India, 4th ed., September 1943), p. 2.
2. *The Jungle Book,* p. 4

8. To the Arakan

1. Compton MacKenzie, *Eastern Epic* (London: Chatto and Windus, 1951), p. 499.
2. Raymond Callahan, *Burma 1942–45* (London: Davis-Poynter, 1978), p. 32.
3. Callahan, *Burma*, pp. 25–26.
4. Barbara Tuchman, *Sand Against the Wind: Stilwell and the American Experience in China 1911–45* (London: Macdonald Futura paperback edition, 1981), p. 213.
5. Tuchman, *Sand*, p. 389.
6. Callahan, *Burma*, p. 83.
7. Tuchman, *Sand*, p. 385.
8. Woodburn Kirby, *History of the Second World War: The War Against Japan* (London: Her Majesty's Stationery Office, 1962), vol. III pp. 34–35.
9. Callahan, *Burma*, p. 59.
10. Jon Godden and Rumer Godden, *Two Under the Indian Sun* (London: Macmillan, 1966). See especially chapter 6.

9. Cut Off at the Pass

1. Geoffrey Evans, *Slim as a Military Commander* (London: Batsford, 1969), p. 86.
2. Henry Maule, *Spearhead General: the Epic Story of Sir Frank Messervy* (London: Corgi Books paperback edition, 1963), p. 211.
3. Callahan, *Burma*, p. 135.
4. Field Marshal Sir William Slim, *Defeat into Victory* (London: Cassell, 1956) pp. 246–47.

10. North to Naga Country

1. Slim, *Defeat*, p. 164.
2. Allen, *Burma*, p. 229.
3. Allen, *Burma*, p. 639.
4. Allen, *Burma*, p. 242.
5. Charlton Ogburn, *The Marauders* (London: Hodder and Stoughton, 1960), p. 91.
6. Ogburn, *Marauders*, p. 289.
7. Richard Rhodes James, *Chindit* (London: Sphere Books paperback edition, 1981), p. 196.
8. Ogburn, *Marauders*, p. 279.

9. Peter Wickham, "The Arakan 1943–44: A Personal Recollection," in *Red Flash* (Journal of the 8th Gurkha Rifles Regimental Association), no. 17, March 1994, pp. 18–21.
10. M. R. Roberts, *Golden Arrow: The Story of the 7th Indian Division* (Aldershot: Gale and Polden, 1952), p. 146.
11. Allen, *Burma,* p. 638.
12. Roberts, *Golden Arrow,* p. 146, quoting L.H.O. Pugh

11. At Kohima

1. *The Jungle Book,* p. 51.
2. Woodburn Kirby, *History of the Second World War: The War Against Japan,* (London: Her Majesty's Stationery Office, 1965), vol. IV pp. 8–9.

12. March to the Irrawaddy

1. Geoffrey Armstrong, *The Sparks Fly Upward* (East Wittering, Sussex: Gooday Publishers, 1991), p. 193.
2. *4/8th Gurkha Rifles News Chronicle No 2* (1945, local distribution only), p. 3.
3. *4/8th News Chronicle No 2,* p. 4.

13. Across the Great River

1. Allen, *Burma,* p. 578.
2. Roger Hilsman, *American Guerrilla* (Washington: Brassey's [US], 1990), pp. 297–98.

14. Enemy on the Run

1. Slim, *Defeat,* pp. 438–39.
2. E. D. Smith, *Battle for Burma* (London: Batsford, 1979), p. 123.
3. Bruce Catton, *Glory Road* (London: White Lion Publishers, Book Club edition, 1977), p. 161.

15. The End of the Chase

1. Slim, *Defeat,* p. 519.
2. John Casey, "Nobel Prisoner of Rangoon," in Britain's *Daily Telegraph,* October 15, 1991.

Epilogue

1. Sadao Oba, "Recollections of Indonesia, 1944–1947," in Ian Nish, ed., *Indonesian Experience: The Role of Japan and Britain, 1943–1948* (London: Suntory-Toyota International Centre, London School of Economics and Political Science, Discussion Paper IS/80/05, 1980), p. 33.

Appendix

1. Allen, *Burma,* p. 637. The overall casualty figures given here are taken from Appendix 1 of Louis Allen's book.

Select Bibliography

Libraries of books have been written on the British in India, on the Indian Army, the Gurkhas, on Burma as a country, and on the World War II British campaigns in North Africa. Fewer books have been written about the campaigns in Burma. This may be because on the Allied side the majority of the troops were not English-speaking and many were illiterate. Our enemies, though highly literate, wrote Japanese. Not many of their writings on Burma have been translated.

We do not claim to have consulted more than a small proportion of the literature. The books listed below are titles that we have found useful and that might be of interest to a reader wishing to follow up aspects of the narrative. This should not be taken as a judgment on books not listed. Some fine ones have been omitted because they have little connection with our story.

The publishers listed are those of the editions consulted and not necessarily of the original editions.

Allen, Louis. *Burma, the Longest War 1941–45*. London: Dent, 1984. Will probably remain the standard account of the Burma War for some years to come, and a very good one it is. Allen was an intelligence officer in Burma. He spoke and read Japanese, so was able to research the story from both sides. He died in 1991.

Armstrong, Geoffrey. *The Sparks Fly Upward*. East Wittering, Sussex: Gooday Publishers, 1991. A soldier's story, well written. Colonel Armstrong commanded the 136th Field Regiment, Royal Artillery, from 1944 to 1945. This was the regiment of twenty-five-pounders that supported the 4/8th Gurkhas for much of the advance down Burma. Earlier he was in action in the Western Desert through most of that eventful year, 1942. See also under "Robertson."

Biggs, Maurice. *The Story of Gurkha VCs*. Winchester: The Gurkha Museum, 1993.

Broadway, M. H. *Order of Battle of Gurkha Units 1940–1946.* Winchester: The Gurkha Museum, 1993. This pamphlet lists all Gurkha formations and the theaters of war in which they served.

Cady, John F. *The United States and Burma*. Cambridge, Mass.: Harvard University Press, 1976. A useful overview, by an American scholar, of Burmese history and politics, with a valuable bibliographic essay.

Callahan, Raymond. *Burma 1942–1945*. London: Davis-Poynter, 1978. An American historian examines the way in which divergent political priorities shaped the strategy of the Burma campaigns, and at the same time gives an account of the fighting.

Chant, Christopher. *Gurkha: The Illustrated History of an Elite Fighting Force*. Poole, Dorset: Blanford Press, 1985.

Collier, Richard. *The War in the Desert*. Alexandria, Va.: Time-Life Books, 1977.

Collier, Basil. *The War in the Far East*. New York: William Morrow, 1968.

Davis, Patrick. *A Child at Arms*. London: Hutchinson, 1970. An account of his war by a young British "emergency" soldier who also served with the 4/8th Gurkhas and whose service through part of 1944 and most of 1945 runs in parallel with the author's. See also "Sheil-Small."

Donnison, F.S.V. *Burma* (The Nations of the Modern World Series). London: Benn, 1970.

Evans, Geoffrey. *Slim as a Military Commander*. London: Batsford, 1969.

Gilbert, Adrian, ed. *The Imperial War Museum Book of the Desert War 1940–1942*. London: Sidgwick and Jackson, 1992.

Hanley, Gerald. *Monsoon Victory*. London: Collins, 1946. Anyone wanting a firsthand, personal impression of the scale of the Japanese defeats at Imphal and Kohima in 1944, and the subsequent retreat of the Japanese back to the Chindwin River, should read this book. It also gives a graphic picture of campaigning through a Southeast Asian monsoon, and is unusual too in its concern with the 11th East African Division in Burma. Written by a war correspondent soon after the events.

Heathcote, T. A. *The Indian Army, the Garrison of British Imperial India 1822–1922* (Historic Armies and Navies Series). Newton Abbot, Devon: David and Charles, 1974. A fine record of the Indian Army in its classical period, full of facts and covering most aspects of its organizational and fighting history.

Hilsman, Roger. *American Guerrilla: My War Behind Japanese Lines*. Washington: Brassey's (US), 1990. One of the few books by an American participant in Burma, and interesting on the extensive irregular warfare that was conducted behind the Japanese lines.

Huxford, H. J. *History of the 8th Gurkha Rifles 1824–1949*. Aldershot: Gale and Polden, 1952. The standard regimental history.

James, Harold. *Across the Threshold of Battle: Behind Japanese Lines with Wingate's Chindits, Burma 1943*. Lewis, Sussex: The Book Guild, 1993. The author was an 8th Gurkha, and seconded at the last moment to Wingate's first Chindit expedition, with which he won an MC. An interesting personal account that also attempts, fifty years after the events, to give an objective assessment of Wingate and his enterprise, both still barbed in controversy.

James, Harold, and Sheil-Small, Denis. *The Gurkhas*. London: Macdonald, 1965. A series of anecdotal accounts of some of the many battles in which the Gurkhas have fought, starting with the Indian Mutiny in 1857. Both authors served with the 8th Gurkhas.

Kirby, Major General Woodburn, et al. *History of the Second World War: The War Against Japan*. London: Her Majesty's Stationery Office, 1958 (vol. I), 1962 (vol. III), 1965 (vol. IV). These massive volumes are the official British histories. They are indispensable for the keen student, with a comprehensive text, full of marvelous maps in several colors, and with a surprising number of photographs.

Lewin, Ronald. *Slim, the Standardbearer*. London: Leo Cooper, 1976. The definitive, and well-crafted, biography of our 14th Army commander. A fine book that does justice to the stature of the man.

McCrae, Alister, and Prentice, Alan. *Irrawaddy Flotilla*. Paisley, Scotland: James Paton, 1978. We could not resist listing this beguiling little book, which traces the history of the Irrawaddy Flotilla Company from 1852 to its virtual extinction during the Japanese conquest of 1941. Both authors were Scotsmen working for the company. Both served in the war.

MacHorton, Ian. *Safer Than a Known Way*. London: Odhams Press, 1958. His account of his extraordinary experiences with Wingate's first Chindit expedition. The author was an 8th Gurkha. He was wounded again in 1945 while with the 3/8th Gurkha Rifles at 20th Indian Division's crossing of the Irrawaddy at Myinmu, southwest of Mandalay.

MacKenzie, Compton. *Eastern Epic*. London: Chatto and Windus, 1951 (vol. 1). The first volume of an intended duo. It was written at the invitation of the old (British) government of India, which wanted an experienced author to write the story of India's efforts during the war "in the form of a popular novel, but strictly accurate as to detail." It is our loss that the second volume was never published.

Mason, Philip. *A Matter of Honour: An Account of the Indian Army, Its Officers and Men*. London: Jonathan Cape, 1974. A marvelous book by a fine writer, and if one had to pick one history of the Indian Army to read, this must be it. The author has that rare ability to present the whole picture through telling selection of detail, and to present analysis of underlying causes interwoven with narratives of happenings.

Masters, John; *Bugles and a Tiger;* London: Michael Joseph, 1956; and *The Road Past Mandalay;* London: Michael Joseph, 1961. Two classics. The author was not popular with all his fellow officers, it seems, but he could fight and he could write. *Bugles* covers his peacetime service with the 4th Gurkhas, 1933–1939. *Mandalay* describes his war service in the Middle East and Burma, which was eventful.

Maule, Henry. *Spearhead General: The Epic Story of General Sir Frank Messervy and His Men in Eritrea, North Africa and Burma.* London: Corgi Books, 1963. Frank Messervy was a character. Everybody loved him. He commanded our 7th Indian Division from July 1943 to December 1944, and then took over 4th Corps, which included the 7th Division, for the 1945 campaign. This popular biography includes many accounts of personal experiences by the men under his command.

Ministry of Defence (1965 edition). *Nepal and the Gurkhas.* London: Her Majesty's Stationery Office. A succinct factual introduction to the geography, history, and people of Nepal, and especially to the Gurkha tribes. It is a Ministry of Defence publication and has been issued in successive revised editions.

Mollo, Boris. *The Indian Army.* Poole, Dorset: Blanford Press, 1981. Generously and delightfully illustrated, primarily about the uniforms of the Indian Army, but with interleaved historical sections.

Moorhouse, Geoffrey. *India Britannica.* London: Harvill Press, 1983. Entertainingly written and well-illustrated short history of the British in India, perhaps as near to an evenhanded account of the love-hate relationship between Indians and British as we can expect from one author.

Mosher, Don. *China-Burma-India.* Alexandria, Va.: Time-Life Books, 1978.

Northey, W. Brook, and Morris, C. J. *The Gurkhas: Their Manners, Customs and Country.* London: John Lane the Bodley Head, 1928. A vintage book now, and written before travel in Nepal became unrestricted, but still worth reading.

Ogburn, Charlton. *The Marauders.* London: Hodder and Stoughton and New York: Morrow, 1960. A well-written, honest, and moving account of the experiences of American Casual Detachment 1688, or 5307th Composite Unit (Provisional), or Galahad, or Merrill's Marauders, by one of those who took part. The unit could surely not have found a better memorialist.

Perry, F. W. *The Commonwealth Armies: Manpower and Organisation in Two World Wars*. Manchester: Manchester University Press, 1968. Includes an interesting chapter on the Indian Army, its expansion in both world wars, and the political and economic background in both Britain and India.

Pitt, Barrie. *The Crucible of War: Year of Alamein 1942*. London: Jonathan Cape, 1982. One of several volumes that form a comprehensive account of the campaigning in the Western Desert.

Pitt, Barrie, ed. *History of the Second World War*. London: Purnell, 1966–68. An attractive mixture of authoritative short articles by many hands, lavish illustration, and copious maps. Issued in ninety-six weekly parts and totaling 3,136 pages. Intended for a mass readership, yet on the whole accurate and balanced.

Roberts, M. R. *Golden Arrow: The Story of the 7th Indian Division*. Aldershot: Gale and Polden, 1952.

Robertson, G. W. *The Rose and the Arrow: A Life Story of 136th (1st West Lancashire) Field Regiment, Royal Artillery, 1939–1946*. Dorchester, Dorset: 136 Field Regiment, R.A., Old Comrades Association, 1986. A privately printed history of the artillery unit that so often supported the 4/8th Gurkhas. The book is based on local records and on many contributions received from surviving members of the regiment. See also "Armstrong."

Rock, George. *History of the American Field Service 1920–1955*. New York: Platon Press, 1956.

Sheil-Small, Denis. *Green Shadows: A Gurkha Story*. London: William Kimber, 1982. Here is another officer of the 4/8th Gurkhas who published his war memoirs. See also "Davis." Denis does not cover his early years in Britain's territorial army. He starts with his commissioning into the 8th Gurkhas in 1942.

Slim, Field Marshal Sir William. *Defeat into Victory*. London: Cassell, 1956. Perhaps the best book written by any senior general in World War II on his own campaigning. It is confined to the war in Burma. Slim was as good a craftsman with words as he was with soldiers, guns, tanks, and airplanes.

Smith, E. D. *Battle for Burma*. London: Batsford, 1979. A brief (190 pages) account of the four-year fighting that gives much more space to the American and Chinese roles than is usual in British accounts. The author served with the Gurkhas in Italy.

Smurthwaite, David, ed. *The Forgotten War: The British Army in the Far East 1941–1945*. London: National Army Museum, 1992. A well-illustrated short account not only of the British but also of the Indian Army in the Far East. Various contributors, with interesting chapters on such matters as "Artillery in the Jungle," "Forgotten Heroines," and "Prisoners of Nippon."

Sykes, Christopher. *Orde Wingate*. London: Collins, 1959. A sympathetic portrait of a controversial soldier.

Toye, Hugh. *The Springing Tiger: A Study of Subhas Chandra Bose*. London: Cassell, 1959.

Trench, Charles Chenevix. *The Indian Army and the King's Enemies 1900–1947*. London: Thames and Hudson, 1988. Not so much a history as a description of the old Indian Army in action through firsthand accounts of its participants, some previously unpublished. There is plenty of detail and there are linking passages, but little analysis. Very readable.

Tuchman, Barbara W. *Sand Against the Wind: Stilwell and the American Experience in China, 1911–45*. London: Macdonald Futura Publishers, 1981. A long book (816 pages), well written, that makes a persuasive case for judging General Stilwell to be a great, if flawed, man. Originally published in 1971 by Macmillan under its subtitle alone.

Tuker, Francis. *Gorkha, the Story of the Gurkhas of Nepal*. London: Constable, 1957. One of the better books on Nepal and on Gurkha history, by an officer of the Gurkha Rifles who became a general—and who can write.

Index